The Christian Mission
Among Rural People

Studies in

THE WORLD MISSION OF CHRISTIANITY

No. I: *Church Growth in Korea*
by Alfred W. Wasson

No. II: *The Medieval Missionary*
by James Thayer Addison

No. III: *The Christian Mission Among Rural People*
a joint study

No. IV: *The Family and Its Christian Fulfilment*
a joint study

No. V: *New Buildings on Old Foundations*
by J. Merle Davis

No. VI: *Religious Liberty: An Inquiry*
by M. Searle Bates

No. VII: *The Highway of Print*
by Ruth Ure

No. VIII: *The Christian Message in a Non-Christian World*
by Hendrik Kraemer

No. IX: *The Rural Church in China*
by Frank Wilson Price

Copies may be secured from
International Missionary Council
156 Fifth Avenue, New York 10, N. Y.

Studies in *No. III*
THE WORLD MISSION OF CHRISTIANITY

The Christian Mission *Among* Rural People

Printed for the
Rural Missions Cooperating Committee
of the Foreign Missions Conference of North America
by
AGRICULTURAL MISSIONS, Inc.
New York

1949

First printing, 1945
Second printing, abridged, 1949

PRINTED IN THE UNITED STATES OF AMERICA
SOWERS PRINTING COMPANY, LEBANON, PENNSYLVANIA

Contents

Foreword to Reprint Edition

THE pertinency of *The Christian Mission Among Rural People* to present-day world conditions and the continuing demand for the book, both at home and abroad, necessitate this reprint. The first printing of 3,500 copies has been exhausted for some months. To maintain the low cost of the first edition, we have omitted the former Part III dealing with source materials related to present Chapters 5, 6, and 7. Since most of these papers were reprints and are still available, we have listed them on pages 206-207 and they can be had on request to Agricultural Missions, Inc.

Events since the military phases of World War II ended have highlighted the importance of rural people to a world at peace. Their allegiance to communistic patterns of thought and action is being sought with increasing success in many parts of the world. Their problems of food, health, and education become more acute. Plans for making technical services available to underdeveloped countries are underway, but this provision is only one of many aspects of a complex problem. Of all people, Christians should know that these rural people not only want but must have more things to live with as well as a new and adequate faith to live by. This is the Christian mission to rural people!

In the lands of Asia, Africa, and Latin America there are some 120,000 organized and unorganized rural churches with 12,000,000 members and about 100,000 pastors, evangelists, and Bible women. In addition, there are tens of thousands of teachers in village schools. These leaders and church groups constitute vast resources for a Christian approach to rural people and their problems, if use will be made of them. No rural worker desiring to make his largest contribution to Christian life in the villages should be without this book.

J.H.R.

Foreword

THE Rural Missions Cooperating Committee of the Foreign Missions Conference of North America has had great satisfaction in sponsoring this study of *The Christian Mission Among Rural People*. The idea of such a study to be undertaken by a group of rural missionaries on furlough grew out of the discussions at the Rural Missions Conference held at Cornell University, January 23 and 24, 1942.

In the years since the Jerusalem Conference of the International Missionary Council held in December, 1928, there had accumulated a great body of reports, interpretations, programmes, and rich and creative experiences by many missionaries in many parts of the world related to the varied aspects of the work of the village church and to rural life and rural living. It was felt that the time was ripe for a comprehensive statement that would bring these experiences and insights into a new focus. This book is the result.

The Christian mission among rural people constitutes one of the very major concerns of the World Christian Movement. In spite of the great advances in industrialization of production, the mechanization of labor, and the growth of great urban centers of population, the majority of the people of the world still live by agriculture or are directly dependent on it. Practically all of Asia, Africa, and Latin America is rural. If we include western Russia, agriculture is the dominant vocation of the majority of the people of Europe. Whether on the basis of the number of congregations or of the number of communicant members, the churches brought into being by the modern missionary enterprise are preponderantly rural. It is hoped that this study will bring new insight, new enthusiasm, and helpful guidance to this part of the total task of the church to make Christ known, loved, and obeyed in the home, on the farm, and in the community.

The Rural Missions Cooperating Committee takes this opportunity to express its profound thanks to the members of the study group: to Mr. Arthur T. Mosher, India, of the Presbyterian Church, U.S.A., who served as Director of the study and as Chairman of the study group; to Miss Lora I. Battin, China, of the Methodist Church; to Dr. Ewing M. Bailey, Egypt, of the United Presbyterian Church of North America; to Dr., now Bishop, Newell S. Booth, Belgian Congo, of the Methodist Church; to the Rev. Elmer W. Galt, China, of the Congregational Christian Churches; to Miss Maud J. MacKinnon, Korea, of the United Church of Canada; and to Miss Alice Murphy, China, of the Congregational Christian Churches.

The Rural Missions Cooperating Committee desires also to express its appreciation to the Mission Boards which made available without cost the services of the missionaries who participated in the study and for their financial contributions which made the study possible.

A special word of thanks is due to Mr. Mosher for the final editing of the manuscript and to Miss Constance Hallock for editing, for preparing the index, and for seeing the volume through the press.

On behalf of the
Rural Missions Cooperating Committee:
MRS. OTIS MOORE, *Chairman*
JOHN H. REISNER, *Secretary*

Preface

THIS VOLUME is primarily for the use of rural missionaries and rural ministers. It is hoped that it will also have value for those in training for these callings and for those responsible for determining mission and church policy and programme and for administering the Christian enterprise.

Its purpose is primarily to provide an over-all picture of the Christian mission among rural people. Increasing specialization among rural Christian workers makes it imperative that each person know enough of the task and problems of workers in other fields to be able to understand his own potential contributions and real limitations, and to be capable of helping to integrate all specialties into a unified programme. Obviously, no volume can achieve this purpose and at the same time give really adequate attention to the techniques and problems of each phase of the programme. We have sought by bibliographies to do what we could towards amplifying the exposition in the text itself.

We wish it might be possible for two developments to grow out of this study.

First, we wish that an attempt might be made to take the principles which are presented here, and to implement them by the development of detailed programmes in each major cultural region of the earth. We feel that it is legitimate to have made a statement such as this volume presents, treating the problem of the Christian mission among rural people without reference to a particular regional culture, even though that necessitates limiting the exposition to broad generalities. However, the successful application of these principles must wait upon translating them into concrete programmes and projects for the rural people of each cultural region. We wish that this might be the starting point for many such studies by groups of Christians within individual regions.

Second, we hope that this presentation will stimulate other workers, either individually or in groups, greatly to expand the sections in the report which for obvious reasons could not be treated fully in our study. This is necessarily a continuing process in the exposition of the total task of the Christian mission among rural people.

While the form of the volume as it stands is the work of our Committee, edited by its Chairman, we must express our great debt to all who have counselled with us. We are greatly indebted to the fifty missionaries, rural ministers, seminary professors, and mission administrators who wrote out critical analyses of the preliminary draft of this statement for our guidance. Our special thanks go to John H. Reisner, both for his help in facilitating this study, and for his leadership through the past fifteen years in promoting the interchange of thought, experience, and acquaintance among rural missionaries which has been responsible for many of the insights brought together in this volume.

We are profoundly grateful to our several denominational boards and to the Rural Missions Cooperating Committee for the opportunity this study as afforded us as a group.

EWING M. BAILEY
LORA I. BATTIN
NEWELL S. BOOTH
ELMER W. GALT
MAUD J. MACKINNON
ALICE E. MURPHY
ARTHUR T. MOSHER,
Chairman

PART I

The Report

Introduction

WHEREVER there is a sufficient mantle of soil, sufficient moisture either by rainfall or by irrigation, and enough light and warmth supplied by the sun, men till the land. Some do not produce enough to furnish sufficient food for their own families; others contribute their products to the life of other people and in return receive for their own use the products of the toil of other men. Some of them live in isolation; others live in villages. Some have adequate homes, educational opportunities, and medical care; many more live in poverty and under the shadow of disease.

Some till their farms with small wooden ploughs and light oxen; others have tractors. Some have free access to as much land as each will cultivate; others find their small inherited farms becoming smaller with each generation. Some must supplement their limited income through work away from the farm. Across most of the fields of the earth farmers fight excessive loss of fertile soil by erosion, while in the valley of the Nile other farmers see the fertility of their fields annually renewed by the silt left by the receding flood-waters of the river. These are the rural people of earth. We would see them know the Christ.

* * *

The importance of rural people arises from two sources: one is the fact that they comprise so large a proportion of the population of the world, and the other is the fact that rural families are large enough to effect a net growth of the population whereas urban families are not. The first of these is important to the Christian mission because it indicates how much of the need of the world, simply on the basis of the number of people involved, is in the countryside. The second is important because of its implications for the best use of the resources of the Christian movement, from the standpoint of its own growth.

When Charles McConnell set about writing a book on the rural task of the church, he chose to call it *The Rural Billion.* This reflected the fact that about one-half of the people of the world are rural. The proportion varies from country to country. In highly-industrialized countries, the rural population may be not more than twenty percent of the total. In relatively unindustrialized countries like India and China, rural people account for about seventy-five percent of all people. In parts of Africa, the percentage of rural people runs even higher.

One-half of the people of the earth being rural, if the Christian gospel is to go "into all the world" it must effectively permeate the rural areas of every country.

The method whereby this may be brought about is conditioned by the second aspect of the importance of rural life, namely, the propensity of rural families to do more than reproduce themselves while city families tend to die out. It is a universal observation that birth-rates are higher in the rural than in the urban sections of a country. Many reasons may be advanced for this. Among them are the facts (1) that children become economic assets in farming areas at a much earlier age than in the city, (2) that the family unit is more highly respected in rural areas, and (3) that birth-rates tend to decline with advancing formal education, and such education has been less widespread in rural than in urban areas.

The result of this higher birth-rate in the country, and of the inability of city populations to maintain their numbers, is that the city populations are replenished and increased by an influx of people from rural areas. It means, moreover, that an appreciable proportion of the leadership of the cities is provided by individuals who come to the cities in late adolescence or as adults, and who have been reared in rural surroundings. Thus, rural people bear the burden not only of training young people for rural leadership, but of rearing many young men and women who will eventually find their way into the leadership of the cities.

This fact, as pointed out notably by O. E. Baker[1] and empha-

[1] Baker, O. E. "The National Welfare and Rural Urban Migration in the U.S.A.," *Christian Rural Fellowship Bulletin* No. 4. "The Rural Family and its Significance to Organized Religion," *Christian Rural Fellowship Bulletin,* No. 43.

sized by many others, has profound implications for the Christian movement. Depending strongly on childhood training for its organized strength, it must face the fact that much of its future urban, as well as rural, vitality depends upon its present rural influence.

One of the most prevalent misconceptions as to possible ways of bringing the Christian spirit into the countryside is the belief that strong city churches can (and sometimes the belief that they automatically *will*) become aggressive agents in taking the Christian spirit to surrounding rural areas. Two factors practically always prevent this. One is that the Christian message to be understood and appreciated must be transmitted in terms its recipients understand, and these terms are different for country and for city. The second factor is that any flow of influence from the city to the countryside, which depends entirely on attraction and personal witness as Christian evangelism does, has to fight against the whole current of population and of interest, which moves from rural to urban areas.

To be sure, urban influences are strong in setting the social standards of surrounding rural areas. But the vehicles of this influence are the newspaper, the radio, the cinema, and the returning villager who has visited or worked for a time in the city. These influences are almost always secular. Very seldom if ever are they strongly evangelical. Therefore, it is unsound to reason from this general influence of the city on the countryside to the proposition that the Christian spirit itself will easily flow in that direction.

It is becoming more and more clear not only that the countryside is the human seedbed of the cities, and the country church the mother and renewer of the city church in a real biological sense; but also that the Christian revelation becomes rooted and flourishes in rural society only as it is mediated through thoroughly rural experiences by men and women who love rural life, even while they know its problems and its pitfalls.

The Report of the International Missionary Conference at Jerusalem in 1928 pointed out that one of the most pressing needs of the Christian movement is that it recognize the necessity for adapting its approach to the class of people it is addressing at the moment. It held that there are three primary groups of people, for each of which a distinct mode of approach is essential. These three primary groups are: rural people, the industrial working classes, and the urban intelligentsia.

No one has been more insistent on a distinctively rural approach to rural people than Dr. Kenyon L. Butterfield. This did not blind him to the equally distinctive challenge of the cities. He wrote:

> To urge upon the Christian enterprise the deep significance of its responsibility to the villages is not to ignore the importance of enlisting educated individuals for Christian service, nor the need of the Christian approach to the problems of urban areas. The winning of at least a portion of a nation's leadership to the conviction and practice of Christianity is essential if Christian ideals are to dominate the thought and life of a people. Moreover, the cities clearly constitute a strategic field for the Christian enterprise. There gather wealth, power, social institutions, influential personalities. As a country becomes more industrialized, so the cities become more powerful and their complex social and industrial problems in greater need of the Christian approach.[2]

We focus our attention in this study on rural people, and note, in beginning, their importance in the world sense. This importance follows from (1) the fact that rural people are *people,* called to be sons of God; (2) the number of rural people—half of the people of the world; and (3) the fact that rural areas are the continuing birthplace of each nation, supplying an excess population which keeps moving toward the cities, so that urban social organizations, including the church, must continually look to young men and women reared in rural surroundings for renewal.

* * *

Eight insights seem to dominate recent experience in rural missions.

I. The peculiar advantages of rural living for the development of a religious outlook.

II. The permeating implications of Christian faith in God for every phase and experience of life.

III. The evangelistic influence of all activities that are conducted in conformity with the Christian spirit.

[2] Butterfield, Kenyon L., "The Christian Church in Rural China," *Chinese Recorder* 62:341-344.

IV. The primary importance of the family in all human development and advance.

V. The central place of the small neighbourhood in social welfare and action.

VI. The formative influence of group worship.

VII. Renewed understanding of the nature of the church: the necessity for it to become a true community.

VIII. The fact that the principle of self-forgetful love applies as fully to the fulfilment of organizations as it does to individual persons—particularly, that it applies to the church.

The task of the Work Committee, having identified these insights, became that of trying: (1) to discover the relationships between them, and (2) to determine the relevance of each to the task of fulfilling in rural life the implications of the life and teachings of Jesus.

It will be noted at once that certain of these insights are peculiar to rural life. Others are more likely to be met in rural areas, but may be present anywhere. Still others are universal. However, all must be considered in this study, for two reasons. First, whether exclusively rural or not, all of them do apply in rural areas. Second, some of those which are most general have been widely discussed with particular respect to the form in which they are met under rural conditions.

The method which the Committee set for itself was substantially as follows: First, to gather the available interpretations of the implications of the life and teachings of Jesus for rural life, and on the basis of these to try to discern what, ideally, should be the outcome of the introduction of the Christian spirit into rural life. Second, to study information bearing on the method whereby the Christian spirit may be brought to bear on rural life; specifically, to examine the thesis that achievement of Christian discipleship and witness to Christian faith in God are inseparable. Third, to attempt through an inductive consideration of the results of the first two parts of the study to derive principles which should undergird the Christian rural programme, and to compare these principles with those advanced in the recent literature on rural missions. Fourth, to select the fundamental books which, in the opinion of the Committee, every rural Christian worker should have and to prepare bibliographies classified according to the outline of the Report itself.

This outline has been followed, in the main. The chief deviation from it has been that three important sections have had to be removed from the body of the Report itself and placed in a later part of the volume in order to bring the main insights close enough together in the volume for easy comprehension. These are the sections on "Implications of the Life and Teachings of Jesus for Rural Living," "Training Leadership for the Christian Rural Programme," and "The Rural Church." These will be found in Part II. The Rural Bookshelf and the bibliographies are contained in Part III.

* * * *

Many people may expect, since this study was undertaken under the auspices of the Rural Missions Cooperating Committee, that it will deal particularly with the problems of what some people call "mission lands," and that it will make recommendations for mission policy.

That we have not dealt particularly with mission lands, grows out of the fact that we have come to this task from responsibilities in China, India, Egypt, the Congo, and Korea. Conditions vary so widely within and between these countries that only a general treatment, free from regional peculiarities, is possible. Moreover, it is our conviction that the church is called to seek goals which are universal, even while it seeks them within the cultures of particular regions.

That we have not made recommendations for mission policy grows out of a similar problem, for each mission society faces unique situations, and each has its own favored type of organization. All, however, have similar goals: to make Jesus Christ known, and to gather his disciples into self-supporting, self-propagating churches. This study cannot outline policy, but it can and does attempt to bring into focus the task which individual Christians and village groups of Christians face in the countryside, and the principles which experience has shown to be fundamental to victorious Christian discipleship in rural life. Understanding of these should be the cornerstone of all mission policy in rural areas.

It will bear repetition that the Committee has conceived its task to be primarily one of bringing scattered insights together, considering each in the light of all of the others, and combining those which are compatible with each other, as valid phases of the Christian message, into a single connected statement of the Christian mission among rural people. This makes the chief task that of showing relationships, and eliminates the possibility of producing either a handbook or an exhaustive treatment of any single part of the subject. We have, however, sought in the bibliographies to gather the most significant materials for giving effect to the Christian programme.

1.

The Background of Rural Life

ADVANTAGES AND VALUES

THERE are certain aspects of rural living which make it congenial to the development of a religious attitude and to appreciation of the Christian revelation. Many of these have been recognized for generations and for centuries. One of the most clear-cut recent comparisons of the effects of rural and of urban living on human outlook to be found in recent rural Christian literature is "Rural and Urban Philosophies," by O. E. Baker.[3]

Some of the advantages of rural life inhere in the processes of agriculture and are therefore supremely the possession of farm families. But the inter-relationships between farm families and other rural families are so close that these advantages flow over into the lives of other rural folk than farmers.

Farmers everywhere deal always with life. They deal constantly with birth and growth, with maturation and death, with competition, parasitism, disease, and adjustment. They prepare the soil, plant the seed,[4] and conserve moisture for young seedlings by cultivation to remove competing plants. They guard against depredation by disease, insects, birds, and beasts. They gather the mature harvest to meet the needs of men. They plough living plants back into the earth to enrich the soil.

These relationships of the farmer within the biological world are fundamental and have far-reaching consequences.

The first living things on earth were plants—many of them in the sea, some of them on the land—carrying in their leaves a magic by which the energy in the rays of the sun could synthesize the non-living elements of earth into living tissue.

[3] *Christian Rural Fellowship Bulletin,* No. 10.

[4] Sells, James Wm., *An Order for the Dedication of the Seed, the Soil, and the Sowers,* Department of Town and Country Work, Methodist Church, 150 Fifth Avenue, New York 11, N. Y.

All other physical life depends on plants, trillions of billions of them, waving in the wind and in the currents of the sea, growing, reproducing, dying (even in their death contributing to the living of others, for through their death new substances, organic remnants, mingle with the elements of earth).

Among these plants, and gaining their sustenance through them, live the animals of the earth. So closely akin to plants are they, even today, that the complex molecule of hemoglobin differs from the equally complex molecule of chlorophyll only in that its nucleus is an atom of iron, while that of chlorophyll is one of magnesium. Animals and plants breathe the same air, drink the same moisture, inhabit the same earth. They live intimately with one another: plants furnishing food for animals, animals carrying pollen from plant to plant, and distributing seeds caught in their shaggy coats. Sometimes one plant lives on another plant. A plant may be a parasite on an animal. They live interdependently in and on the soil: minute bacteria drawing nitrogen out of the air or feeding on the refuse of dead plants, earthworms burrowing through the soil, rabbits digging their burrows, and insects making their homes.

Man is part of this biological world.[5] He gains his sustenance through plants and animals. He suffers disease from the invasion of his body by other forms of life. He, in turn, disrupts the pattern of living of animals and of plants. Slowly we learn that the whole pattern of human culture is integral with that of biological life. We see the doom of certain civilizations in the acceleration of soil erosion as men destroy the natural balance of plant cover and of animal associations. Many of the most fundamental problems, opportunities, and satisfactions of men grow directly out of this relationship between man and the rest of the living world.

In our generation, particularly in the industrial civilizations of Europe and America, close contact between man and the natural life on which he depends has been broken. The nature of the toil of many men and women has become such that they congregate in cities, buying their food from distant regions, and piping their water from distant reservoirs. Even the tasks of homemakers have been commercialized to such a degree

[5] "We are parts in a living sensitive creation. . . . The living creation is not exclusively man-centered: it is biocentric. . . . We have genetic relation with all living things." Bailey, L. H., *The Holy Earth,* p. 23.

that much of the food of a family comes to it already processed and in such a form that one cannot readily identify the plant or animal from which it came. In much of urban life the presence of growing children in the family and a bit of garden around the home are the only remnants of close contact between man and the growing, biological world of which he is a part, and on which he is utterly dependent.

Of all people, farmers deal most constantly and directly with a variety of these relationships with the natural world.

This contact with the growing world has a wholesomeness which has been recounted many times. It is in the poetry of Wordsworth; it was emphasized to the point of exaggeration by Rousseau. There is unquestionably a healing in the rush of flowing water, in the soughing of trees, in the unhurried succession of leaf and flower and seed. David Grayson even promised some day to tell the story of a spinster saved by three flower pots.

But the contact of rural people with the natural world is not primarily one of esthetic appreciation. Farmers are not spectators, like hikers tramping through the country in search of recreation. They are enmeshed in the natural world. A sudden change in the weather, which to the spectator brings only invigoration, may spell disaster to the ripening crops of the farmer. The man on the land sees his fortunes rise and fall with those of the living world about him. His economic dependence on the varying weather, on the control of disease, on the uncertainties of the harvest may at times almost blot out appreciation of the ways of nature. Moreover, in many parts of the world, there are financial and political phases of farming which can divert the attention of rural people from the natural life of the farm. Fluctuation in prices of farm products, taxation policies which favor the residents of cities, land tenure practices which give little security to farmers who do not own their land, may have this effect. But still in the background there is the daily contact with plants and animals, and intimate knowledge of their ways, growing out of the close connection between every farmer and the natural world of which he is a part.

Farmers everywhere are constantly aware of the impersonal forces of the natural world. The chlorophyll of plants draws energy from the light of the sun. Rootlets penetrate the earth in vain unless rain falls to bring the inert elements of the soil into solution. If the weather be too damp and cool, fungi may infect the growing crop; if it be too dry and hot, the leaves wither and the plant dies. The farmer knows these forces intimately and he finds that they are but little in his control.[6] They bring him a rich harvest when their combination is fair. They destroy the handiwork of his toil when sudden or unusual changes occur. He relies upon the dependability of some fully as much as he fears the vagaries of others; for the angle of the sun at his latitude is certain, the responses of certain plants to day-length and to sunlight are constant, and the compensation of better response by one crop to a change which inhibits another is sure.

Man does not exhaust the handicraft of God in an environment where, through the centuries, weak acids and thermal changes break down rock into the raw materials of soils, where every thimbleful of earth is inhabited by myriad forms of life, where bacteria transfer nitrogen from the air to the soil, where green leaves build sugars and starches out of water and air and the light of the sun, where fruiting reacts to ratios of carbon and nitrogen, and flowers respond to the length of the day. In this growing world, in this interdependence of life, man obviously is but a part, and the man-made portion is but a small fraction.

Therefore, while the farmer may develop a considerable self-reliance so far as independence from other men is concerned, he can never come to feel independent of majestic forces beyond himself which affect almost every move he makes as a husbandman. He can never feel himself to be more than a co-operator. He is confronted constantly by evidence of a creator, a greater power, "Another," beyond himself, whose ways he cannot control and therefore to whose ways he must adapt himself.

Farmers tend to sense their debt to the past and their obligation to the future. Particularly where there is a heritage of continuous occupancy of one farm by successive generations of the same family, the farmer has a strong sense of the continuity

[6] So the animist in Africa and India directs his magico-religious rites toward placating the "spirits" which he believes can direct the forces he cannot control.

of life, and of his connection with the past and with the future. The soil he tills was left him by his father and must be conserved for the family of his son.

Farmers have faith in the future. No matter what tragedies come, this faith does not die—not faith in an easy future, but in *a* future. Floods may drive them out, drought may destroy their crops, dust storms may bury their soil or carry away its richness, but they return to replant and to rebuild, knowing that of seedtime and harvest there is no end.

Farming is a family occupation. It is almost impossible for farming to be carried on by an individual person. It must always be a joint activity, and it has almost universally been a family activity. A farmer has to have a wife. There are tasks on the farm suitable for all ages, so that children may very early become economic assets, and elderly people remain capable of participating in the life of the farm long after they would be forced to retire if they lived in the city.

The farm home is usually the center of the farm business. The farmer may be in and out of the house frequently during the day. He need not go away from home to reach his daily work. This strengthens family life, because the father is with his family, and because the children see the father at his work and are able to work with him in many tasks.

Where farm families live on isolated farmsteads, the isolation from other families means that the family is thrown together not only in work but in recreation. Such isolation has its disadvantages, but it does strengthen family ties.

The small neighbourhood persists in rural life. Farmers cannot congregate in large cities. The resources with which they work cannot be stored in a small room, nor can the processes of agriculture be piled one above the other in tall buildings. Space is essential to farming, and the presence of the farmer at frequent intervals throughout the day and often the night is essential in the management of livestock. Thus, small neighbourhoods persist in rural areas. This is true whether farmers live in isolated farmsteads or in villages.

In the city, people form contacts chiefly with their own kind, with those who are congenial. They may not even know the names of people living next door. In the countryside, it is one's neighbours with whom one must work, must play, must live.

Farming embraces, and does not divide, the whole of life. The observation is often made that farming is a way of life rather than a way of making a living. Urban conditions tend to divide life into compartments. One has business associates and social friends. Men of the city often pride themselves on keeping these two separate. In the more highly industrialized parts of the world efforts have recently been made to "commercialize" farming, to put it "on a business basis." Many leaders doubt the social (to say nothing of the economic) wisdom of replacing the family farm with a corporate type of agriculture.

Throughout most of the rural world the family farm remains the dominant type of organization. On this family farm and in the agricultural village, play, work, learning, and worship—for each individual, for the family, and for the neighbourhood—are interwoven in a manner rare among urban people. Life is whole in the countryside.

These, then, are advantages and values of rural life on which the Christian programme may build and which it may utilize. (1) Farmers deal constantly with living things, with the biological world of which they are a part. (2) Farmers are constantly aware of the impersonal forces of the natural world, forces which witness to a power beyond them to whose ways they must conform. (3) Farmers have a sense of the continuity of life; they realize their bonds with the past and the future. (4) Farming is a family occupation. (5) The small neighbourhood persists in rural life. (6) Farming embraces, and does not divide, the whole of life.

DISADVANTAGES AND HANDICAPS

Rural living offers great opportunities, but it has disadvantages and handicaps, as well. A recognition of these is important in the development of the Christian rural programme. However, an important distinction between the nature of the advantages and the nature of the disadvantages is this: *the advantages of rural life are inherent, while the disadvantages are largely avoidable!*

Rural people have a minor voice in political administration. In most countries and in most generations, even where rural people have had rights of suffrage equal to those of the people of the city, the administration of government has tended to be dominated by the cities. There are obvious reasons for this. One is the fact that social contacts are more continuous in the cities. It is easier for people to congregate and to organize for political purposes. A second reason is that urban people are more inclined to place dependence upon political expedients than are rural people. They think more in terms of contracts, of "arrangements," of organization, whereas farmers look upon the natural factors affecting plant growth and animal health as being the most important forces determining their welfare.

One of the frequent injustices consequent on this dominance of the cities is the use of tax income derived chiefly from agricultural land for purposes which are of major benefit to urban people. Another is the tendency for freight rates and tariffs to be designed to benefit urban industries, at the expense of farmers. These are among the factors responsible for the current demand by farmers in the United States for "parity," a reasonable correspondence between the prices of those commodities which farmers buy and of those which they sell. In a country like India, which is over 75% rural, this dominance is mirrored in freight and tariff schedules favorable to industrial producers at the expense of the general consuming public.

That this handicap of subordinate political influence need not plague rural life is attested by the numerous examples of rural people having organized for purposes of political influence. The peasants of Denmark achieved dominant political influence in the late years of the last century, and farmers of the United States have considerable political power today. Nevertheless, urban people may always have relatively greater political power than country people.

It is important to keep in mind that certain of these handicaps of rural life invade the life of the church itself. There is a tendency for city churches to dominate denominational policy, aided by the same impersonal factors which result in the general political dominance of cities. Christian groups thus face the peril that, while the rural churches are chiefly responsible for Christian nurture and for church expansion, the policies of Christian groups are determined by those predisposed to over-value the relative importance of urban activities.[7]

[7] One who saw an early draft of this manuscript wrote: "I would like to know how many official bodies in the denominations promoting the Foreign

That this difficulty is not limited to countries largely urban and industrial is evident from a recent communication from the National Christian Council of China, putting the strengthening of city churches first on the list of emphases, on the mistaken grounds that Christianity spreads chiefly from the cities to the surrounding countryside.

Danger of becoming drugged by overwork. This danger is not peculiar to rural people. Miners are exposed to it, as are all people who have to perform heavy tasks of manual labor. Increasingly, too, we recognize that urban people in occupations requiring close and sustained attention face the same danger as those whose tasks require great physical exertion. But rural people, especially those who live in isolated farmsteads, are particularly exposed to this danger. Entirely too many rural people fall into the class typified by "The Man With The Hoe." Some are forced into it by the extreme poverty in which they live. Others with no such necessity fall into habits which absorb all of their energies in toil.

In cases of overwork for which extreme poverty is the reason, the remedy is such a revolution in agricultural and homemaking methods as will transfer the burden of toil to animals and to mechanical sources of power. Where the reason is any other than this, the provision of attractive neighbourhood activities can do much to alleviate this danger. There is involved here a problem in trusteeship of time and of abilities, discussed on pages 152-156. Rather than being an inherent weakness of rural life, this danger of overwork is a matter of allowing a virtue to be carried too far.

Paucity of leadership and artistic talent. Repeatedly, it is pointed out that rural life suffers from a paucity of talent for leadership in local activities. To the degree that this is the outcome of neighbourhoods being small, it is unavoidable. Obviously, there will be fewer talented musicians, fewer eloquent speakers in the small than in the large community. Moreover, certain urban occupations call for more constant exercise of the faculty for getting along with people, for participating in

Missions Conference (of North America) have any actual dirt farmers as members? In a given organization, local, district, state, or national, does the ratio of farmers in the executive or policy-determining bodies anywhere near approach the ratio of farmer membership in the total?"

social functions, than does the ocupation of farming. Participation in neighbourhood activities is, in a sense, "extra-curricular" to the tasks of farming, whereas it is inherent in many of the tasks of the city.

At the same time, it should be recognized that leadership in a rural neighbourhood is more difficult than it is in urban activities. In the village, all of one's life is known to many people. Any domestic or occupational weakness reduces a person's influence in local affairs. A higher quality of life is thus necessary in rural than in urban leadership because rural life is not segmented, people are well known to each other, and they must live together year after year and decade after decade.

While each neighbourhood has fewer people on whom to draw for leadership, civic ability usually increases or decreases with the civic burden which must be carried. For this reason, some rural neighbourhoods are finding it possible, through thorough-going cooperative organization of much of their life, to meet their own need for competent civic leadership.

Every group has its leader. A weakness of the Christian programme has often been its failure to reach and develop those who are the natural leaders of rural groups.

Tendency to imitate the city. This is both a danger and a result of other handicaps. We are becoming increasingly aware that, as literacy and education increase in rural areas, and as rural people move into industrialized cities, standards of urban culture are held up as the ideal, rather than distinctively rural values. The African going to work in the mines of Johannesburg takes back to his village standards of an urban-industrial civilization. The American farmer attending the cinema is confronted chiefly by urban ways and urban standards. Even the rural schools are, in many cases, developed along urban lines. As a consequence they tend to train youth for urban living, rather than for life on the farm.

Here, clearly, is a handicap which is not inherent. The city will always have a special lure for some people. But a rural culture which realizes its own values and makes these the touchstone of its educational and esthetic activities can eliminate, in large degree, this handicap of rural life.

H. Paul Douglass in his book, *The Little Community,* struck at the root of this problem in calling on the little towns to be fine little towns instead of trying to become miniature cities. The same challenge needs to be made to all of rural life.

Lack of social contacts. Whether or not this handicap exists depends chiefly on the type of rural organization. In regions where farms are large, families live on isolated farmsteads, and transportation is poor, it is a real handicap of rural life. However, most of the rural people of earth live in agricultural villages or on farmsteads which are fairly close together. In both these cases, there is no lack of social contacts.

Lack of social institutions. It is often pointed out that rural people have less adequate resources than city people in the way of schools, hospitals, medical care, etc. Where true, this may be due to a variety of causes, and therefore dependent on a number of cures. If the reason is political weakness, increased political participation and cooperation is called for. If the reason is partly poverty, even while the poverty is itself partially due to lack of these facilities, all-around improvement must be part of the remedy. It may be that acceptance of urban standards has encouraged rural young people interested in education and medicine to abandon the village for the city. If so, these misplaced standards are in error.

Very few people are entirely rural. Most of the people of the earth are a composite of rural and urban influences. Some, in an agricultural economy which is almost entirely self-sufficient, are almost exclusively rural. Some others, deep in the heart of industrial cities, are almost exclusively urban. But most men and women are partly rural and partly urban in outlook and in background. American farmers are close to the elemental background of plant and animal life and of the impersonal forces of nature, but they also have the contact with machinery, the use of non-human power, the dealing with financial credit, and the social contact through radio, newspaper, and national civic participation which are characteristically urban. Farmers in North India spend most of their waking hours among rural influences, yet they also identify themselves, to varying degrees, with the urban neighbourhoods in their vicinity.

SUMMARY

The Christian mission among rural people must take full cognizance of the background of rural life. It must recognize the *importance* of rural life, both because of the large proportion of the people of the earth who live in the countryside, and because of the fact that it is the rural families who populate and re-populate the cities. It must recognize the *inherent advantages and values* of rural life, in order that it may nurture, develop, and build them. It must know the *dangers and weaknesses* of rural life, so that these may be overcome.

2.

The Christian Message: For the Whole of Life

HOWEVER many glimpses of the ways of God one may meet elsewhere, the acquaintance with him and with his ways most needed by men is to be gained through Jesus Christ. "That God exists is testified by reason, conscience, and nature with its wonders. But *who* God is—God Himself must tell us in His Revelation."[1] Evidences of God are all around one in the countryside, and so are grand opportunities for great living, once the import of these opportunities has been revealed and understood. Thus, *Christ stands between the witness of the natural world to God and the fulfilment of man and the natural world in the purpose of God.*

We have noted in Chapter I something about the men and women to whom this Christian revelation comes in the countryside. Each of them is a bio-psycho-socio-spiritual organism; biological in the form and function of his body; psychological in the concepts conjured up by his mind (to affect, in turn, his actions and his dreams); sociological in his solidarity with his fellows in their joys, their sorrows, their sins, their achievements; spiritual in his longing to understand his place in the world, and in his potentiality of transcending the plane of physical living; and an organism in the intricate interaction of each of these with all of the others.

A recent statement by William A. Smart, in his Lyman Beecher lectures at Yale, seems to put in words of our day an essential element of the Christian message to these rural people. Jesus, in revealing God, he says, ". . . made men discover a new dimension in life. He made them conscious of their places in an eternal kingdom of spirit. They dared claim kinship with God, to know themselves immortal. It was not a matter of

1 Brunner, Emil, *Our Faith*. New York: Charles Scribner's Sons, 1936, p. 6. Used by permission.

believing in God's existence but rather of being lifted up to his level."[2] *Lifting people up out of the limitations of animal life,* away from susceptibility to death *into life which is eternal,* this is the redemption, the salvation, of rural people accomplished through the revelation of God's purpose in Jesus Christ.

John Mackay expressed the same understanding in words which further develop its meaning when he wrote, in *A Preface to Christian Theology,* "Redemption, the participation of man in the life of God, is thus found by the seeker to be the meaning and the goal of Biblical truth."[3] *The participation of man in the life of God* thus becomes the invitation extended to men through Jesus Christ.

It has been pointed out repeatedly through the centuries that this invitation to participate in the life of God does not mean that the Christian is to live in a spiritual instead of in a physical world. Rather, he is to live in this spiritual-physical world while trying to look at all people and at all problems with the eyes of God. He is to treat people as children of God, and as potential sons in the spirit. He is to shape things to meet the needs of man.[4] When he participates in the life of God and looks at the world with God's eyes, his body, his time, his abilities and skills, his cultural background, his material possessions, his income, all become resources to be husbanded for the benefit of God's children, and he sees each of the sciences and the arts, each profession and vocation, in its true light as an avenue for glorifying God.

Having met the Christ, farmers put their ploughs into soil which they recognize as God's soil, using draught animals and mechanical principles recognized as elements in the working of God, to produce food for men, women, and children now recognized to be creatures of God, called to be his sons and

[2] Smart, William A., "Old Wine in New Bottles," in *Preaching in These Times,* New York: Charles Scribner's Sons, 1940, p. 138. Used by permission.

[3] Mackay, J. A., *A Preface to Christian Theology,* New York: The Macmillan Company, 1941. Used by permission.

[4] "One of the most curious of all heresies in Christianity has been the tendency to place spirit over against matter. . . . In between the religions which would deny matter outright and those which would deify and worship natural and 'fleshly' impulses, stands the Christianity which would neither deny the material nor worship it, but which would seek to control it for the highest and best life of men." McConnell, Francis J., *Human Needs and World Christianity,* New York: Friendship Press, 1929, p. 45.

daughters in the spirit. Having met the Christ, rural women manage households in the light of the understanding that these are the most important workshops, the most significant social groups of earth, for these households are where children are moulded and where the lasting human satisfactions which sustain parents are achieved. Having met the Christ, rural boys and girls study in schools which they see to be instruments for seeking out the ways of God, for understanding the structure of his universe in order to cooperate with its ways, for appropriating the heritage of their people and the revelation of their Lord, for helping them in their growth toward the fulness of the stature of mature children of God. All have learned that the means which Jesus used were at least as important as the ends which he sought. His was the winning strength of forgetting himself in loving others, of overcoming evil by the sheer power of the good, the joy of letting go of the lower to grasp the higher.

Moreover, this participation in the life of God includes participation both in creation and in redemption. Nicholas Berdyaev calls attention particularly to the first of these:

> Christian anthropology should unfold the conception of man as a creator who bears the image and likeness of the Creator of the world. This implies that man is a free and spiritual being capable of rising above nature and of dominating it. . . . Man is both a fallen and a sinful creature, split into two and longing for wholeness and salvation, and a creative being called to continue the work of building the world and endowed for the purpose with gifts from above.[5]

Thus all of the creative tasks of the farm, home, and village, are fields for participating in fulfilling God's purposes. God is not dead; he is living. God has not ceased creating; he is ever creating. He is using the seeds of the field, the rain and the sunshine, the instincts of men and women, and the processes of growth. Wherever men offer their wills to him, he uses, as well, men's minds, children's kindnesses, and mothers' loyalties. Men and women who learn of God through Christ may become co-creators with God, and the opportunities for this co-creation extend through the whole range of life's interests and activities. They are found in the field, in the home, in

[5] Berdyaev, Nicholas, *The Destiny of Man,* London: Centenary Press, 1937, p. 65.

neighbourhood gatherings, in civic participation, and within the world-wide fellowship of Christians. In this fundamental sense, the Christian message is for all of life. Let us recall here our observation in Chapter I on the values of rural life, that cultivation and husbandry, concerned as they are with seed and birth and growth and regeneration, make understanding of this cooperation in creation particularly easy for people who live in the countryside.

In all contacts among people, there is the second opportunity for participation in redemption—for cooperating with the Holy Spirit in drawing men to God through sacrificial love, and for redeeming organizations and secular programmes by revealing the functions they might be fulfilling in the purposes of God. We have been more mindful of that portion of this role which deals with individuals than we have with the call to redeem groups and to cooperate in creation.

Creation and redemption: always these are linked in the Christian revelation of the purpose of God. Each is partial without the other. God's call to man is to participate with him in both.

God's redemption of man in his son Jesus Christ is, thus, a release from the sin, the self-centeredness, of man, and an initiation of man into fellowship in God's own eternal, creative, and redemptive activities.

Because man and all the materials of earth are involved in these purposes of God which Christ reveals, it is clear that in revealing God, Jesus revealed man. He came as a flash of lightning which, in illuminating the heavens, lights the earth as well. In delineating the purpose of the Great Spirit, he defines the function of material resources. In establishing fellowship between God and man, he establishes the norm for healthy relationships among men. In introducing the music of eternity, he tunes to a high pitch the significance of each moment of time. In literal truth, the revelation of God in Jesus Christ transforms the whole of life.

WHAT ARE THE IMPLICATIONS OF THE CHRISTIAN MESSAGE FOR THE WHOLE OF LIFE?

> We have frequently said that Christianity is not just a theology but a way of life. . . . Then we left the phrase "Christianity a way of life" hanging in mid-air until it be-

came just as much of an abstraction as the theology which went before it.[6]

This challenge is well founded. Must we simply say that Christianity is "for all of life," and leave it at that? Or is it possible to be more specific, to discern some of the specific attitudes and actions which are demanded by Christian discipleship? Is it possible to make explicit some of the attitudes which we hold to be implicit in the Christian gospel itself? Much of the writing in the field of rural missions in the past generation is made up of attempts to do exactly this. This literature reveals that certain areas of rural life have received a great amount of attention while others have been virtually ignored.

It is convenient to divide the opportunities and problems of rural life into three categories in discussing the implications of the life and teachings of Jesus for them. These are: (1) implications for social relationships, (2) implications for trusteeship of resources, and (3) implications for inner experience.

In trying to discern these implications, one may simply state the general principles which the Christian spirit would seem to call for within a given area of life, or one may go beyond these general principles to particular concrete problems and incidents in rural life. In the remainder of this chapter, we shall treat the general principles which seem to represent the Christian spirit in each of these areas of life, reserving for Part II[7] the expansion of what seems to be the consensus of Christian thought as to definite implications of the Christian spirit for particular rural problems.

It cannot be too strongly urged that in exploring these implications of Christian faith we are not playing around on the periphery of the legitimate interest of Christians, but are seeking to discern constituent portions of this gospel itself for rural people in our day. Christ continues to insist that spectators cannot learn the secrets of God. Even today his reply to the questioner is, Come and see. Come out into the whole of life, treating each person as I treat him, using all materials as I have revealed to you that God would have them used,

[6] Green, Shirley, "A Church Program for the Rural Community," *Christian Rural Fellowship Bulletin*, No. 62.

[7] See page 135.

growing in fellowship with the Father within your own heart. *Only when you do this, moving out into the whole of life upon our Father's errands, will you begin to know the Father who sent me.*

Implications for social relationships. Since men and women everywhere are potentially sons and daughters of God, Christian faith has definite implications for all social relationships. It has been said that three-quarters of the teaching of Jesus has to do with the relations of men to one another,[8] and "in almost every New Testament Epistle, while the first part deals with some Christian truth, the last part of the writing deals wholly with social rights and duties—the stout stem of doctrine blossoming out into practical ethics. . . . No modern treatise on social science is more obviously and directly concerned with social obligations and abuses of every kind than are those New Testament letters which set forth Christ as the Master of mankind."[9]

Whether it be within the family, within the neighbourhood, or within the broad brotherhood of men across the earth, the implications of the gospel for relationships among men are those following from the recognition of all men as equal in the sight of God, regardless of position, ability, caste or class, sex, race, or attainments.

The primitive relationship between human beings is one of subservience of the individual to the interest of the group, coupled with almost complete lack of concern for the welfare of other groups. In primitive society the individual is of secondary importance; it is the group which is primary.[10] "Personal freedom," "individual initiative," "personal rights" are little known and rigidly limited concepts among primitive peoples and even in some highly developed civilizations. Ask a villager, plodding along a path in India, who he is, and he will respond not with his own name but with that of his caste.

But in such cultures this dominance of the interests of the group over those of the individual tends to stop at the boundary of the clan, or tribe, or caste. All other tribes are beyond con-

[8] Faunce, W. H. P., *The Social Aspects of Foreign Missions,* New York: Missionary Education Movement, 1914, p. 18. Used by permission.

[9] *Ibid.,* p. 20.

[10] See the section on "The Individual and the Tribe" pp. 24-30 in *Out of Africa* by Emory Ross, New York: Friendship Press, 1936.

sideration. They are the Samaritans, the outcastes, the barbarians. Within the group there is submergence of individual personality and exaltation of the group; between such groups there is often indifference or enmity.

The Christian spirit fosters two seemingly opposite tendencies. On the one hand, it declares the sovereign worth of each individual, as distinct from the group of which he is a part. On the other, it widens the circle of men within which the liberated individual ought voluntarily to subordinate his personal interests to those of the group, until it includes all men everywhere. While recognizing and seeking to retain the valid contributions of the family, the neighbourhood, and the state, the Christian spirit emphasizes individual sovereignty and calls for voluntary loyalty to the whole human family. Christians in Africa and in the Orient have the unique opportunity of trying to gain the values of individual freedom and world-wide sympathy and loyalty without losing the values of social solidarity and group responsibility found in the larger family and in communal groups, but so nearly lost in Western countries. In achieving this synthesis, they will overcome both excessive individualism, on the one hand, and the inertia of a binding traditionalism that smothers personal rights and growth, on the other.

This is the general principle of which the implications of the gospel as to the relationships between men under different circumstances and in different capacities are applications: individual sovereignty with voluntary loyalty to the whole human family. The groups of men, such as the family, the guild, the neighbourhood, the nation, become opportunities for achieving brotherhood in different ways and in different degrees.

Current writings and experience in the Christian movement identify and analyze five types of social relationships for which the will of God is to be sought. First come relationships between members of the family. Next are three types of relationships within the local neighbourhood: relationships between individuals, relationships of individuals to groups, and relationships between groups. Finally, there are the relationships of the wider social order. All of these are significant contacts between sons and daughters of God, and it becomes part of the task of rural Christian discipleship to seek the judgment of the Christian insight upon each of them.

Our recognition of the necessity for Christian judgment is of longer standing for some of these types of social relationships than it is for others. Our understanding of the implications of the life and teachings of Jesus for social relationships *within the family* and *between individuals within the local neighbourhood* are long-established but in danger of being neglected. Our understanding of the implications for *relationships between individuals and groups, between groups in the local neighbourhood,* and for those *within the wider social order* are the subject of considerable concern by some but are evaded by others.

We are always in danger of making one of two mistakes. We may slight the implications long-established (honesty, chastity, humility, etc.) in our preoccupation with modern insights ("social consciousness," security of tenure, equality of opportunity, etc.), or we may ignore the latter, justifying ourselves by the comment that they are immature. The first error is fatal in that it abandons insights essential to true interpretation of the Christian message and to the achievement of Christian discipleship. The second is vicious in that it distorts and emasculates the Christian message by its own ignorance of burning contemporary moral issues in rural life.[11]

Implications for trusteeship of resources. "And man shall have dominion over the fish of the sea, and over the birds of the heavens, and over the cattle, and over all the earth, and over every creeping thing that creepeth upon the earth." Jesus, by implication at least, accepted and built upon this principle out of the Old Testament. In other words, the soil, the plants, the animals, and all of the non-living things among which the farmer and his family live are *resources* to be utilized in the development and enrichment of human life.

Toward all of these resources the Christian attitude is that of *trusteeship*. Individual men of a particular generation did not create the materials of the earth with which they work, nor were those resources created for their particular generation alone. Each of us stands in a great succession, born upon an earth and into a culture developed before his time and needed by his children and by his children's children. Each of us, there-

[11] See the summary of recent Christian judgment in these fields of rural social relationships on page 137 ff.

fore, is a trustee, administering for the common good of all people resources which he has had little or no hand in creating, and therefore little or no right to control in pursuit of his own advantage. Rights of "ownership" can have validity only in so far as they contribute to a wise utilization of non-human resources for the common good (or as they make it possible for persons to remain free rather than to become themselves "resources" which other men may manipulate and control).

There has been a growing re-discovery, within recent years, of Old Testament teachings with respect to trusteeship of resources. This is partly due to the fact that the ethical principles of the Old Testament are almost entirely in terms of rural life and of rural resources. More important, in all probability, is the fact that the insights of the Old Testament with respect to God's will for the relationships between men and the resources of his world were so sound that Jesus found little need to revise them. About social relationships he could use the approach that "ye have heard it said by them of old times . . . but I say unto you." With respect to trusteeship of resources, the insights of them of old times had been correct.

It is perhaps this very fact which has to such a large degree eclipsed consideration of the will of God for the handling of resources. Perhaps in preoccupation with the New Dispensation, with that which was unique in Jesus Christ, with that which distinguished the new Christian community from its Jewish ancestry, the valid revelations God had given of his will before-times came to be neglected.

Today these insights are being rediscovered, and men are realizing that God has a purpose for *all* of life, not just for relationships between people but for attitudes toward resources: toward *material resources,* toward *abilities and skills,* toward *cultural resources,* toward *the human body,* toward *time,* toward *income.* The historic revelation of that will is recorded chiefly in the Old Testament, so we go back to it today to study its message afresh and to search for practices which are valid for the needs of our day; just as the Year of Jubilee, the Principle of the First Fruits, tithing, and the rules for land utilization described in Deuteronomy were for those times.

It might be pointed out that certain Oriental, African, and primitive American cultures contain splendid traditions of trusteeship particularly with respect to land, and are (in this regard) more sound than the over-emphasis, in European culture, on the prerogatives of private ownership. The ancient Hindu village owned its land in common and parcelled this land out to families according to their needs, with provision for periodic re-distribution, along lines very similar to those followed by the Hebrews. The Congo village of today grants temporary rights to cultivate; land is now owned outright by individuals or families.

"The earth is the Lord's, and the fulness thereof" is an insight much more widespread than the Hebrew tradition. That man is meant to have dominion over the other creatures of earth is less universally comprehended. Particularly does Hindu philosophy, with its belief in transmigration and its consequent uneconomic attitude toward barren cattle and field pests, deny divine sanction for such dominion.

Such traditions of sound trusteeship of agricultural resources as are found in indigenous cultures should be fostered, and, where necessary, restored. They are fully Christian in import.

It seems strange that so much of the discussion of stewardship (trusteeship) among Christians should have been concerned with the utilization of income, for *the fundamental resources are not income but are* (1) *material resources,* (2) *abilities and skills,* (3) *cultural resources,* (4) *the human body, and* (5) *time.* It is these, first of all, of which men are to be trustees. Where they are free to choose their vocations on the basis of the way in which their aptitudes and skills can make the greatest contribution to the common good, they will seek to assume trusteeship over such available resources as will help them to make that contribution. The amount of "income" which each receives as the result of this trusteeship depends upon the economic institutions of the society in which he happens to live. This income often will bear little relationship to his contribution to the common good. But whatever it is, it does itself constitute an additional resource. The repeated and numerous references to stewardship of income in our churches have been unfortunate only in so far as they have diverted attention from the necessity for trusteeship of the more fundamental resources.[12]

The implications of the life and teachings of Jesus for trusteeship of resources have been in a sort of "no-man's-land"

12 *See* summary of recent Christian judgment in the field of trusteeship of rural resources on pp. 149-151.

in recent years. On the one hand, there have been many rural leaders who have seen the relevance of these problems and have been concerned about their neglect. These people have been particularly concerned about the problems of soil conservation, of wasted time, of cultural losses. On the other hand there have been some who have failed to see how these matters are integral to the Christian gospel itself, and who have tended to try to rule them out of the Christian programme.

Arthur T. Mosher stated the need for realizing the importance of this phase of the Christian gospel in "The Kingdom of God and Rural Reconstruction":

Our interpretation of the Gospel records must include an emphasis on Stewardship including health, time, productive resources, and personal ability, as well as cash in hand. I doubt if this has been given anything like as thorough interpretation as have implications of personal morality. One gets the impression that most references to stewardship precede or accompany opportunities for contributing money to various causes. Important as these are, they by no means end the implications . . . as we would all agree.

I feel this weak spot in our program very keenly. It seems to me that this is the foundation in the Christian Gospel for many activities into which allegiance to Jesus Christ has forced us, yet which, because of the lack of a fuller explanation of stewardship in our presentation of the Gospel, have been forced into a secular position. . . .

There is a neglected bud on the tree of the Christian program, out of which it was intended that there should grow the branch of Christian stewardship. The branch of stewardship will bear the fruit of health, nurtured by a knowledge of the rules of hygiene and sanitation, and by the practice of scientific medicine. It will bear the fruit of efficient production of material goods for the use of God's children, nurtured by technical skill and the desire to use most fully our talents of time and of productive resources. It will bear the fruit of highly trained and consecrated workers in many fields, motivated by the desire to be good stewards of personal abilities. Unless or until that branch develops as it should, the tree of the Christian program does not truly represent the Christian Gospel. Our Christian program in rural areas must include, in its interpretation of the Gospel in terms of village living, an increased, and realistic emphasis on stewardship of personal abilities of time, of productive resources.[13]

[13] Mosher, Arthur T., "The Kingdom of God and Rural Reconstruction," *Christian Rural Fellowship Bulletin*, No. 56.

Implications for inner experience. Inner transformation of the individual is an important outcome of entry into the life of God through Jesus Christ. The Good News is to be worked out in every relationship with men, with ideas, with materials, —worked out by individuals in whom and by groups in which it is itself working a transformation. The language of the Great Commandment is in terms of inner decision and commitment: "Thou shalt love the Lord thy God with all thy heart and with all thy soul, and with all thy mind." Jesus was making explicit that which was already implicit, when he added, "And the second is like unto it, Thou shalt love thy neighbor as thyself."

To the degree that any person enters the discipleship of the Master, he finds his life centering in the will of God. He accepts that will as the most important consideration in all of his affairs. This does not weaken his own initiative and power, but rather gives these a place in the great encompassing plan of God for mankind, and thus he finds new meaning in the smallest happenings of life. Acceptance of the purpose of God as the dominating goal of all that he does makes it possible for him to relate everything that happens to him to the larger plan of God, and to the lives of others. Even in hardship, disaster, suffering, and death his commitment is eternal—given unreservedly to God who lives and suffers with him.

The inner secret of life for Jesus was the consciousness that God was with and in him all the day and every day. The gospel should bring rural people into this same realization of the presence of God. For God is not less with the farmer as he performs his daily tasks than when he is worshipping in the village church. "Lo, I am with you always." As each farmer grows in discipleship this becomes more clear to him and he feels God's presence in the fields as he tills the soil, in the mill as he grinds his grain, in the privacy of his family circle, and as he carries or hauls his produce along the dusty highway to market.[14]

To this continual presence the disciple responds in worship and in commitment to apply the implications of the gospel throughout all of life. He commits himself to following Jesus, realizing that with his first commitment he neither comprehends all, nor is perfected in all of his ways; but that as he

[14] Brother Lawrence, in *The Practice of the Presence of God,* remarked that a kitchen is as appropriate a place for worship as is an altar.

faces toward the goal which Jesus sets before his followers, he may expect to learn as he follows, and to find more and more inner strength coming from God's spirit to empower him for the tasks of discipleship. Jesus felt the need of frequent withdrawals for the special vigil of prayer, but all the day long, preaching, moving along the paths, healing the sick, he was in that intimacy with the Father which is essentially prayer.

To this co-living God makes response in significant ways. He sheds light upon life's meaning and upon man's rôle in the universe. He gives direction in daily living: in personal contact of the spirit of man with the spirit of God, in fellowship with Jesus Christ, through people who are trying to study and show the will of God, in the expression of God's will in the Bible.

The Christian recognizes that God is working in the processes that he sees all about him and in those that are within him. Jesus saw the activities of his Father in the lilies and in the grass. His followers recognize "the miracle and mystery"[15] of God's hand and thought in the reproduction of human, plant, and animal life. They may detect his creating and sustaining hand in the development of their children. They may come to realize that in applying scientific methods of agriculture, in observing in the home the laws of hygiene, sanitation, and sound nutrition, in protecting soil against erosion, and in supplying irrigation water to thirsty crops, they are cooperating in the ways of an ever-living, ever-creative Father.

Just as God works with man and man with God in the production of food, so is God present in the processes of thought, in the expression of feelings and emotion, and in faith. When one thinks, feel, wills, he is not alone. God is in him, not domineering, not dictating, but cooperating. As the Christian comes to realize that the thinking and willing and feeling of human beings are channels through which God works for the building of the Kingdom, he can cooperate joyously in the faith that God will use his cooperation for his own high purpose.

Man's work in garden or field or at the forge, and woman's work in preparing food or in attending to the needs of her children, are lifted from the plane of drudgery when one sees in them the element of fellowship in work with the Creator of

[15] Ziegler, E. K., "A Christian Rural Life Philosophy," *Christian Rural Fellowship Bulletin,* No. 67.

all things. God works among his plants and animals, and so does man. God provides healing processes for diseased or torn tissues, and man's skill can hasten these processes. God has uses in nature for rain and wind, cold and heat, sunshine and darkness, and man can study and practise to make these more effective. George Washington Carver once said, "The things are already there. God, working through my hands, brings them to light."

As man works with God, he grows closer to him.

Jesus lived at peace with himself because of the completeness of his commitment. There was no faltering nor confusion nor uncertainty in the manner of his daily living. His inner satisfaction came from his complete understanding of the meaning and purpose of life, through his oneness with God in knowledge and in fellowship. He lived in constant obedience to the implications of this relationship for all of life. He recognized how revolutionary these attitudes and their consequences were to self-centred men. He felt the joy of being obedient to the heavenly vision, amid the violent opposition and persecution of a world of men to whom such a vision was largely foreign.

His peace, the "peace of God," was not the peace of repose, but the poise of purposeful endeavor. Jesus lived with agitation and turmoil and trouble all about him, involving him personally, and involving those whom he loved. But he met all these with majestic strength and confidence.

A river is the most perfect parable that nature offers of the meaning of Christian peace. A river, not a stagnant pool; the Jordan, not the Dead Sea. For what is a river? It is a flowing way. Waters that come tumbling down a thousand hillsides, purposeless and unchannelled, and ofttimes agents of destruction in an unhappy countryside, find their way at last into a single river bed. From the moment of confluence, where they commit themselves to a common channel, their bed is made. They are at peace. The channel will lead them by many a strange way to the sea, which is their goal. In the upland plateaus the waters flow perchance through sunlit meadows, "quiet," like those in the shepherd's Psalm. Anon they disappear in a dark mountain gorge, plunging headlong in swirling eddies through "caverns measureless to man." Farther on they rush to the brink of a cataract and, in foam and thunder, shoot across its brow. Then, like the waters of Niagara, they continue their lordly way till they reach the sea.

But through all the changes of its chequered way, the river is at peace, for its bed is made.[16]

It was such peace that Jesus promised to his disciples when near the close of his days on earth he said, "Peace I leave with you, my peace I give unto you. . . . Let not your heart be troubled, neither let it be afraid." From the acceptance of God's will and purpose as omnipotent in the affairs of men there comes to the disciple this simple and rugged peace. New commitments to meet new situations bring renewal of contentment: not a contentment which sees no wrongs to right, but a contentment which knows that striving is not in vain. Greed for wealth and lust for personal power lose their force. The fear of failure and of frustration is broken. In their places comes a glad recognition of a loving Father who desires the welfare of his children, yet who depends on them to cooperate with him, and to turn, of their own free will, to accept his love. This transformation is the key to integrated personality and to that freedom which makes constructive living possible.

In Christians of the countryside, these results of Christian discipleship on inner experience merge with characteristics to which all rural people are heir.

The slow and patient processes of nature: the germination of the seed, the long summer days that must pass before the wheat gleams golden in the sun and the fruit is ready to drop from the bough, these speak not of ruthless haste and hectic living but of patient waiting for the things of God. Patience is a quality of soul more easily possessed by those who live on land. Confidence and hope of the "harvest abundant" as the result of faithful toil are present in the farmer's heart as he watches the corn ripening in the sun and the fruit taking shape on the branch. The fisherman, too, casting his net into the sea knows that there are "times and seasons" and that he must patiently but hopefully await the draught. Poise and quietness enter the heart as faithfully, year by year, the farmers of the world follow the seasons.

Jesus was heir to this heritage of the countryside. He was born in a stable, with farm animals nearby and shepherds tending their flocks by night on the surrounding pasture-lands. He grew to manhood in a village, becoming intimate with the fields and hills around him. His baptism was in the flowing

[16] Mackay, *op. cit.* p. 129. Used by permission.

stream of the Jordan, and it was through the open heavens that God spoke: "This is my beloved son." He called his disciples from the waters of the lake of Galilee to be fishers of men. Under a fig tree and sitting at the receipt of custom they heard his call to "Follow me." His pulpits were almost entirely wayside spots, close to fragrant fields, or sunlit sea, or sloping hillsides. Stirring words that have echoed through the centuries were given to a woman at a well, to fishermen bringing their boats to land, and to little children who gathered around his knee. His transfiguration took place on a mountain top and his acclamation as king on an open highway, with flowers and palm branches flung before him.

The narrow path to Calvary was open to the heavens. The cross on which he died was taken from a tree of the forest. Jesus was mistaken for a gardener when he first appeared to Mary after the crucifixion. It was on the road to Emmaus that he left the hearts of the disciples burning within them. He was made known to his disciples by the breaking of bread beside a lake. Close to the village of Bethany he ascended unto his Father.

He loved the quiet countryside, the lake of Galilee, the hills of Judea, the tranquil valleys, the lilies blooming by the wayside. The beauty of the sunrise heralding a new day of life and opportunity; the flaming sunset showing forth the glory of God; the purple twilight with its promise of rest from the labor of the field; the starry heavens; and the beauty of the sea and sky and land, of waving grain, of still waters, of tranquil woodland, all give a sense of God's unfailing power and divine love, and help man to develop strength and serenity of spirit.

We covet painting, music, sculpture, and good literature for rural people, but they are not indispensable. In the country, nature paints beautiful pictures, birds and the wind and streams provide music, and all about are God's open books. With or without art from men's hands, the souls of country-men may be enlarged, with that fulness of appreciation of the great intangibles that Paul had when he wrote, "Whatsoever things are true, whatsoever things are honourable, whatsoever things are just, whatsoever things are pure, whatsoever things are lovely, whatsoever things are of good report, if there be any virtue, and if there be any praise, think on these things."

SUMMARY

The Christian message is one for all of life. Because it brings to earth the will of God for men, it reveals the relationships which God would have prevail between all men, in their families, as individuals and as groups within their neighbourhoods, and in their relationships in the wider social order. It reveals the way in which God would have men regard the resources he has given them: bodies, time, abilities, cultural resources, and material things, and it determines standards for trusteeship of income. The experience of having God revealed through contact with Jesus Christ, and of seeking to follow his will for all of life, works changes which can amount to transformation in the inner lives of Christians.

In the light of such a comprehension, how futile it is to try to segregate the "religious needs," or the social or economic or physical needs of man! Man, rooted in the physical world of soil, plants, animals, society, birth, and death, is called by a seeking God to become his child in the spirit. Truly, such a gospel is for all of life!

3.

Christian Achievement and Witness: Through the Whole of Life

ACHIEVING Christian discipleship and witnessing to one's faith in God are phases of the same process. They are inseparable. Both are present in all of the activities and attitudes of life. In this chapter, these activities are analyzed to discover what contributions each makes to this dual role of the Christian life.

JESUS CAME LIVING

Jesus came living; seeking, as God is always seeking, for sons and daughters to participate in his own life. It was life that Jesus was proclaiming and it is only by life that life may be created.

Jesus came working, taking up the stubborn stuff of earth and fashioning it to meet the needs of men, sowing seed in the springtime that the harvest of God's green kingdom might feed the bodies of men, taking part in the tasks of the family and, very likely, assuming major responsibility for family support as Joseph laid down his tools.

Jesus came being friendly, tarrying in the home of Lazarus in simple companionship, dining through the evening in the home of Simon, refreshing his comrades by washing their road-worn feet, and gathering children about his knee because he loved them and enjoyed their company.

Since life is a spending and a recuperation, Jesus came re-creating: toiling through the daytime, then slipping away at night to rest; pouring out his spirit to those whom he loved, then disappearing into the shadows to meet his Father and to have that spirit restored, replenished, re-created. Of course the strength went out of his body when the woman touched his garment! That is life. Jesus knew the secret of re-creating that strength. As leaves of plants utilize the light from the sun to transmute chemical elements into the stuff of life, so Jesus learned to utilize the spirit of the Eternal to recreate the ever-wasting spirit of man. Jesus came praying. And Jesus came re-creating the bodies of men, repairing the damage done by disease and by despair, building the health of men because he knew the interdependence of the body and of the spirit, valuing the body which is the instrument of the spirit's contact with the life of earth.

Jesus came living: living on earth by eternal standards, loving men actively and consistently even through the experiences of repudiation and execution, revealing thereby the atoning power of such living in the sight of God, conquering death for his followers as individuals and as a church.

Jesus came living. Shall anyone say that it was only when he spoke that men learned of him? Or did Peter, long after the Master had gone, remember the morning Jesus could not be found because he had gone out into the hills to pray, and learn of him by remembering? When Matthew wrote into his account the incident of the children, it was Jesus's words which he recorded, but it was words embodied in the incident; for what caused him to remember those words so many years later except the vivid recollection of what Jesus had done, except that impressive vignette of living, the brushing aside of adults, of disciples, to recognize children and to memorialize their dignity?

Jesus came living: working, being friendly, cooperating, health-building, studying, teaching, recreating, worshipping, preaching, witnessing—activities never to be separated in life, facets of one purpose, phases of one process. They are separated arbitrarily here to try to discover what each is capable of contributing to the tasks of the Christian programme; to that first task which is that of setting the stage, preparing the hearts of men that God may touch them as with a spark, converting them into his sons in the spirit; and to that second task of expressing, in all of the affairs of men, the discipleship of the Christian community. These two—achieving Christian discipleship, and human witness to Christian faith—are the same process: that of Christian living.

WORKING

However much their work may be lightened by planning and by mechanical improvements, it is by physical labour that farmers finally accomplish their tasks. It is by toil that the sod is turned, the seed sown, the weeds removed, the harvest cut, and the grain threshed, providing food for the sons of men. It

CONTRIBUTIONS OF WORKING

a. Primary contribution–accomplishment of worthy tasks to meet the needs of men
b. Concomitant contributions
   1) Realization of cooperation with God in creation
   2) Fuller comprehension of God
      a) God's power
      b) God's love
   3) Sense of achievement
   4) Contribution to health: physical, mental, emotional
   5) Appreciation of duty rightfully to use all resources
      a) Natural
      b) Income
   6) Toughening of moral fibre through discipline

is by toil that hands are made skilful in the performance of daily tasks, in the alleviation of pain, in the baking of bread, and in the management of an orderly household. When that toil issues in a trusteeship of resources well accounted for in production of goods to meet the needs of people in sending out sons and daughters clothed, strong, and trained to acquit themselves creditably in the world of men, it has made real contributions to Christian discipleship.

Frank Price, missionary to the rural church in China, tells of the experience of a young Chinese minister helping, with his own hands, build a village house of worship.

The city minister told me that the few hours with those farmers, toiling with his hands for God, and having a part in the making of the little church, marked a high spiritual experience in his life. . . . *The Kingdom of God comes in the rural vocation* when the human-divine significance of the rural vocation is seen and felt and expressed. We work for God! We work with God! A Christian farmer can say that not only when he is building a village chapel but in all his daily labor. . . . 'We are fellow-workers with God.' Where is that more evident and true than in agriculture and in the various occupations of rural life? No wonder that in China and in all agricultural lands the religion of the people, the popular faith, is closely associated with the work of the farmer and the natural forces with which he must deal. In our Christian faith God's kingdom comes as we see the sacredness of our task; as we consecrate all labor on the soil, all nurture of growing things, all of our tiny part in ongoing creation, to God, the Source of all life, the Everlasting Creator; . . . This is not a truth we make, but a truth we discover—that we can be partners with God in the creating of His world.[1]

It is by working that this lesson is finally driven home.

There are many ways in which farm and home work may contribute to one's comprehension of God. The toil involved in the production of a single crop or in the care of a flower garden hints at the limitless power of God exhibited by his universe. The value a farmer puts on a bit of his own handiwork—a crop of corn, an improved variety of fruit—hints at the love of God for his creation. And when some bit of his construction has gone awry or comes to destruction, the farmer experiences in faint fashion the pain which the waywardness of men can cost a loving Creator. When parents labor day by day with loving hands and hearts that their child may be fed and clothed, they, too, may come to understand more clearly the tenderness and care of God for his children. If that child, grown to manhood or womanhood, departs from the traditions of the home and casts his or her lot with the dissipated or with the profligate, the parents come to understand more fully God's forgiveness. Faint as is the image, these experiences give the concepts of the power and love of God's emotional rootage, and therefore greater meaning.

The sense of achievement in having spent one's self in a worthwhile task is itself a valuable contribution to the poise of a personality.

We are so accustomed to these essentials—to the rain, the wind, the soil, the sea, the sunrise, the trees, the sustenance—that we may not include them in the categories of the good things, and we endeavor to satisfy ourselves with many small and trivial and exotic gratifications; and when these gratifications fail or pall, we find ourselves helpless and resourceless. The joy of sound sleep, the relish of a sufficient meal of plain and wholesome food, *the desire to do a good day's work and the recompense when at night we are tired from the doing of it,* the exhilaration of fresh air, the exercise of the natural powers, *the mastery of a situation or a problem—*

[1] Price, Frank W., "The Kingdom of God in a Rural Community," *Christian Rural Fellowship Bulletin,* No. 33.

these and many others like them *are fundamental satisfactions, beyond all pampering and all toys,* and they are of the essence of goodness. I think we should teach all children how good are the common necessities, and how very good are the things that are made in the beginning.[2]

Very often, the conditions under which the products of the farm are sold tend to destroy any feeling of service in meeting human needs. David Grayson, in *The Countryman's Year,* tells the story of setting off to market full of pride in the honey which he is taking to be sold. By the time prospective buyers have criticised its qualities in every possible way in order to beat down the price, all of Grayson's happiness is gone. This practice of depreciating a product's quality in settling on a price is common to many cultures. Any change of marketing practices which allows the seller to retain pride in his product is to be supported. In some instances, the development of cooperative marketing can achieve this.

Physical labour, if not in excess, makes a positive contribution to the health of the body and of the mind. It may reveal an interest or aptitude previously undreamed of which may become the basis of one's vocation. When a worker has put time and effort upon a bit of material, making from it a thing of beauty or of utility, his appreciation of beauty in form and design is stimulated. Workmen who take pride in doing their jobs well and find satisfactions in the creation of beauty are likely, in turn, to become more appreciative of beauty elsewhere. The worker may come to dislike shoddy or cheap products and to decry the waste involved in spoiling good material by poor workmanship. This may result in a new appreciation of the duty laid upon man to use every resource at his disposal for the highest use to which it can be applied. We may safely assume that honest craftmanship, beauty and simplicity of design, and thrift in the use of time and materials were revealed in the carrying out of each task committed to Jesus during his boyhood and early manhood.

Income has a new meaning when it is received in payment for aching muscles. No other meal is so appreciated as one earned by physical labour. The boy who must work for his spending-money more readily develops an attitude of trustee-

2 Bailey, L. H., *The Holy Earth,* new edition. New York: Christian Rural Fellowship, 1943, p. 7. (Italics not in the original.)

ship than the boy who receives an allowance unattended by definite duties. The farm boy usually has plenty of duties, but not all farm fathers utilize the opportunity to link these with money income for the boy so that he may secure practice in the trusteeship of income.

For men and women who today work with their hands in guiding the plow, in making the furrow true, in plying the plane at the carpenter's bench, in washing and mending clothes for the family, there is involved a discipline resulting from the acceptance of responsibility and the honest and careful completion of a task that toughens the moral fibre.

BEING FRIENDLY

How often we read in the Gospels that Jesus was "moved with compassion" for the people. "He saw a great multitude, and he had compassion on them, and healed their sick." He was continually being friendly along the pathway of his life.

The most worthy purpose of friendliness is simple comradeship. To find a kindred spirit and to give oneself in comradeship is one of the rewarding and creative experiences of life. Rural people have abundant opportunity for such friendship: for neighbourliness in giving help when there is illness or an

CONTRIBUTIONS OF BEING FRIENDLY

a. Mutual benefits
   1) Mutual comradeship
   2) Recognition of human solidarity
   3) Growing conception of people around the world as the family of God
b. Contributions to the friendly person
   1) Experience of love and sharing
   2) Enriched faith in a loving God
c. Contributions to the befriended person
   1) Need met
   2) Realization of goodness of one's fellows
   3) Awakened faith in God
   4) Enlistment in befriending others
   5) Compensation for handicaps
d. Contributions to the observing community
   1) Christians embody some of the spirit of their master
   2) Demonstrates Christian conviction that love is a greater force than hate

extra burden of work in one home, for befriending each other's children, for companionship in common tasks and common interests.

Certain benefits of being friendly are common to all involved. These include the feeling of comradeship. Again, both learn more about our human solidarity. "All ye are brethren" is no longer just a phrase, but a demonstrated fact. The love displayed in the compassion of Jesus becomes known as God's energizing love in his disciples and at the heart of his church. As the circle of friendship widens, the larger conception that all people around the earth are the family of God begins to take on reality.

There are rewards to those who consciously exert themselves in friendly ways. In their own experience they gain the fruits of having shared with others. "It is more blessed to give than to receive." Acts prompted by love, especially when sympathy has been quickened by sorrow, perform the alchemy of increasing love. And the experience of loving and being loved that comes with friendliness enriches faith in God and man. Every good deed of Jesus was to him a spiritual experience. In it he was doing his Father's work and revealing his Father's love. And so his followers, in every helpful act, are working with God and experiencing the presence of his spirit.

There are contributions of friendliness to those befriended. There is first the contribution of the friendly act itself, perhaps the meeting of some baffling need of body or of mind and the consequent release from pain or anxiety or fear. This may lead to recognition of the goodness of one's fellows. In a culture where spontaneous friendliness is not common, it may well awaken faith in the goodness of a God whose children are helpful; and this faith in the goodness of God may lead to the influence of God's spirit and to a desire to know him. Thus the way may be opened for conversion to Christian faith and discipleship.

Finally, a natural result of being befriended is enlistment on the side of the friendly. Gratitude tends to prompt a desire to repay the favour. This repayment frequently will be not to the befriender, but a "passing on" of friendly service to others. Paul had the true Christian spirit when he wrote to those in Rome that he was "debtor both to Greek and barbarian, both to the wise and to the foolish," and was ready to go to them in Rome and pay his debts. Freely had he received; freely would he give.

In so far as Christians are friendly, reaching out to help the sick and the handicapped and the unevangelized of earth, they indicate to the world that they embody some measure of the spirit of their Master. And the Christian practice of extending a helping hand to reform rather than to corrupt, to mediate where there is strain rather than to incite envy and strife, to redeem and restore rather than to retaliate, demonstrates the Christian conviction that love is a greater force than hate, and that evil may be overcome only by good.

In every community there are to be found individuals with physical or mental handicaps—those who tend to fall behind in any race of life unless others have a heart for their interests. It is friendship which they need: friendship which will buoy them up in spirit, increase their self-respect, and re-equip them with the tools of participation in the life of the community, above all, friendship which will increase their ability to meet life with their own resources. It is chiefly in Christian circles that the social conscience has become aroused and enlightened to make friendliness with such persons a matter of special concern and study, in order to help them in the best way.

"Henceforth I call you not servants; for the servant knoweth not what his Lord doeth; but I have called you friends; for all things that I have heard of my Father I have made known unto you."

"By this shall all men know that ye are my disciples, if ye love one another."

COOPERATING

Working together, cooperating, achieves economical use of specialized skills, of time, and of effort. People are not endowed alike, nor do they have equal opportunity to cultivate skills and abilities. All the way from very primitive society, where one man fashions bows and arrows, another tans hides, and another carves wood, to the most complex order of our day, experience has taught the economy of division of labour and of pooling of effort. This becomes still greater when consciously coordinated in cooperative living.

Cooperation yields great material gains. A modern nation conserves its forest resources, its water power, its bird and animal life, its minerals, all through measures of cooperation. Most of the voluntary cooperative projects of rural communities are on a scale far less impressive, but they follow like principles and yield analogous gains. Illustrations may range all the way from a neighbourly gathering to build a hut in the tropics or an earthen house in India or China, through cooperative exchange of work in harvest fields or kitchens, to well-organized credit or marketing societies. Many such types of cooperation allow men to perform tasks which cannot be performed at all by individuals working singly, but which become simple when tackled by a cooperating group.

Cooperating can enrich comradeship and foster social solidarity, very much as being friendly does. The friendly atmosphere of shared effort can foster both self-respect and mutual appreciation.[3] Men lose some of their idiosyncrasies in learning to work together; each begins to appreciate the others' contribution. The wider the scope of cooperation, the more clearly the reality of the common brotherhood of all men is understood.

Society *is* cooperation. All men *are* interdependent. Each man and woman *does* contribute to, and depend upon, others. Too much of rural life, however, is so organized that each does his bit while by himself, then takes his product to be exchanged

CONTRIBUTIONS OF COOPERATING

a. Contributions of cooperating
   1) Economical use of skills, time, effort
   2) Performance of tasks not possible singly
   3) Comradeship and social solidarity
   4) Social understanding
   5) Alleviation of mass suffering
b. The church as Christian cooperation
c. Basic qualities essential to cooperation

in the market for money or for other goods and services. While this does not destroy interdependence in fact, it greatly weakens realization of it. On the other hand, where parts of rural life are so organized that this cooperation is inescapably apparent, with several people gathered in one place working together at a

[3] See discussion in Felton, Ralph A., *What's Right with the Rural Church*, pp. 32-36.

common task, it becomes much easier to understand the real interdependence of our common life.

A fifth contribution of cooperating (really a special case of the second) is the possibility of dealing with mass suffering. Individual effort is helpless in the face of this problem. Yet lack of privilege caused by geographical location, or by racial discrimination, or by the economic structure of society, affects whole masses of people. Sudden calamities strike whole communities—epidemics, earthquakes, droughts, floods, insects, economic depressions, invasions. It is friendly service through cooperative agencies of philanthropy and of social planning that can meet these larger misfortunes. It is through such cooperative friendliness, as well as in personal, intimate, individual contacts, that followers of Christ demonstrate the spirit of their Master.

These gains from cooperative effort are common to all peoples, whatever their cultural forms and whatever their religious outlook. It is one of the valid facets of the Christian insight that it recognizes the cooperative nature of life and affirms that this social cohesion must prevail even in man's approach to God. The church is a process of cooperation. It worships corporately. It organizes in order to serve its neighbourhood. It meets for fellowship and re-creation. How weak it becomes when its worship services degenerate into an assembly of individuals met to hear a preacher! How strong it becomes when its members meet together to worship God, and when they plan and work together to take the spirit of Christ into all of the activities of the neighbourhood! Paul's oft-used figure of the community of believers as one body, all members one of another, all contributing diverse abilities to a common task, is one we need constantly to recall and to reflect.

There are factors which facilitate working together in rural towns and in the open countryside. Many families live all their lives in one neighbourhood. They know each other and each others' affairs intimately. Their tasks are sufficiently similar that they know how to help each other. All recognize the importance of getting certain jobs done quickly at critical seasons of the year, and many of the tasks of each are spread across fields and pastures in plain sight of his neighbours so that they know when he is in need of help.

However, cooperation depends upon the development of

certain positive attitudes and abilities. The same close association which can foster comradeship can also lead to friction and to quarreling. For neighbours to rise above petty irritations and selfishness requires humility and self-discipline. Each must learn to respect the opinions of others, and to be generous when opinions cannot be reconciled. The closed mind is a deadly enemy of cooperative effort. Patience when others make mistakes, and a sense of order that can fit individuals into an effective pattern, are essential qualities not easily learned. Friendly criticism and protest must be combined with loyalty to the cooperating group. Each must learn the profound truth Jesus taught and exemplified: the joy of sacrifice for the good of others. These demands upon the spirit made by cooperation have led to many such statements as that by M.M. Coady in his *Cooperation and Religion*[4] emphasizing the moral basis of cooperative effort.

Particularly in Western countries, farmers have been noted for their individualism, their self-reliance, carried oftentimes to the point of glorification of solitary as opposed to cooperative effort. This is an attitude which must be changed if cooperation is to be achieved.

HEALTH-BUILDING

"And Jesus went about in all Galilee . . . healing."

"Wouldst thou be made whole?"

"Thy faith hath made thee whole."

Soundness of body, mind, and soul; that is health. How important, then, is health-building among the phases of living, among the activities by which Christian discipleship is achieved! It is important because each is responsible for his own body and faculties, and it is important in the Christian's relation with his fellows, since any contribution to their health is of the essence of friendliness, of loving sympathy.

From the earliest days the Christian church has associated itself with the ministry of healing. This was not only because the care of human health made it possible to demonstrate Christian compassion in a vivid way, but because the church thus associated itself with the entire range of human need. Nor is it true that the ministry of healing had to do only with physical health, for we

[4] *The Commonweal,* October 6, 1939. Reprinted as *Christian Rural Fellowship Bulletin,* No. 50.

know how definitely one form and another of religious ministration has been used through the ages for the restoration of complete health, spiritual and mental, as well as physical.[5]

Positive health is more than freedom from disease. It implies a body full of energy, an individual full of the joy of living and reaching out to take his place in the life of the world. In a sense the human person is like a highly cultivated plant. For fullest development he must be protected from other forms of life which will become parasites on his body if given the opportunity. Preventive inoculations forestall illnesses caused by disease bacteria just as seed treatment reduces disease infestation of plants. Spraying ponds to control mosquitoes, thereby preventing malaria, and spraying fruit to prevent disease infestation, are similar in purpose. Thus we return again to the intimate relations between men and the animals and plants with which they share the earth. By positive health development through attention to nutrition, recreation, rest, we intensify the life of the individual and increase the resistance of the human body to some of the organisms which cause man pain and illness. By disease prevention we "cultivate the human environment" eliminating deadly parasitism by other forms of life so

CONTRIBUTIONS OF HEALTH-BUILDING

a. Primary contribution: health, an effective tool
b. Concomitant contributions
   1) Realization of the interdependence of physical, mental, and spiritual life
   2) Recognition of the inseparability of individual and community welfare
   3) Demonstration of Christ-like compassion

that men's bodies and faculties may reach the fullest possible development. By treatment of disease we remove harmful organisms and other bodies which have gained access to the human system; and by providing rest, proper nourishment, and a mind at peace, we allow nature to rebuild tissues.

Health: An Effective Tool. The primary contribution of

[5] Hume, E. H., M.D., LL.D., Director of Christian Medical Council for Overseas Work.

health-building to achieving the implications of the Christian gospel is health itself: soundness of body, mind, and soul. The first and most intimate resource of which the disciple of Christ is trustee is his own body. Health-building is the implementation of this trusteeship, and health is an important tool of Christian discipleship.

Interdependence of Physical, Mental, and Spiritual Life. In the task of health-building we discover how completely the body, the mind, and the spirit are not only inter-related but fused together throughout our life on earth. Physical pain affects the mind and the spirit, and attitudes affect physical well-being for good and for ill. "When the Psalmist says, 'By thee I run upon a troop, And by my God do I leap over a wall,' the scientist tells us he is stating a physiological fact as well as describing a religious experience. He brings us down to abrupt prose by saying his faith had so stimulated the adrenal glands that he could accomplish hitherto impossible feats."[6]

Some years ago a medical missionary went for an extended visit into the countryside in China, holding clinics in each place. Always, at least one woman, with hand on her chest, complained of *men ti huang*. To that worker *men ti huang* meant "lonesome," and she did not understand the complaint. Thinking that her knowledge of the dialect might be faulty, and that the gesture might indicate indigestion, the medical worker went over the countryside distributing soda mints for *lonesomeness*. But at the last village visited, a woman came to say, "Do you know, teacher, that since I have become a Christian, I am no longer 'men ti huang!' " Then she knew what it meant. Lonesome? Yes, it meant lonesome and more than that —longing for something better than their self-centered, futile

[6] Doctors vary in their estimate of the percentage of people who pass on mental and spiritual sickness to their bodies. In a group of Johns Hopkins doctors, a psychiatrist said that 40 per cent of the cases that came to their clinics were mental and spiritual in origin. But the surgeons present insisted that the percentage was probably 60 per cent. A pastor friend of mine, while being examined by a very able doctor, remarked, "Doctor, I wish I had the equipment for dealing with people that come to me as you have for dealing with those that come to you." The doctor replied, "Forty per cent of the people who come to me should not have gone past you." While he put the percentage at 40 per cent, an outstanding neurologist put it at 30 per cent, and another able doctor put it at 85 per cent with only 15 per cent physical. —Jones, E. Stanley, *Abundant Living.* New York and Nashville: Abingdon-Cokesbury Press, 1942, p. 5. Used by permission.

lives, a depression so deep and strong that it had become a physical distress.

A doctor in the Congo dared not operate on a person whom he knew to have a guilty conscience because the patient, fearing witchcraft from the wronged person, was likely to die in spite of all possible care, a victim of his own emotional instability.[7] In Africa it is so much expected that there will be invocation of spiritual aid in dealing with spiritual causes of disease that when this is omitted it seems incongruous. Dr. C. Chesterman cites an old deacon who "prayed in a hospital waiting room, 'We pray Thee, O God, that the Holy Spirit may join himself to these needles and thus enter our bodies and heal us.' "[8]

When suffering, as so often happens, has resisted superstitious treatments for months and years, the relief afforded by scientific treatment, explained to the patient and his family in words they can understand, brings a liberation both from the bondage of ill health and from the more terrible bondage of fear of the evil spirits which they believed had caused the suffering. Dr. R. E. Hoffman writes that "the purpose of medical work is to show the people that there is a better way of dealing with disease than their old superstitious way, and to get them to revise their wrong concepts and attitudes toward disease and toward life."[9]

Many a farmer takes more pains with the feeding and care of his stock and poultry than of his children. He needs a Christian concern for health in his home as well as in his stable.

Recognition of the Inseparability of Individual and Community Welfare. Immunization against disease serves both as a control of imminent outbreaks and as an opportunity to teach the modes of prevention and the causes of disease. Ill health is not just an individual matter. Even in cities where considerable control is possible, communicable disease cannot be controlled by legislation apart from education, and certainly in the country the most effective means is health education.

7 Davis, W. E., "Ten Years in the Congo," reviewed in *International Review of Missions,* Vol. 29, 1940, pp. 410-411.

8 Chesterman, C., M.D., "Attitudes Toward Medical Service," *International Review of Missions,* Vol. 26, 1937, p. 383.

9 Hoffman, R. E., M.D., F.A.C.S. "Efficiency in the Task of Medical Missions," *Journal of the Christian Medical Association of India, Burma, and Ceylon,* January, 1940, Reprint, p. 60.

The practice of rural sanitation, where Christians working with interested neighbours actually improve the village well, get rid of rats, hunt down and destroy mosquito larvae, work out methods of sewage disposal, and cooperatively develop other health projects, not only makes the neighbourhood a safer place in which to live; it teaches the inseparability of individual and community welfare.

Demonstration of Christ-like Compassion. When Jesus walked the paths of Galilee, those along his way were impressed by his constant compassion for those who were ill, and by his consistent desire to see them made whole. Around the earth, where his followers have gone, the same has been true. His disciples feel the compelling necessity to succour, to heal, and to build health. It is one of their distinguishing characteristics. Medical service of high standard which is given in the spirit of love, whatever the patient's financial status or social position, is a convincing testimony for Christianity. Often this impresses relatives and friends more that it does the patient engrossed in his own misery.[10] Someone tells the story of Indian women who walked quite a distance beyond a government-operated clinic to a Christian clinic for treatment. Asked by the Christian attendants why they did not stop at the nearer clinic since the medicine was just the same, the women answered, "The medicine may be the same, but the hands are different."

The presentation of Christ is a part of the ministry of health and healing.[11] This should be by medical workers themselves, who are conscious of cooperating with God in developing healthy bodies, and able simply and informally to report this consciousness to those whom they serve. For Christ is the power as well as the prize, and faith in him is a powerful contributor to optimum health. How many people have echoed the cry, "If I may touch but his garment, I shall be whole." And when made whole, how many there are who want for others the same wholeness. Many, if still called upon to suffer, achieve through him the triumph of spirit over weakness and pain.

10 Hoffman, R. E., *op. cit.*

11 "Until you know what it is to suffer, with Christ, more at the sight of souls that are spiritually diseased than at bodies that are physically diseased, you must not be a missionary."—Hall, Ronald Owen, *The Missionary-Artist Looks at His Job,* New York: International Missionary Council, 1942, p. 61.

STUDYING

"What think ye?" was Jesus' common question of his followers. He expected them to think, to study through to a solution of their problems. Studying is an essential part of Christian living.

Study in the Countryside. Multitudes of rural people are continually asking questions about the goals and about the methods of the tasks which face them. This is not limited to Christians; but a striking difference is noted when comparisons are made between places where Christianity has long been a force and sections where it is comparatively new, and also between Christian and non-Christian farmers where Christianity has been only recently introduced. Traditionalism looks on thinking as sin: one is not supposed to think but to do as one has been told and to follow the traditions of the past. Christian living demands a willingness to experiment, a desire to improve. This is most easily recognized with respect to the use of tools and material resources; it should be applied as well to

CONTRIBUTIONS OF STUDYING

a. Increasing competence
b. Improved service
c. Attitude of expectancy
d. Devotion to improvement

other resources, to the social relationships of life, and to inner development. This requires study: careful and continued investigation by some, and a thinking approach to life by all.

The Contributions of Studying. From study there comes a growing competence in all relationships—with God, with people, with things. Studying is more than thinking God's thoughts after him. It is a definite process of cooperation, of working together with God in an additional realm. God is active in the thinking of people. The Christian thinker is conscious that he has the help of God as he works out his problems. In a very real sense we can say that when we think, God has a chance to get his thinking done.

It is the person who thinks, searching for the best ways of

acting, who develops competence and confidence in his relationships with people. Skill in making one's trusteeship fruitful may come in part from utilizing the experience of the past as expressed in the traditional way of doing things, but it is tested, corrected, and completed by thought and study.

Thinking also makes its contribution to the life of others in the improved service that results from studying. The gradual improvement of seeds and plants has come from studying. So has the development of machinery from the stone hoe and the rough wheel of early days down to the present. Improved methods of cultivation and of caring for livestock have all come because someone, oftentimes a workaday farmer, studied and asked questions and was not satisfied until better answers had been found.

A person who has the habit of thinking about what he does has an attitude of expectancy that enriches and gives meaning to his life. Thinking is the best way to get out of the rut of routine; it turns one's thoughts to creation, to construction, and to serving. The real thinker always hopes and very often expects to find tomorrow different from today.

Devotion to improvement is a characteristic contribution of thinking. It is true that this may be overdone, bringing dissatisfaction with one's present lot, but Christian living implies a "divine discontent" with things as they are. This studious discontent is the atmosphere of creative living.

TEACHING

Jesus well merits the term by which he was known in Galilee, "the Great Teacher." *He began with his pupils where they were, forced them to work out the point of the lesson for themselves, and gave them the opportunity to put into practice what they had learned,* lest it slip away.

CONTRIBUTIONS OF TEACHING

a. Develops skills
b. Leads to the acquisition of knowledge
c. Influences attitudes
d. Facilitates learning which is inherent in all the activities of life
e. Embodies the life and personality of the teacher
f. Respects and develops individual potentialities

Life is a continuous process of "becoming." It is always faced by new situations, new possibilities. To these, it makes its response. "Apparently the basic pattern of life is that of a responsive organism in the midst of a provocative environment."[12] An individual *learns* from these experiences: the child who burns his finger learns to avoid fire, the boy who falls from a tree learns to be more cautious, and the girl who discovers that the human voice can be improved by training determines to appropriate the experience of others in singing her own song.

This learning process, this "becoming" of life, can be hastened and broadened by deliberately confronting people with the accumulated experience of others, at a time when they can apply this experience to a new situation. This conscious cooperation with the learning process is called *teaching.*

What can teaching accomplish in the Christian rural programme? (1) It can develop skills. (2) It can aid in the acquisition of knowledge. (3) It can contribute to the development of attitudes. In all of these it draws on the flower of achievement and of understanding in the past experiences of men. Thus the achievements of each become the common property of all mankind. We convey our thoughts in words wrought out of the long history of the race. We cook our food and heat our homes with fire which man conquered thousands of years ago. It is by teaching that these achievements are passed on from generation to generation. We use iron in a thousand ways by processes developed through generations and constantly accumulated and passed on by teaching. We rally to the ideal of political freedom, born in a distant ancestor or society, enriched by repeated attempts to achieve it. Cooking, building construction, music, agriculture, medicine, government, all of these and many others are the slow accumulation of human achievement, to be passed on to each new generation by teaching. Many of these depend, in turn, on the mastery of certain "tool" subjects: mathematics, writing, and logic.

Develops Skills. Teaching can facilitate the development of skills: such simple skills as putting on one's clothes or cleaning one's teeth, such complex and difficult skills as designing a

[12] Buttrick, G. A., *Preaching in These Times,* New York: Charles Scribner's Sons, 1940, p. 9. Used by permission.

farm implement or constructing a programme of group worship. There are skills involved in almost every phase of Christian discipleship. There are skills to be gained in caring for the human body, in combatting disease, in maintaining positive health. There are skills involved in the trusteeship of agricultural resources, in the selection of seed, in the care of livestock, in the prediction of market demands and prices, in the control of soil moisture, in the breeding of animals, and in the grading of produce. There are skills in the management of the home: the planning of meals, the arrangement of rooms, the preservation of foods, the care of children, and the entertainment of friends. There are skills in the practice of the personal devotional life: skills of concentration, of receptivity, and of regularity. There are skills in the art of teaching itself: the gaining of interest, the centering of attention, the evocation of constructive participation, the guarantee of adequate practice and continuation. Developing these skills is one of the contributions of teaching.

Leads to Acquisition of Knowledge. Teaching can lead to acquisition of knowledge, and knowledge, again, is a useful and often essential instrument to Christian discipleship. It may be knowledge of the normal functions of the human body essential to sound habits of eating, or the detailed knowledge of anatomy necessary to surgery and medical treatment. It may be knowledge of the cultural resources of one's people, in order that the good may be utilized and the drab properly evaluated. It may be knowledge of the development of the soil, of the food and water requirements and of the parasites and insect pests of particular crops, in order that a system of agriculture insuring permanent fertility may be designed. It may be knowledge of the properties of metals and of the mechanical reactions of soils essential to the manufacture of agricultural implements; knowledge of the tool subjects, the multiplication tables, the alphabet, the interpretation of statistics, the rules of composition, or the laws of logic; of the life and problems of one's brothers around the earth who are vitally affected by every change in political and social policy in one's own country. It will surely be knowledge of the Christian tradition, of the Old Testament history of the Jewish people, of the life and teachings of Jesus, of the story of the Christian church from the day of Pentecost in Jerusalem down through nearly two thousand years, of the world-wide and life-wide sweep of the Christian movement and of the Christian community today. And, for those who will themselves be teachers, it will be knowledge of the laws of learning. Aid in the acquisition of knowledge is the second of the contributions of teaching.

Influences Attitudes. The third contribution which teaching can make is that of influencing attitudes. Very largely it is the whole teacher in person who achieves this, and not the material, however "attitudinal," which he presents. No professional teacher can escape having such an effect on his pupils, just as no parent, no employer, no companion can escape it. So strong is this influence in some teachers, many of whom attempt only to teach skills or only to impart knowledge (and some of whom decry any conscious desire to go beyond this), that their students, long afterwards, ascribe to them credit for major influence in determining lifelong attitudes.

This contribution of teaching comes through careful planning, as well as indirectly, just as in the case of knowledge and of skills. Good teaching involves conscious planning on the part of the teacher towards influencing the growth of attitudes. It recognizes that very often the most important result of teaching is its influence in this direction.

Attitudes are also influenced by the direct teaching of knowledge and of skills. Knowledge of the consequence of sound and unsound health habits influences one's point of view toward the body. Knowledge of the origin of coal and oil, of the life histories of hardwood and softwood trees, and of the development of soils may well create a new respect for natural resources. Skill in creating music usually increases one's appreciation of music created by others. Particularly, direct teaching may mould the outlook of the student when the subject matter deals with personality—biography, sound novels, strong plays, great poetry. Preeminently, the story of the life of Christ may determine the convictions of those who study it.

From two standpoints, then, teaching is inseparable from the inclusive activity of life. On the one hand, its purpose is the facilitation of learning, which goes on apart from, as well as because of, teaching. Life is itself a "becoming," and the human organism learns from every interaction with its "provocative environment." Teaching, to be effective, must therefore be an integral part of the activities of all of life. It is strengthened by every utilization of actual problems in the course of daily living. These are much more effective opportunities for teaching than are those created in the classroom.

In the second place, teaching is inseparable from living because of the importance of influencing attitudes. It is the personality of the teacher, of the parent, of the playmate reacting to concrete situations which is the controlling influence here. The need for teaching attitudes demands that every teacher, parent, minister, scoutmaster, and companion "live the life."

Teaching is fundamentally a process of aiding the growth of people. If it is to make its full contribution to living that is fully Christian, there must be respect for the unique potentialities latent in each person. There is a type of totalitarian teaching which develops selected and specialized skills, imparts selected and censored knowledge, and strives to subordinate these to standardized attitudes. Teaching contributes to Christian living when it aids the life of each individual and community to blossom forth with its distinctive contribution to the realization of the full implications of the life and teachings of Jesus.

RE-CREATING

Man's oft-repeated cry is for new life, fresh strength, for a new chance. "Create in me a clean heart, O God, and renew a right spirit within me." The Psalmist sang of the Good Shepherd, "He restoreth my soul." The need is answered in the new birth, the re-integration of life around a new center, but it must also be met by the day-by-day refreshing that comes through the right kind of recreation.

Jesus appreciated the value of re-creation. Our gospel stories tell of his frequent withdrawals into the hills and deserts for prayer and meditation. When his disciples returned from their first missionary tour he said to them, "Come ye apart and rest awhile." We see him at feasts and wedding banquets, not only of the socially-accepted, but also in the homes of the socially-scorned. His parables and the illustrations in his talks show his notice of children at play and his interest in and knowledge of nature. He frequently used stories of social affairs to drive home his points, as in the story of the slighted invitation to the marriage feast. Much of his time was taken up in bringing re-creation of physical and spiritual life through healing.

There must be periods of spiritual regeneration following periods of spiritual expression and drain, rest after exertion, solitude after social contacts. This regeneration, recovery, and withdrawal are "re-creating." True recreation is that which

CONTRIBUTIONS OF RE-CREATING

a. Brings renewal
b. Promotes harmonious coordination: physical, personal, social
c. Provides opportunity for creative expression
d. Fills life full: the wholesome displaces the anti-social

makes life over, which renews strength and faith. Recreation is found in worship, in creative activity, in play, in exercise, in recovery of health, in reading, and in rest.[13]

Not all so-called recreation is re-creative. To be of the greatest value it should be along lines that call for a decided change from one's work, and that exercise those muscles and those aspects of mental and social life which have been neglected. There is recreation in a change of activity. Too often, people resort to "spectator" amusements which only stir their emotions, when they might better be engaging in physical exercise or in some creative activity different from their usual tasks.

Many scientific experiments have proven that adequate rest is necessary for the worker to do the most and best work. Here lies one value of the Sabbath. "The Lord's Day was made for the Lord's children." God in his love has ordained it to meet man's physical, mental and spiritual needs. It has existed from the beginning of Jewish history. Now, it is a day that Christians keep in memory of the risen Christ. It is one of humanity's most valuable possessions, one which needs to be redeemed in Western lands, and one of the greatest benefits to be brought to lands where it has been unknown. It is the day of special worship, the day in which to discover the meaning and destiny of life, to make real the great spiritual values, to find inspiration

[13] The contributions of worship and healing have been treated in other chapters, so, although they are vital forms of recreation, they will not be discussed here.

and creative power to live. It is God's clear answer to our cry for new life and fresh strength; that is, for re-creation.

Festivals, like punctuation marks in a sentence, add interest and meaning to life. Where the meaning of non-Christian festivals is not wholesome and uplifting, these may be given new and Christian content or a Christian festival may be substituted.[14]

Recreation Brings Harmonious Coordination. There is an elemental satisfaction in the harmonious coordination of the body when it is strong and active as God intended it to be. Poise and confidence come partly through the complete control of the body, an instrument ready for any task.

This same healthful attitude is developed in groups through play activities. Within the church circle, play builds friendliness and good fellowship; it unifies the group and brings a sense of solidarity and loyalty, erasing artificial differences and divisions. A recreation programme often brings outsiders into happy contact with the church. It should never be used as "bait," but simply to bring joy: the joy that comes from the unity and harmony of the playing group.

Most leaders have learned to lead by leading. In directing games, recreational activities, and other group projects they have found how people react, how to influence them and how they work together most happily.

The elements of good sportsmanship and coordination, learned at play, really re-create life when practised at home and at work. Cooperation, teamwork for the good of all, obedience to rules, unselfishness, giving others a fair chance, holding no grudges, clean living, cheerfulness, and self-discipline are important by-products of constructive recreation.

Recreation Promotes Creative Expression. It is when people are playing, free from economic pressure, that they turn to those activities they like the best. Often this discloses unrealized aptitudes and abilities. Right vocations have been found through "riding a hobby." Avocations develop initiative and ingenuity and add richness and interest to life.

Some of the most rewarding avocations have been found in

14 "The Life of the Church," Madras Conference Report, Vol. IV, p. 20. In making this substitution, care must be taken that Christian festivals not become so commercialized and over-organized that they lose their Christian significance.

carrying on old native handcrafts that have been largely superseded by the use of machine-made products. Many a man has found deep satisfactions in carving, modeling, painting, pottery-making, furniture-making, or in flower or vegetable gardening, even though he could have purchased a superior product on the market. Quilt- or lace-making, embroidery, and weaving have satisfied the love of color and the desire to make something beautiful that lies in the soul of every person. Music, drama, and story-telling have preserved the traditions of the past and brought joy to many.

Is it not because we are made in the image of the Great Creator that creative expression brings us such deep joy? As we love that which we have made, not for its perfection, but because we made it and it is part of us, we sense that God can love us as we are, not for our achievements, but just because we are his children.

Filling Life Full. Wholesome recreation can displace antisocial activities. If people are busy with fine and clean sports, interests, and hobbies they will not be interested in gambling, drinking, and other questionable pastimes. If facilities are available and young people have early developed a taste for the right kind of recreation, objectionable interests and activities can be "starved out."

The small Occidental family, with its diverse interests outside the home, needs family-centered recreation to keep the "sense of family," to unite the members of the family in common interests and understanding. "The family that plays together stays together. Today this family is not based as strongly on dependence on each other for material things as was true in the past, but rather the present-day family is held together by satisfying relationships within the home."[15] The large composite family of the East needs home recreation perhaps even more. Most quarrels in these families have their roots in monotony and boredom. The family that plays happily together can work more happily together. Wholesome fun reduces friction.

Through reading[16] a person can share in the experiences of men of all ages and can find guidance, companionship, and

[15] Jones, Alma H., *Family Good Times, op. cit.* See also handbooks published by the Cooperative Recreation Service, Delaware, Ohio.

[16] For this reason major attention must be given to teaching the billion illiterates of the world to read!

understanding. He may roam the seven seas. He may store his mind with the beauty of the Psalms, the stories of Jesus, and incidents from the whole story of mankind.

Through association with the works of God in nature, a person finds a deeper understanding of God himself. Through quiet meditation for which there is opportunity in the countryside, he can attain tranquillity. If a man has eyes to see and a responsive heart, he can find balance and poise, daily recreation, in the life of the countryside.

WORSHIPPING

Worship is communion with God, whether in constant communion with the Presence that is always with us, or in periods of private prayer, or in the gathering of the home circle, or in the definitely arranged and organized worship within the church.

Communion with God. Such experience with God is, itself, the end that man seeks. It is the realization of the prayer of Jesus "that they also may be in us." And the yearning heart of God has fellowship with children who love him. For God and for man the great contribution of worship is the consummation of communion. God gets what he wants more than anything else—children in loving fellowship. And man realizes his greatest need—contact with his Father.

Consciousness of God in Life. Those who really worship receive abiding contributions which grow out of the experience of communion.

Worship develops the consciousness that God has entered and is entering continually into all of life. The interpenetration of worship with the activities of everyday living makes

CONTRIBUTIONS OF WORSHIPPING

a. Primary contribution—communion with God
b. Consequent contributions
   1) Consciousness of God in life
   2) Strength from the worshipping group
   3) Emotional grounding of Christian ideals
   4) Development of stability
   5) Motivation of change in personal and social life

explicit the presence of God in the lives of individuals and groups: he is not a God intervening in a land foreign to him.[17] He is always present.

No one can habitually seek communion with God in worship without coming to feel keenly the contrast between the holiness of God's will and the sorry corruption of our common life. This engenders an increasing sense of dependence upon God, both for renewal of courage and insight, and for grace to forgive our woeful failure to make his will our own. Such dependence increases the desire for communion, and deepens man's feeling of humility and limitation in contrast to the holiness and power of God.

Strength from the Worshipping Group. When group worship expresses what is really held in the minds of the worshippers, when it is indigenous to their village experience, it develops a group consciousness which gives strength to each member. In effective rural group worship, the enduring values of family and community living are expressed, the possibilities of concerted action are realized, and the reality of the world-wide church comes to a focus. The local body recognizes its place in the great fellowship of the Universal Church engaged in praise and prayer. It may be few in numbers but it is part of the Ecumenical Church, gathered from every tribe and tongue and people and nation, some in heaven, and some on earth.[18]

The liturgy of the church in receiving new members should be worded so as to stress the fact that Christian discipleship involves membership, not only in the local fellowship, but also in the fellowship of the whole ecumenical church. When communicants receive the sacraments they should be conscious of the fact that they are touching hand with fellow Christians all over the world. They should feel that they are kneeling at the altar with Christians of the whole world. When they take part in the Lord's Prayer, when they use some of the great hymns of the church which are the common heritage of all, when they read passages from the Scriptures, or when they utilize any other common element of worship, or bring offerings for the

[17] Brightman, Edgar S., "The Christian View of Nature," Delaware Conference, 1943.

[18] *Christian Action in Africa,* New York: Foreign Missions Conference of North America, 1942, p. 31.

extension of the programme of Christ in the world mission of the church, the whole church comes into focus.

Group expression by itself influences the beliefs, attitudes, and practices of individuals. When that expression comes in worship with the powerful sanction of its relationship to God and the overtone of communion with the Divine, the strengthening of one's own individual conviction is much greater and is lifted to a higher level. To realize this contribution, Christian ideals of social relationships must be a definite part of the ritual and liturgy of the regular worship of the church.

The Emotional Grounding of Christian Ideals. Effective worship results in emotional reinforcement of ideals and attitudes. There is a sense of God uniting the group in a brotherhood in which Christian ideals are to be made operative. "Through the experience (of worship), we find new power to win the victory over every form of evil and sin in ourselves and in our environment. We find release from anxiety, bad habits, fear, and those attitudes and traits which make us un-Christian in personal character and community and family relationships."[19]

In worship there is a heart approach to God, an emotional comprehension of what is true. To the knowledge that certain ways of living ought to be and that certain ideals are valid, worship adds the feeling that these must be achieved. Worship pours the whole warmth of the emotional life into striving to make those ideals and ways of life an assimilated part of the living person and of the group.[20]

Development of Stability. Worship develops stability in groups which worship as a body. This is due both to the assurance that fellowship with God gives, and to the integrating character of worship. The stability of the family may be built around the family altar, and a community can strengthen its

19 Ziegler, E. K., *Christian Rural Fellowship Bulletin,* No. 70.

20 "The heart and the life of the Christian religion is worship," says F. Whittaker, in "Worship in the Indian Church," *National Christian Council Review* (India) 59, 1939 p. 250, and then he quotes the Tambaram statement: "We have learned . . . that in carefully guided common worship, groups of new believers best learn to apprehend with heart and spirit the truths in which they are instructed, and that such worship proves to have a liberating effect on those who all their life were subject to the bondage of ignorance and scorn."

corporate stability and heal its divisions by worshipping together. Rajaiah D. Paul says, "It is very important that co-operation should begin in Christian Worship."[21] The stability of the Christian church across international lines is very largely due to the fact that all over the world worship services link local groups into a world brotherhood with one Father.

Stability of personal life translated into poise and assurance comes to the individual who walks with God. He who can live in fellowship with the Eternal can take his place among men.

Motivation of Change in Personal and Social Life. "The changed and enriched lives of individual Christians, their deeper love for each other, their spirit of brotherhood, their eagerness to witness for Christ, and above all the radiance of their personal Christian character are the major products of the emphasis on real worship."[22] "The experience will give us new ethical insights, clarified vision, spiritual energies, serenity of spirit, and both vision and dynamic for enlightened social action."[23] Such results as these follow only that kind of worship which is entered into with reverence, and with such corroding attitudes as jealousy and spite and contention purged away.

Ever since J. Waskom Pickett's study of the Christian Mass Movement in India[24] there has been a factual basis for the statement that worship improves social customs and relationships. As Bishop Pickett points out, these by-products are not easily produced when worship in a very vital sense is not a part of the Christian programme. In bringing the individual close to God, such worship makes men more conscious than before of the need for these changes, and gives power to make them.

Worship impresses upon people the necessity of putting "God's earth more completely at the service of all mankind"[25] and also aids to "produce the character needed to make the new world."[26]

[21] *National Christian Council Review* (India) 61, 1941, p. 438.

[22] Ziegler, E. K., *A Book of Worship for Village Churches,* p. 21. Agricultural Missions, Inc.

[23] Ziegler, E. K., *Christian Rural Fellowship Bulletin,* No. 70.

[24] Pickett, J. W. *Christian Mass Movements in India.* New York: Abingdon Press, 1933.

[25] Wallace, Henry, Delaware Conference on Christian Bases of World Order, 1943.

[26] Dr. Schairer, Delaware Conference on Christian Bases of World Order, 1943.

It is necessary to remember, however, that the essential purpose of worship is communion. The consequent contributions of worship are not achieved by seeking them. They only occur when one's whole attention is absorbed in communion with God. "Worship has psychological value in the formation of character. But the true purpose of worship to which all else is ancillary, is worship."[27]

PREACHING

"It is not ye that speak, but the Spirit of your Father that speaketh in you."

Since the day of Jesus, our race has said, in effect: There is a mystery encompassing this shadow-show of earth. Ever and again we feel His touch (or think we feel) and hear His footfall. Yet we are busy tilling the reluctant soil, healing bodies, building homes. Man goeth forth to his labor unremittingly until the evening. But we cannot escape the mystery: there is an unseen realm of which this seen realm is but the blurred reflection. In Jesus that unseen has come alive. We would see Jesus. We would understand that Book of His people with that strange, redeeming sense of God. Through Him we would have traffic with the Eternal. Yet the traffic of earth holds us. . . . In answer to that need and cry there have always been those who have felt themselves called to that very task. . . . It was as if a voice said to them, ' . . . You know by every high surmise that the world is Mine. Yet man will not come to Me that they may have life—though their denial is their wilderness. You must bring them to Me. . . . And you, you are Mine, shoddy though you know yourself to be. You have seen the light of the knowledge of the glory of God in Me, and you must tell them what you have seen.'

So preaching arose.[28]

Preaching is intended to be a prophetic instrument of God's voice to his people, lifting man's soul to God, turning his attention to the problems of the world and to the application of Christian truth in their solution, and presenting Christ to those who do not know him. The subject of preaching is the revelation of God in Jesus Christ, recognizing the continual leading of the Spirit in the heritage of world-wide Christianity. The contribution of preaching grows out of this interpretation

[27] *Christian Action in Africa,* p. 32.

[28] Buttrick, G. A., *Jesus Came Preaching,* p. 7. New York: Charles Scribner's Sons, 1931. Used by permission.

CONTRIBUTIONS OF PREACHING

a. Gives thinking content to experience; evaluates and interprets experience in the light of the will of God
b. Shares the faith, convictions, and appreciations of the preacher
c. Challenges to decision and commitment
d. Shows the inter-relationships of life

of God and his will to the congregation and the leading of them in conscious relationship to him.

Gives Thinking Content to Experience. In the first place, preaching stimulates thinking about everyday experiences at a time when God and his will are at the forefront of men's attention. Preaching considers the experiences of life in connection with the thought of God. The sermon can relate experiences to faith, can elevate them and interpret their significance. It is a leading in meditation upon one's own life until the significance of one's experience becomes clear in the light of Christian faith, and until the implications of that faith for all of life become evident. The thought-life of the hearers comes to be built around the idea of the rule of God in human affairs. In the countryside, preaching can discuss the significance of the farmer's experiences of seed-time, marketing, soil management, and village education (in addition to experiences common to both rural and urban people) in the presence of the thought of God.

Shares Faith, Interpretations, Appreciation, Conviction. Preaching is, in addition, a sharing of faith, of interpretation, of appreciation, of conviction, of experience, by one who feels that he has found God and who has meditated prayerfully upon his will.

> "But come you," this wistful race says to its preacher, "and we will set you free from toil. You shall study the Book. You shall listen in the Silence. You shall toil in the fields of the Spirit. Week by week you shall bring us the harvest of the Unseen."[29]

Not all who preach can make preaching their primary concern, but no one should preach who does not have time adequately to prepare for it, and who does not have a distinctive con-

[29] Buttrick, G. A., *Jesus Came Preaching*, p. 7. Used by permission.

tribution of life and thought to bring. Some of the finer rural preaching has been done by sensitive spirits who were at the same time active farmers, diligent students of the Book, and disciples of the Christ, thereby combining understanding of rural life with knowledge of the God of Jesus Christ.

Preaching is a witnessing by one within the fellowship of the congregation as to the love, and power, and purpose of God. The preacher brings the fruit of his own experiences to the congregation in the form in which he feels God would have them reported.

These shared ideas and beliefs deal with the concept of God, with the problem which people face, and with the teaching of Jesus in regard to life in the family, at work, and in every other phase of one's activity. The commitments which are shared in preaching make it easier for each hearer to make the daily decisions and commitments which are necessary in his own life.

Challenge to Decision and Commitment. Preaching can challenge men to the act of decision and commitment which is essential to Christian discipleship. The right kind of a sermon always evokes from the congregation a renewed decision for loyalty to Christ and a determination to let his will prevail in all of the affairs of life, especially in those with which the sermon has particularly dealt. A woman in West China said, after a moving sermon: "He preached so that the sweat ran out of us! Beginning now, I am going to do these things; I am going to live as God expects his children to live!"

Shows the Inter-relationships of Life. In the fourth place, preaching integrates life. Preaching takes the separate experiences of life and shows their inter-relationships in the total life of the individual and of mankind. How many of the influences of our daily lives tend to make us consider problems separately, as though they could be judged by criteria peculiar to them and without relation to other problems! Preaching can bring these problems together in the sight of God, giving them their due proportion in the totality of life. This it may do by the established procedure of expository preaching, for the great records of the Bible are the accounts of men and events within the history of an entire people living consciously under the scrutiny of God.

Faith is deepened by the note of assurance never lacking from the right kind of preaching. Preaching links this faith to the events of daily life. Following the example of Jesus who, in preaching, used the ordinary, humble circumstances of daily life, the sermon can take ordinary affairs and impregnate them with spiritual meaning.

The sermon also may integrate the emotions and the will. Through an emotional enrichment of life, devotion and decision are inspired: devotion to God, devotion to one's task, devotion to the service of others, devotion to the ongoing programme of the church in all its phases.

The mandate of preaching includes all of the implications of the gospel, and its genius is that it respects the inter-relationships of these, their fundamental unity, in the life of Christian discipleship. Preaching illuminates the significance of working, befriending, health-building, re-creating, etc., as facets of discipleship, and evaluates their importance in the life of the spirit.

WITNESSING

"And ye shall be witnesses unto me . . . unto the uttermost part of the earth."

The decision to make God central in one's life, to seek his will for every phase of life, commits one to full Christian living. Jesus pointed out that there is a quality of this Christian living which makes it necessarily a witness to the grace of God. Christian living has the quality of light. "Let your light so shine before men that they may . . . glorify your Father which is in heaven." Every life inevitably is a witness; if it be a God-directed life, its witness will be to God.

The Life of Love. In his *Letters of a Modern Mystic,* Frank C. Laubach wrote: "My job here . . . is to live wrapped up in God, trembling to his thoughts, burning with his passion. And, my loved one, that is the best gift you can give to your town."[30] All that we have been talking about in this chapter is part of that demonstration of the life of love. The Christian witnesses to God through *working* with God to accomplish the tasks of men. He witnesses through the comradeship that comes, when

30 Laubach, F. C., *Letters of a Modern Mystic,* New York: Student Volunteer Movement, 1936, p. 15. Used by permission.

a life of *being friendly* links the spirit of Jesus to the solidarity of humankind. He witnesses through that quality of working together that achieves results in *cooperating*. He witnesses

CONTRIBUTIONS OF WITNESSING

a. Varieties of witnessing
   1) The life of love—God-directed living
   2) The confession of the lips—an inner necessity—
      a) to reveal the source of one's faith
      b) to complete the witness of living, and because
      c) faith is strengthened by sharing it
b. Witnessing prepares the way; conversion is the work of the Holy Spirit

through providing for individual and community welfare in *health-building*. He witnesses through the development of knowledge, skills, and attitudes in teaching. He witnesses through the enrichment of resources in *studying*. He witnesses through the renewal, coordination, and creative expression of life in *re-creating*. He witnesses through the act of communion in the experiences of *worshipping* that bring the consciousness of God into life, and that develop power, emotional rooting, stability, and motivation for improvement. He witnesses through backing life by thoughts from God in the sharing, challenging, and integrating work of *preaching*. That is, he witnesses in all of these, *if through them he is living the life of love.*

Such living demonstrates the power of the Spirit of God to transform the human soul; such men and women testify to others out of their own experience that the gospel of Jesus Christ is the power of God unto salvation.

There should be a continual consciousness that in all these phases of Christian living the individual is making God known to others and in the finest way asking them to share in that life. This is the fuller evangelism that seems to extend the "good tidings of joy which shall be to all people." In the face of the hunger and need of the multitudes, Jesus turned to his disciples and said, "Give ye them to eat." An outgoing discipleship today gives others life, life in its fulness, life of the quality of the love that Jesus manifested. Through all the phases of living the witnessing Christian tells of the "great things the Lord hath done" for him.

The Confession of the Lips. We have discussed that phase of living known as preaching. Not every Christian is called to preach but each should be impelled to round out the total witness of his life by revealing the source of the faith which is in him and by commending it to his friends. "Men do not light a lamp and put it under a bushel." When one's whole life and world have been transformed it is good news, news which is too good to keep. So oral or verbal witnessing is an integral part of Christian living. It springs from the fulness of the heart. Only in seeking to share one's faith with others does that faith become full, and when so shared it plays its part in drawing men to Christ.

In sharing their experiences, Christians are drawn together and may strengthen one another's faith. When a person opens his heart and speaks of his deeper meditations and experiences and aspirations, these become more vivid and meaningful to him, and help to encourage others. Jesus' prayer "that they may be one, even as we are one" comes closer to fulfilment as Christians share the religious experiences of their own lives. Such interchange fosters sympathy and helps to prevent misunderstanding.

The necessity for including oral telling of the Good News and verbal expression of one's own Christian experience in the witness of total Christian living lies in the incompleteness with which even the best of our attempts at "living Christ" are attended.[31]

Jesus continually "lived the life," "went about doing good," and it was the well-attested quality of his living which insured the ring of authenticity when he spoke of the Father. Yet he did *speak* of the Father. "The real answer (to the question of method of witness) is in that unity between word and action which is typical of the Gospel. For there word is action. 'The Word became flesh.' And action is word. The Book of Acts is the name for a description of the Apostolic witness. . . . In fact, the two are so closely connected in the life of Jesus and of the

[31] "And who are we, to believe that the kind of life that we can demonstrate is so utterly transparent that by itself it should draw men to God?" Visser 't Hooft, W. A., *None Other Gods*, New York: Harper and Brothers, 1937, p. 173. Used by permission.

Apostles that we cannot separate them. . . . Actions confirm words, and words clarify actions. . . . We must re-discover this original unity, and make sure that our actions do not belie our words, and also that they do not remain dumb and meaningless."[32]

The Compulsion of Faith. The integrated witness of word and action and attitude gives expression to a Christian's own inner experience of life with God. Feeling the conquering power of faith in his own life, the Christian is impelled to tell the Good News. So from him others see the vision, and are drawn towards discipleship. Witness springs from faith; it engenders faith. The early church was born of the witness of the disciples and apostles. It is called to propagate itself in the world by continuing witness to each oncoming generation. The medium of witnessing is Christian living, flowing through the channels of special preaching services, of song, of drama, of personal evangelism, of parish visitation, of the written tract, and by means of healing, teaching, health-building, working, studying, befriending, cooperating. The effectiveness of each of these is always in proportion to the genuineness with which love is expressed and to the presence of faith in God and in his purposes.

In all witnessing, men help to prepare the way; conversion is the work of God.

[32] Visser 't Hooft, *op. cit.* p. 173. Used by permission.

4.

The Family and the Christian Community

WE HAVE stressed the fact that the activities of life are not separate, but are merely facets of an integrated and interdependent whole; namely, of *living*. The world is not made up of separate workers, befrienders, worshippers, teachers, cooperators, and health-builders, but of *people,* who perform and participate in these activities, usually in two or more activities at one and the same time, making the division of life into compartments a foolishness and a stumbling-block.

Health-building is at the same time work and befriending and cooperation, and may be worship when carried on in the consciousness of cooperating with God through utilization of divinely-appointed processes. An individual's work affects his faith; his faith affects his health; his cooperating may become a teaching; and his re-creating may become an oblation.

Man is an individual-social paradox as well. None of us is a person apart from his social environment. We are inescapably social. This means that in the same way that the activities of an individual person are indivisible, the activities of different persons within primary social groups are interacting, overlapping, and indivisible.

THE FAMILY

It is supremely in the family that we see this interaction, this interdependence, this solidarity of life within the social group. The faith of the father conditions the outlook of the children; the development of the children influences the faith of the parents. The child learns when the parent teaches; the parent learns from the reactions of the child. One child may be in a mood to play, when the welfare of the family requires that he be working. The illness of another child upsets the planned activities of the mother.

Nowhere is the imperative of social adjustment and the fact of social solidarity so apparent as in the family. It is not the fault of the children when the father becomes ill at a season of the year critical to farming operations, yet all must suffer the consequences. The husband may not be responsible for his wife's failure to become a skilful home manager, yet he is limited by her shortcomings. And when a new insight comes to daughter or father or son or mother, he discovers very often that its values cannot be achieved by his decision alone and that changing a mental or physical or spiritual habit or custom often necessitates influencing the whole family.

So in a way similar to that in which the life of each individual is indivisible, the life of the family is indivisible. *Family life demonstrates the solidarity of mankind, while being the primary area in which the life of man is lived.* All mankind is bound together by interactions exactly like these in the family. One of our problems lies in the fact that the distances which separate us often deceive us into believing there is little connection, and that we as nations, or as regions within a nation, may go our own way with impunity. All mankind *is* a family in its inter-relationships and its solidarity. The same adjustments and sacrifice of personal interest to group interest which are necessary in the family are imperative to citizenship. Therefore the family is doubly important; as the scene of dominant social influences on growing children and on parents, and as a school in which the demands of world citizenship are exemplified.

To an unusual degree, farm life centers all activities in the family. The father does most of his work close to the home, and throughout much of the year he is in and out of the house repeatedly through the day. In some cultures, the farm-wife helps in the field (or is primarily responsible for the field work); in many, she cares for garden and livestock; in all she is intimately involved in the farming occupation. Many farm tasks are such that the children may participate in them. Where farmers live in isolated farmsteads, children have relatively more contact with brothers and sisters and parents, and less with other playmates.

A farm family works as a unit, eats together, and often plays and worships together. Even non-farm families in rural villages retain strong family ties. It is in the cities that work, play, worship, and study are decreasingly family-centered in character.

The significance of this strength of home influence in rural life is that it indicates the tremendous importance of home and family training in the Christian programme.

Learning by Living in the Home

Not only does the family demonstrate the fact of social solidarity, but it is *the most important laboratory in which life is learned and wrought out.* Here life is broken down into small enough compass that each individual can see the effects of his own actions and attitudes on the common life of the family. He is introduced to the problems of social adjustment as the same family stays together year after year. Civilized life is maintained and made possible by the ability of people to get along with one another, which is first developed in children by the home.

Fellowship with God is most easily experienced first in the religious life of the family. With his growing sense of values, the child realizes that his parents turn in trust and expectancy to some power greater than themselves. Religious attitudes are more often caught from association with elders than acquired through deliberate teaching. Because home life is genuine and continuous, touching almost all aspects of life, that which the family values highly makes a deep impression. If the members of the family really respect magic, or money, or social position as the greatest good, the child will tend to accept their judgment. If a loving God is the center of the home, the child will naturally look to him.

Habits formed at home largely determine character and ideals. Any acts of conscientious effort, cleanliness, courtesy, truthfulness, unselfishness, or taking the consequences of one's acts; or, on the other hand, any acts of extravagance, envy, evasion, or carelessness, if practised at home, soon tend to become personal characteristics and to leave a permanent impression on the behaviour patterns of each member of the family.

These fundamental facts about family life are true for all people, Christian and non-Christian, religious and non-religious alike. Social solidarity is universal. Being the primary social group, the family is everywhere the most powerful influence in the learning and development of children.

For each Christian, acquaintance with Christ, and, through him, with God, increasingly becomes the supreme loyalty of his life. Not himself, not even his family, but God, is the center of the universe. God's will is to be done. God is to be served. God is to be loved with all of one's heart and soul and mind, on this earth, within the web of natural life. The family then becomes the most important grouping in this web of life.

In the strict sense, the phrase "Christian family life" must remain an unattainable ideal. Our approximation to it will be closer, however, if we recognize that the ideal is unattainable. For it is only as each individual realizes how his own self-centredness invariably taints his actions and his attitudes that he may be saved from a self-righteousness which, on the part of individuals, is one of the greatest impediments to approximating Christian family life.

For the *Christian* family, there is added to the interactions between the activities of each person's life and to the interactions between members of the family, the fact that each individual is seeking to live his life, individually and in the family, in the sight of God. Thus *the family becomes the pre-eminent group,* bound together in work, in worship, in health-building, in learning, and in teaching, *in which Christians live and learn to live together,* each respecting the others, each seeking the welfare of all, each suffering in the common sorrows, each rejoicing in the common joys, and each trying to do the will of God.

The Pattern for Wider Social Relationships. Family life, influenced by the life and teachings of Jesus, becomes the pattern for the association of Christians in the whole of life. Life in community will always demand adjustments. There will always be differences in desires to be reconciled. Affliction will forever strike individuals in such a way as to disrupt the plans and call for the sacrifice of others. And the most enduring satisfactions, the highest exaltation as well as the deepest sorrows, will grow out of life in community.

Greater progress in handling many of the broader social problems waits on the day when, in speaking of society as a family, emphasis is placed on this necessity for sacrificial adjustment. Here is a lesson which the church needs to learn. Men and women are too prone to keep searching for the wholly congenial congregation, and to participate in the church for what it can give them. They are often unwilling to make the costly identification with the family of believers which is necessary if Christian fellowship in the church is to be achieved.[1]

Genuinely dedicated to Christ and to the service of the neighbourhood, the home can be a powerful evangelizing agency. Often one home in a village or town has become the nucleus of a new church through the use of the home for Christian meetings, Bible study, or inquirers' classes, and through the entertaining, as guests, of Christian workers, friends, strangers or those in need. Many churches have first been sheltered in homes as was that in the home of Philemon.

Home Responsibility. When this supreme importance of the family is recognized, Christian parents will look upon their home as their primary responsibility, and the church will put the nurture of Christian homes high among its objectives.

It is ultimately the individual which is sovereign, not the family. Yet every sovereign individual lives *en famille,* and this social solidarity both forms him and is a primary field for his Christian discipleship.

THE CHRISTIAN COMMUNITY

The second major social organism of Christian living is the local Christian community, the group of persons within the neighbourhood, who are bound together by a common loyalty, and who are seeking to approximate the kind of life to which God calls all men.

As rural people around the earth respond to the call of Christ, they find themselves "lifted up." Their feet are still in the soil, their hands on the plough, their human abode in the family, and their daily lives laid among their fellows of the neighbourhood, but they have been transformed in outlook by their contact with Jesus Christ. Through the centuries, as this has happened to people, men and women have sought fellowship with those in their vicinity who were like-hearted. As they have so come together they have discovered that where two or three are gathered together in his name, there is their

[1] This is an element in the condition which brought forth one of the statements of the Madras Conference: "It is part of the obedience and sacrifice which Jesus demands of us that we accept participation in the humiliation and suffering which membership in the church may often mean in actual practice." Vol. 2, p. 272.8. See also opening paragraphs of Presidential Address of George A. Buttrick to Federal Council of Churches, December, 1940.

Father in the midst of them.[2]

As this group gains cohesion, it discovers that increasingly the wider neighbourhood comes to look upon it as "representing" the Good News which Jesus came to proclaim. The individuals of the group may be ever so imperfect and ever so fully aware of their own shortcomings, but they find the group looked upon as representing the "Body of Christ," whether or no. As a result, the group finds itself compelled, both by the discipleship to which its members are pledged, and by the attitude of the non-Christian neighbourhood toward it, to represent Christ in that neighbourhood.[3]

"Behold, how these Christians love one another." Repeatedly, through the years, this has been said of groups of Christians. When it has been said it has been because, in a society not widely noted for its brotherliness, the followers of Christ, in spite of continuing imperfections, have been drawn together by their common allegiance, in their common worship, and in their joint concern for their fellowmen. Wherever this quality of fellowship has been achieved, it has been a powerful witness in the society in which it has been set. Instances of it in the first century are recorded in the New Testament. Gibbon speaks of it in his study of the spread of Christianity in the Roman Empire. Pickett records its witness in modern India. Obviously, by no means all groups of Christians achieve this quality of fellowship, but it is a powerful witness of those which do.

Because every person is an individual-social being, one of the basic longings of men is for fellowship. It has been pointed out repeatedly in recent years that the rise of totalitarian philosophies has had at least some of its roots in this unsatisfied

[2] "The great Church of God is an uncommon fellowship of commonplace men." Hogg, "The Function of the Christian College," *International Review of Missions* 23:116.9.

[3] It is recognized that here the "true church" of those genuinely dedicated to Christ is spoken of as synonymous with the particular local congregation, and that this actually is usually invalid. "The Church is at once wider and narrower than what we call the churches. It is narrower because large numbers who belong to the churches as we know them are not members of the Body of Christ; for their Christian profession, and their church membership, is of a purely conventional character. The Church . . . is also wider than the churches that we know because many sincere Christians who live lives devoted to Christ have none the less, for one reason or another, never found a spiritual home in any of the existing churches." Mackay, *op. cit.*, p. 163. Used by permission.

yearning of men for fellowship, for the feeling of *belonging* within a congenial group of people striving for something greater than themselves.

It is against this background that Dr. Visser 't Hooft has urged the necessity for the church to become truly the Christian community.[4]

> The main task of the Christian Community, and the greatest service which it can render to the world, is . . . to *be* the Christian Community, for the real tragedy of our time is that we have on the one hand an incoherent mass of individual Christians, and on the other hand powerful impulses toward new forms of community, but no Christian community. Christians today do not form a true community; and the communities which shape the new world are not Christian. It is only when Christians discover that their faith is a community-building faith, and when the community-builders discover that true human community can be based only on a faith in a superhuman community, that we may hope to get out of our present chaos. . . . Before we gain the right to demand that individualism should be ousted from the social order, we must overcome individualism in the ranks of the Christian churches.[5]

If man, individual-social paradox that he is, is to become Christian, it is essential that he find himself part of a Christian community.[6] That Christian community is the church, as well as the family. To learn to live together—worship together, work together, befriend together, within the bounds of a common commitment to the will of God—is to come into the kind of inheritance on earth for which Christ prayed for his disciples. "By this shall all men know that ye are my disciples, if ye love one another.[7]

Love *one another!* How desperately crucial it is that this

[4] The word "community" is used in this report only in the continental sense of a group of people united by common bonds of loyalty, fellowship, and tradition. We have used the word neighbourhood to denote all the people living in a geographical area.

[5] Visser 't Hooft, *op. cit.,* p. 70.

[6] ". . . The full outworking of the Christian life is possible only in the fellowship of a like-minded community; and the transforming richness of the Gospel is not wholly expressible without that communal participation." *Christian Action in Africa,* p. 117.

[7] A discussion of the development of the Christian community through the Old Testament and the New, from Abraham to the church, is contained in the first eight chapters of *The Bible as a Community Book* by Arthur E. Holt, New York: The Womans Press, 1920.

be a mature love. It has been said that mature love between a man and a woman does not consist of gazing affectionately at each other, but of looking outward in the same direction, together. For the Christian community in a neighbourhood to be a *Christian* community this quality is essential. Drawn together by the love of God, it must undertake to express that love in serving its neighbourhood and its world by its programme of those services which Christians can render only through cooperative action. To be a Christian fellowship is to be a serving fellowship.

Different denominations within a neighbourhood may, like Christian families, serve the personal needs of small groups; but like the family they must always be conscious of their oneness with others in Christ. It is important that denominational groups within a neighbourhood learn to live and work together. They need to form a community which, in turn, becomes a unit in the world-wide Christian fellowship.

The ideal, of course, is a situation in which everyone within a neighbourhood is a member of the Christian community. There are strong reasons why this is more nearly possible in rural neighbourhoods than elsewhere, yet it is very seldom attained. The "uncommon fellowship of commonplace men" usually comprises only part of the people of a neighbourhood.

Like individual discipleship, this quality of fellowship is embedded in life. It is in following Christ that the church learns; in following him into work, into being friendly, into health-building, into teaching, into all of life. *This venture of the rural Christian community into all of life becomes the comprehensive Christian programme in rural areas.*

FUNDAMENTAL PRINCIPLES

OF THE COMPREHENSIVE CHRISTIAN PROGRAMME IN RURAL AREAS

In Chapters V, VI, and VII, nine fundamental principles of the Comprehensive Christian Programme in Rural Areas are formulated and discussed. They are brought together here for ready reference.

1.

Presenting the Christian gospel in its entirety demands a variety of activities operating in every area and interest of life.

2.

The Christian programme must be carried on preponderantly by volunteer workers. All Christians should participate in the programme and all should be trained for their responsibilities.

3.

A pastor or other trained leader is needed, exemplifying the Christian life, enlisting and guiding the people of a neighbourhood in their Christian living, helping to interpret and interrelate Christian activities, and connecting the local Christian group with the world-wide church.

4.

Advisory and training specialists, fully aware of the breadth of the gospel, and in intimate contact with rural life, are needed for leadership in specialized fields and for training and assisting volunteer workers.

5.

The Christian community, the church, is the Body of Christ in the rural neighbourhood, and therefore responsible for mediating the Christian programme (recognizing that its message is life as revealed in Jesus Christ, and that the method of propagating this life, as well as of achieving it, is Christian faith and Christian living).

6.

The Christian community has a responsibility to make its prophecy, its interpretation, its judgment as broad as all activi-

ties of the neighbourhood, by whomever administered, and to make the programme it administers as broad as the needs of its neighbourhood not otherwise met.

7.

The field of the comprehensive Christian programme is the entire neighbourhood, including its regional and world interrelationships.

8.

The organizational form of the church must vary from region to region with the social culture and economic resources of the people who are its members.

9.

Permeating all of the activities of the church should be an attitude of love—sympathetic and forgiving, yet persevering and unswerving—like that manifested by Jesus in all of his living and in his death on the cross. The Christian community should maintain this attitude at any cost.

5.

Activities of the Christian Programme In Rural Areas

IN THE preceding three chapters we have considered three facts. First, that the Christian message has implications for all of life. Second, that achieving Christian discipleship and witnessing to one's faith in God are not two separate activities but are the same and inseparable, and that these are achieved through all of living. Third, that every person is an individual-social being, inescapably a part of his family, of the neighbourhood in which he lives, and of mankind, and that Christian discipleship must be realized within these social relationships. We have noted that of these relationships the most fundamental is the family, and that the primary social agency in and through which Christians may cooperate is the Christian fellowship.

These insights are the underlying basis of the growing concept of the Comprehensive Christian Programme in Rural Areas. They explain why it is that when Frank Price writes back from China, stating his philosophy of Christian rural work,[1] he speaks of seeing village life as a whole, of helping to meet rural needs, and of taking part in rural reconstruction. It explains why the items in a programme for the rural church, in North China,[2] developed under the North China Christian Rural Service Union, include worship, literacy, homes, health, agriculture, home industries, gospel extension, religious education, church building and equipment, primary schools, and recreation. Because the Christian gospel has implications for all of life, and because every activity of living is at the same time an expression of discipleship and a witnessing to Christian faith, *presenting the Christian gospel in its entirety demands a variety of activities operating in every area and interest of life.*[3]

1 "A Philosophy of Christian Rural Work," M.S. No. 93, Agricultural Missions, Inc., New York.

2 "Training and Guiding Lay Leadership in the Village Church," by Alice E. Murphy, M.S. No. 157.

3 This is Fundamental Principle I

A comparison of the contributions of different phases of living, discussed in Chapter II, will indicate how necessary this variety of activities is to the Christian growth of the neighbourhood. Preaching can interpret the role of skilful trusteeship of the land, but it cannot develop the techniques of this trusteeship. Teaching in the rural school can influence the attitudes of pupils by contacts growing out of the hours spent in school, but it cannot eliminate the influence of contacts in the home. Health-building can provide a tool for effective discipleship and can illustrate loving concern for other people, but it cannot produce the emotional stability which is one of the contributions of worship. Each activity of the neighbourhood group, as of the individual, has its own function and makes its own contribution. It is only by the well-integrated combination of these that the abundant life which is the Christian message can be expressed in the neighbourhood, through the full living of the Christian community.

It is of supreme importance to understand that where the Christian programme includes many different activities it does so not out of an expansive desire to embrace all good rural programmes, but because these are essential to achieving and witnessing to the Christian revelation.

Out of the experience of Christians across the earth has come a measure of agreement as to the activities which need to be carried on, and as to the fundamental emphases which must characterize these activities. In this chapter, our purpose is to list these activities, and to summarize the emphases which ought to characterize them among rural people.

For the time being, nothing is said as to the particular agency which should be responsible for administering each activity. This depends to such a degree upon what organizational resources are available within the neighbourhood that no rigid rule can be discerned. It will be obvious from a glance at the list of activities that, while some of them are almost universally the responsibility of the church, many are conducted, particularly in industrialized countries, by other agencies. While this makes thorough integration of all activities more difficult, it will be seen that all of them may become phases of the Christian programme in rural areas, even when not conducted by the church, by contributing to the realization of Christian objectives.

WORSHIP

Here we think particularly of corporate worship. In Chapter II we tried to analyze the contributions which the act of worshipping may bring. Now we are concerned with the qualities which ought to characterize the group worship of rural people.

There are a number of people who have made significant contributions to our thinking on this subject in recent years. Prominent among these are Edward K. Ziegler, Bishop J. Waskom Pickett, and the late Bishop of Dornakal. Mr. Ziegler has published three small books on this topic within the last six years: *A Book of Worship for Village Churches,*[4] *Country Altars,*[5] and *Rural People at Worship.*[6]

In the Foreword to Mr. Ziegler's first book, Bishop Pickett wrote as follows respecting the worship needs of those who cannot read:

> The problem of how knowledge of the truth as it is in Christ can be imparted to new Christians has baffled many ministers, evangelists and teachers. Much of what is said in sermons and lessons makes little or no impression on the minds of typical illiterate villagers. The types of worship service which have evolved in Western churches since literacy has become common do not meet the need of illiterate villagers in India. Services that are centered in the pulpit and in which congregational participation is provided only, or chiefly, through reading, do not, and cannot, engage illiterates in the worship of God, and no one seems to be helped much by coming to Church to see the preacher worship God.
>
> For illiterate Indian Christians a rich liturgy is almost a necessity. They do not have access to the Word of God. Unless their parents were Christians during their childhood their minds are stored with Hindu or Moslem lore, much of which hinders the development of a Christian mind and personality. What is said to them does not meet their spiritual needs unless they receive it and make it their own, and their minds have not been trained to receive and absorb. The liturgical service with its repeated use in worship of materials that express the eternal verities of the Christian faith has special values for them. These derive not alone from the acquaintance the liturgy gives with the truth but from its deposit in the subconscious

[4] Agricultural Missions Inc., New York City, 1939. 35 cents.

[5] Commission on Worship of the Federal Council of Churches of Christ in America, 297 Fourth Avenue, New York City, 1942. 15 cents.

[6] Agricultural Missions Inc., New York City, 1943. 35 cents.

mind of materials out of which personality is reconstructed and made more like unto the mind of Christ.

While Pickett was stating the need of illiterate or newly-literate people, the same need for meaningful worship which is pertinent to the life of the village is common to all.

During the survey under the direction of Bishop Pickett, which resulted in the publication of the book, *Christian Mass Movements in India,* it became apparent that there are certain specific beneficial changes wrought by congregational worship of Christians in villages where they are surrounded by non-Christians. Ziegler recalls these with brief comments[7] as follows:

A Notable Increase in Self-Respect. The old debasing inferiority departs. Manhood is restored, and new and unsuspected powers are discovered in the lives of those who for thousands of years have had to be the victims of the old caste system and its disabilities. No longer do these worshipping Christians feel that they are mere beasts. They are conscious of becoming the children of God, and as His children they rise to walk in newness of life.

Greater Occupational Variation. Those Christians who by the old caste system were bound for life to certain degrading traditional occupations have through this newness of life and new self-respect found that there are new and better fields of work opening up to them. Their sons are entering and conquering new types of occupations and the professions.

Unselfishness. With the development of real worship comes a marked increase in the eagerness of the village Christians to share the blessings of the new life with their neighbours, relatives, and friends. This unselfish sharing spirit leads them to share with those who had oppressed them as well as with those unfortunates upon whom they themselves had looked with contempt. The implications of this for evangelistic witnessing are clear.

New Respect from Other Communities. The Hindu and Mohammedan neighbours of worshipping Christians have far more respect for them than they have for those who do not worship. The dignity of Christian worship wins real respect for the worshippers.

Cleanliness and Appreciation of Beauty. Where regular and satisfying worship takes place, there is a transformation in the outward appearance of the place of worship, the worshipper himself, and his home and surroundings. Cleanliness and love of beauty come with it. Village Christians soon discover that they cannot worship God in the beauty of holiness and a dirty shirt, nor with uncombed hair.

[7] Ziegler, Edward K., *A Book of Worship for Village Churches,* p. 21.

Nor can they contentedly go back from worship to a house and grounds that are filthy and unkempt. So the result of worship is cleanliness and beauty, flower gardens, and clean clothes.

Importance of Women in Church Life. Vital Christian worship has given the village churches a new sense of the dignity of womankind, and has brought them to the front in many aspects of church life and work.

Love for Education. The man who attends regular Christian worship in which every worshipper can and should take active part cannot contentedly remain illiterate. Nor can he tolerate illiteracy in his family or in his church or village. Worshipping Christians love to learn, and they send their children to school.

Better Marriage Customs. It has been found that the evil of child marriage and conformity to old tribal customs or heathen rites are far less among the churches that have regular vital worship.

Less Participation in Heathen Festivals. Wherever emphasis has been placed upon the observance of joyous Christian festivals and satisfying and life-giving worship, there has been little tendency to participate in the degrading aspects of the heathen festivals which are so large a part of the social life of the village.

It will be seen that these beneficial social changes are not the mere theorizing of someone with devout hopes, nor the idle dream of wishful thinking, but are the changes actually observed where a strong program of worship is now being carried on. These social changes may be called some of the by-products of Christian worship. It has been found that to produce these by-products, it is not enough to have a strong program of religious teaching, nor to have high standards for admission to the church or to the communion. These changes come about more largely through the instrumentality of Christian worship than through teaching or pastoral care, or any other factor.

To point out these contemporary studies in the field of rural worship is not to gainsay or to displace the rich fruits of Christian worship through the centuries. But here is Christian practice, Christian ritual, in the making, on the frontiers where the Christian spirit confronts non-Christian life,—and in the countryside, where live one-half of the people of the earth.

It is only a coincidence that the sources we have noted above all come from India. A glance through *Rural People at Worship* will indicate that these successful ventures into the creation of worship materials reflecting the full implications of the Christian gospel for rural people have been widespread across the earth. Here in rapid succession we have a Planting Festival from

Angola, a Prayer for the Land from the Oxford Conference on Faith and Life, an order of service for Rural Life Sunday from New York State, and a Dedication of a Chinese Village Home. Many of these are easily adapted to other lands than those in which they have originated. How rural worship in America might be enriched through the use of contemporary rituals of fellow Christian farmers in Africa, China and India![8]

Out of these experiences there emerge the following conclusions as to what should characterize rural worship:

Fundamental Emphases in Rural Worship

1. The language, the imagery, and the content of rural worship should be in terms of rural experience.
2. Worship programmes should be correlated with the agricultural seasons as well as with the Christian year. Seed-time, first-fruits, harvest, and similar seasons should be occasions for special appropriate worship services.
3. The content of worship programmes should be as broad as the implications of the life and teachings of Jesus for all of life, in order that implications intellecutally accepted may develop emotional rootage in the life of each Christian and of the group. Rural worship should hallow all rural activities of home and field and village.
4. Rural worship should utilize particularly the esthetic values of the neighbourhood in setting, architecture, and elements of worship.
5. All worship requires discipline: of the place of worship to minimize distractions, of the group to avoid confusion, and of emotion to achieve wholesome balance.
6. Participation of the whole congregation in worship requires training in worship, in the meaning of Christian symbols (linguistic, visual, audible), and in the materials of worship.
7. Worship activities must be so planned as to combine dignity with a friendly *esprit de corps* of the worshipping group.
8. Rural worship must recognize the centrality of the human family in Christian living, and must be designed to express the faith of Christians of all ages.

(See Bibliography on Rural Worship, pp. 197-8.)

[8] A collection of prayers from many lands, some of which are and some of which are not, rural, is to be found in Fleming, Daniel J., *The World at One in Prayer,* New York: Harper and Brothers, 1942.

PREACHING

Our literature is much less rich in specific treatment of the subject of rural preaching than it is in studies of rural worship. Comments on it are scattered here and there. If rural preaching is to provide the contributions attributed to it in Chapter III (see page 69) for rural people, it must have two primary characteristics. First, it must speak in terms of the problems and opportunities of rural people. Second, it must be phrased in language which is meaningful to them.

Some of the problems of rural people which need to be touched upon in preaching are of course the same as those of people living in the cities. The character of God is the same everywhere. Many problems of social relationship and of the inner devotional life are the same for all people. Even in discussing these the preacher should learn to use as illustrations those examples which are rural in their setting. Other problems are distinct to rural people, problems connected with farming, with the home life of the farm family, and with the small rural neighbourhood. Preaching which is to bring the Word of God to rural people must do so in terms of these everyday situations.

If the preacher is to make himself understood, and is to wield vital influence with his spoken word, he must plan and prepare his sermons with the speaking habits of his people clearly in mind. In most parts of the world, the majority of country folks are still illiterate, or so nearly so that they read very little. These people use a restricted vocabulary concerning household affairs, fields and crops, bargaining and marketing, and traditions and folklore. Even where rural people read a great deal, these are the topics and interests which engross most of their attention. To fit his sermon to his hearers, then, the preacher should so steep himself in their vocabulary that he will use their words naturally. This does not mean that he should be careless in speech, as some of them are apt to be. All people have standards of good speech. Many rural people in banter and gossip use language which they know is slipshod, but they recognize and respect dignity of expression. It is the task of the rural preacher to use language which is dignified and at the same time familiar to his hearers.

Fundamental Emphases in Rural Preaching

1. Preaching should be in terms of the experience of the congregation, giving the rural and village settings of the Bible, speaking of the enduring values in rural life, showing the implications of the family character of Christian life, calling attention to the continual activities of God in the countryside, and interpreting all of these in the light of the revelation of God in Jesus Christ.
2. Preaching should contribute to a sense of the unity of the life of individuals and of the neighbourhood, and of the interdependence of men and societies.
3. The preacher should preach as a worshipper among worshippers.
4. The preacher should always be aware of his responsibility as a mouthpiece of God, recognizing that preaching is a part of worship through which God seeks to speak to the worshippers.
5. Many sermons should come to birth in the fields and homes of the parish, as a result of the pastoral contacts of the preacher.
6. Rural preaching programmes should result from long-time planning which takes into consideration:
   a. the agricultural year
   b. the church year
   c. the progressive meeting of the needs of the neighbourhood
   d. the special problems of different age groups in the congregation.
7. Preaching should honour the membership of the rural neighbourhood in the wider nation and in the world family of nations, bringing the problems and opportunities of world citizenship before the throne of God.
8. Rural preaching demands continued and thorough study and consecration, in order that the preacher may be qualified to interpret God and his will to the worshipping congregation.

(See note in Bibliography on Rural Preaching, p. 198.)

PASTORAL ACTIVITIES

"A brilliant sermon, splendidly delivered is, in itself, not enough to build the spiritual life of a church and of a neighbourhood. The rural church needs a pastor who is a shepherd of his flock."[9] Our insights on rural pastoral activities come from many countries. Probably the most revered rural pastor of recent times was John Frederic Oberlin, who spent his lifetime in a

[9] Perdue, Mrs. Calvin, "The Kind of Rural Church I Would Like to Have in My Community," *Christian Rural Fellowship Bulletin,* No. 57.

small parish in Alsace. His life has been recorded in a biography by Augustus F. Beard.[10] Recent articles from Christian workers in China, Africa, and Japan stress the importance of this activity. One of the most appealing portrayals of that which a country pastor may achieve is in *A Plain Farmer's Religion*, by Amy Atwater.[11]

It might be pointed out that the rural neighbourhood offers the best opportunity for pastoral work, for it is here that the pastor is in a position to know most intimately the details of the everyday lives of his parishioners. It is the strength of pastoral work that in it the minister may come to grips with concrete personal problems, and bring the Christian spirit to bear not only in the more generalized applications of preaching, but to the personal problems of individual people.

Fundamental Emphases in Rural Pastoral Work

1. The pastor should use the informal contacts with the people of his parish to discover their needs, their aspirations, and their temptations. These are the backgrounds against which his sermons are heard, and the needs which form the object of his ministry.
2. He should use his pastoral contacts to interpret individual needs and contributions in the light of the will of God. This can often best be done "in the stream of life," in the home, in the field, and in the shop.
3. He should recruit for active participation in the activities of the church.
4. He should aid young people in making vocational choices which will achieve wise trusteeship of abilities and resources.
5. He should lead his people to confess their faith in Jesus Christ as Lord of their lives.
6. He should guide the people of his parish into the practice of inter-family fellowship, recognizing that pastoral fellowship is a function of all Christians, and particularly of church officers.
7. He should remember that friendliness is a phase of his pastoral programme. As a member of the fellowship of believers and a man among men, he is called to the same comradeship with other people of the neighbourhood as anyone else.

10 Beard, Augustus F., *The Story of John Frederic Oberlin*, New York: Christian Rural Fellowship, 1946.

11 *Christian Rural Fellowship Bulletin*, No. 19.

CHURCH SCHOOL EDUCATION

Church school education is one of those activities of the comprehensive Christian programme in rural areas, which are almost universally conducted by the church. One of the peculiarities of the increasing attempt to orient the Christian programme to the full needs of rural people has been that, while new activities have been added, the old activities have been carried on without the modification which the new emphasis requires. Thus, while we have had a great deal of study of the role of the rural school, there has been very little attention given to building a programme for church school education of rural people.

The best published discussion of church school education adapted to the needs of rural people is that of Newell S. Booth in his book, *Serving God in the Sunday School,*[12] growing out of his experience in Africa.

Fundamental Emphases in Rural Church School Education

1. It should provide the learning experiences essential to knowing the Christian gospel and its full implications for rural life, and to gaining the necessary attitudes. It should also aid in acquiring the skills of Christian living.

2. The emphasis should be on learning for life so that *actual practice* will result, leading to raising the level of individual, family, and neighbourhood living.

3. Teachers should be *recruited* who are really living the gospel; they should be *trained* in all possible ways, particularly through learning on the job under the right kind of *supervision;* they should use all the *varied teaching methods* and not merely lecture or preach.

4. There should be a regular time for the study of materials, and a setting of *worship* linked with the life of the countryside, and also for the development of techniques for fellowship with God in individual, family, and public worship.

5. A consciousness of active, responsible membership in *the worldwide fellowship* of Christians should be formed by impression through study courses, literature and special programmes and given expression in worship, intelligent sharing, and actual participation in the local activities of the world mission.

[12] Booth, Newell S., *Serving God in the Sunday School,* London: Society for the Promotion of Christian Knowledge. 1937.

6. Studies and worship should bring to the school the heritage of world-wide Christianity made familiar and enriched by *elements indigenous to the students*: suited to their age; close to their rural life and activities and growing out of the cultural background of the land in which they live.
7. The church school should reach both children and adults. However small the group may be, guidance should be given to each in relation to his age and experience. *Graded age grouping* is particularly necessary because rural life frequently groups people vertically in families without much contact horizontally by age.
8. All the units of a church school should be *coordinated into an inclusive whole.*

(See Bibliography, p. 198.)

GROUP ACTIVITIES FOR FELLOWSHIP, RECREATION, AND SERVICE

Three situations call for the formation within the Christian community of smaller groups banded together for particular purposes. One of these is the need for intimate comradeship within small, congenial groups. The second grows out of differences in ability and interest which incline individuals toward one of the activities of the church more than toward another. Coupled with this second is the third, namely, that for performing many of the tasks of the Christian community a small group can operate more effectively than a large one.

Sometimes it is taken for granted that the need for group activities within the church only arises in large congregations and in regions where the Christian community has been long established. This is not true. Many rural churches in the United States have suffered through neglect of the need of adolescents for group activities. Many new congregations in Asia and Africa have been invigorated by programmes of group activities for different age groups and for different interests within the newly created community.

Fundamental Emphases in Group Activities

1. Every group activity should be designed both to achieve some worthwhile purpose within the Christian programme and to contribute to the development of each member of the group.
2. It should be democratic both in selecting the projects and ob-

jectives of the group and in the execution of all activities of the group.

3. It should be integrated with the total Christian programme in the neighbourhood.
4. Each group adviser should be chosen for his or her ability to bring out the latent abilities of members of the group, and to suggest activities and procedures without dominating the thinking and decisions of the group.
5. New groups should be organized whenever there is a "felt need" to be met, and disbanded whenever the purpose of a group has been fulfilled.
6. Group activities should be Christian in their dependence on God and on prayer.

(See Bibliography, p. 199.)

THE RURAL SCHOOL

Few phases of the comprehensive Christian programme in rural areas have received as thorough and competent attention as has the rural school. A glance at the bibliography for this section indicates that extensive studies have been made and recommendations formulated for countries on every continent.

On some points, particularly with respect to teaching methods, these recommendations are not all in agreement. There is, however, very nearly unanimous agreement on four central principles.

First, it is agreed that the school must be a neighbourhood school, conceiving its functions in terms broader than those of classroom teaching of children. The rural school must become, as the name of the new schools in Mexico states, "The House of the People," of all of the people of the village, for in a sense the school must educate the *village,* both as an end in itself and as a necessary phase of teaching individuals.

Second, a tendency universally pointed out is for schools to be urban in pattern and for curricula to stress urban opportunities and achievements, whereas rural schools ought to be designed to develop appreciation of rural opportunities and values. Schools are springing up around the earth today which are, in reality, rural schools, rather than urban schools in the open country.

Third, while the methods suggested for coping with the problems are varied, there is general recognition of the difficulty inherent in complete elimination of religious training from the school curriculum. To function as a constructive element in the comprehensive Christian programme, the rural school must be organized or supplemented so as to utilize the learning of the school experience as a phase of developing Christian discipleship.

Fourth, Christian educators, along with all other current educational thought, are stressing the importance of designing the school experience to contribute to the growth of individual persons rather than merely to transmit the subject matter of many separate fields of knowledge.

These four principles are expanded in the following fundamental emphases.

Fundamental Emphases of the Rural School

1. Learning should be considered as co-extensive with living, continuous participation in life, and the pupil treated as a living, growing organism in constant interaction with all the life of the neighbourhood. Formal, subject-centered, merely transmissive teaching with passive learning is not effective.
2. Agricultural tasks, problems of village improvement, family service, should be the actual media of instruction.
3. The programme should be definitely planned to help the pupils appreciate the real values of rural life rather than urban tenets of success and value. A rural school that leads away from the soil and the village misses its function.
4. The centrality of the family in the growing of the individual should be recognized: anything that separates the child from his family should be avoided; all that brings cooperation with the home should be sought.
5. Education must recognize the cognate functions of science and religion in developing a really freed person, for "science dominated by the spirit of religion is the key to progress."[13]
6. The curriculum must grow out of the soil, using indigenous materials: folk-ways, festivals, proverbs, stories, songs, customs, appreciation of nature, the spiritual heritage of the countryside—the values indigenous to rural life so endangered by the mechanization, urbanization, and complexity of modern life.

[13] Millikan, R. A., *Science and Life,* Boston: Pilgrim Press, 1924, p. 51.

At the same time those that come from the interactions of the present must be utilized.

7. Progressively the rural school should consider the whole neighbourhood as its field and be integrated with all agencies that aid in the educational process: the home, the farm, the church, civic life, economic groupings and activities; so that the neighbourhood may become a real community and receive true community education.
8. Even in the small, remote, rural villages, education must be global in its outlook, linking that neighbourhood to the world of which it is an integral part.

(See Bibliography, pp. 199-200, and Papers, p. 206.)

HEALTH ACTIVITIES

Health activities become an essential activity of the Christian programme through the necessity for trusteeship of the human body, and through the dictates of a loving concern for all, many of whom are suffering or handicapped.

In some places, health activities are carried on chiefly by private physicians and hospitals and most people are able to pay for the treatment they require. In other places, governments make provision for medical care; and, in many regions, including those in which private physicians and hospitals provide medical treatment, health education is a government function. These services can be integral parts of the Christian programme, no matter who administers them. To make sure that they achieve this character, the Christian community should interpret the role of these services and relate them to other phases of the programme.

Rural areas are least well provided with health facilities. Often private doctors and hospitals are so few that, if adequate health activities are to be carried on, the church must itself administer them. It is doing this in China and in other places where need is great.

Fundamental Emphases in Health Activities

1. It is the responsibility of the church to help make the recent advances in disease prevention, healing, and mental hygiene available to the unreached majority of rural people.
2. Health activities must go beyond curative measures and dis-

ease prevention to the development and maintenance of optimal health.

3. Since much of poor health is due to ignorance, health education must be among the activities of the Christian community. This should be achieved through courses at every level in the school, and through study groups, public demonstrations, and all other tools of adult education.
4. As part of health education, the training of volunteer health workers is important.
5. Christian health agencies should cooperate with government health agencies, both to avoid duplication of effort and to infuse government agencies with a Christian interpretation of their task.
6. Health activities are interacting with many other phases of the Christian programme and should be integrated with the whole programme.
7. Christian health workers should be able and eager to interpret their work as cooperation with God in bringing health and healing.
8. Health activities should be of the highest quality, utilizing the simplest administration, buildings, and equipment consistent with such quality.

(See Bibliography, pp. 200-1, and Papers, p. 206.)

TRAINING FOR HOME AND FAMILY LIFE

The importance of training for home and family life grows out of (1) the central function of the home, both as the primary training ground for living-in-society and as the primary environment in which Christian attitudes are to be achieved (emphasized in Chapter III), and (2) the relatively favourable opportunities for full family living which rural conditions create (discussed in the Introduction).

How fully this activity is being appreciated and studied is evidenced both by the extent of the bibliography and by the fact that a report, similar in scope to this entire report, is now available.[14]

Here, again, the Christian movements in the "lands of the younger churches" are taking the lead and showing the way. The centrality of this activity *in the programme of the church*

[14] *The Family and its Christian Fulfilment.* New York: Foreign Missions Conference, 1945.

is readily apparent in those lands. It is recognized that no merely secular consideration of home and family life can be sufficient. Nor can training for Christian home and family life be achieved by adding "religious education" to secular "home and family study." The whole approach and attitude must be different, recognizing the spiritual sovereignty of each individual in his personal communion with and obedience to God, coupled with an attitude which looks on the home and on family life as instrumentalities for glorifying God.

Fundamental Emphases in Training for Home and Family Life

1. In view of the central importance of family life in child training Christian parents should recognize the home as their primary responsibility.
2. To equip parents for their task, the Christian programme should stress the elements of Christian home and family life at all age levels and throughout its activities.
3. Training for home and family life must emphasize the claims of the family group as over against excessive attention to the individual, while maintaining status and responsibility for each person.
4. Pre-marital counselling, with major emphasis on the Christian concept of marriage, and with counsel in marital adjustments and in the skills of parenthood, should be available to all.
5. Training for home and family life must at all times stress the need for finely adjusted balance between the material and spiritual needs of the child.
6. The value of shared family worship must be emphasized constantly, and worship programmes provided in which both child and parents participate.
7. While preserving the strength of family ties, the greater loyalty must be to God and to the common welfare of mankind. Familism of an extreme type must be revealed as selfish and narrow.
8. The inter-penetrative relationship of the church and the home must be emphasized. Christian nurture of children is a joint responsibility of church and home. Only full cooperation of both can be fully satisfactory.
9. In order that the home may exemplify the fact that the Christian gospel is for all of life, training for home life should call attention to all of those interests and activities involved in full Christian discipleship.

(See Bibliography, pp. 201-2, and Papers, p. 206.)

AGRICULTURAL EDUCATION

While the principle of 'education for all of life" must remain the touchstone of the programme of the rural school, the importance of technical agricultural training in rural education, and the extent to which this training has become secularized in recent years, make it deserving of special attention.

The task of this training is to develop awareness of the agricultural process as one of productive trusteeship, and to develop competence in the techniques of agriculture, while keeping these within the framework of Christian discipleship. It should include adequate attention to the non-economic aspects of rural living.

Since the applications of these standards are different in the agricultural school (the task of which is primarily to train farmers), and in the agricultural college (the task of which is primarily to train agricultural teachers, extension agents, and research workers), these two types of education are discussed in separate articles later in this volume.

Fundamental Emphases in Agricultural Education

1. Agricultural education should be cooperation in training human personalities growing in rural life, particularly (a) in the techniques of trusteeship of *agricultural* resources, (b) in *rural* social relationships, and (c) in the spiritual values of *rural life.*
2. Agricultural education should emphasize that all agricultural processes are activities of God.
3. It should emphasize the oneness of the farmer with the life processes all about him.
4. The nature of trusteeship, the roles of conservation and of utilization, must be given thorough consideration.
5. Agricultural education must stress the necessity for including family and neighbourhood participation in a Christian trusteeship of time and abilities.
6. Agricultural education for those who are to farm must be carried on mostly in the neighbourhood where farmers live; central agricultural schools and colleges contribute chiefly to the training of teachers, research workers, and agricultural executives.
7. Agricultural education must stress the fundamentals of life-long learning in agriculture: (a) development of powers of observa-

tion in detecting problems, (b) the habit of seeking counsel and of benefiting from the experience of others, and (c) the practice of thinking one's problems through to a solution.

8. Agricultural education must recognize and study the interrelationships between the country and the city and between agriculture and industry. It must, as well, recognize the international effects of agricultural policies.

(See section on Training Industrial Experts, p. 180.)

LITERACY EDUCATION

When Charles McConnell wrote his book on rural people, he called it *The Rural Billion.* When Frank Laubach wrote last of his literacy work, he called it *The Silent Billion Speak.* These two billions are not precisely synonymous, for there are many rural people, particularly in Europe and North America, who are literate. But, in general it is the dominantly rural countries in which there is the most illiteracy.

That literacy is not an end in itself is recognized by Dr. Laubach's statement that increasing literacy may "bless or blast mankind." Literacy is a tool, which can be used for good or bad ends. The first experience of learning to read is almost universally wholesome, however, for it brings a feeling of self-respect and of "belonging" which the illiterate does not have. *To encourage constructive use of this new ability to read,* literacy campaigns should utilize materials of a comprehensive adult education programme.

Wherever some people are illiterate, an early phase of the Christian rural programme must be literacy education. So many avenues of growth and self-education are opened by ability to read and write that, from this standpoint alone, the time spent in literacy education is time gained in the long run.

Fundamental Emphases in Literacy Education

1. People must be taught first to read the language which they speak in daily life.
2. The lessons must appeal to the eye, the ear, the hand, and the mind, in order to help the memory. From the very beginning, reading should be for meaning, not merely for sound.
3. The desire to read, and faith that one can learn to read, must be aroused.

4. Charts and primers must be simple, and lessons short and easy.
5. Plenty of interesting literature must be available for the newly literate to read from the very first. It must be both pleasurable and profitable to the reader.
6. The source of the compassion which leads one to teach another person to read ought to be made explicit by the teacher's own Christian testimony.
7. The beginning work in literacy in any area should be intensive, to test the methods, then extensive after methods have been proved.
8. Within literacy campaigns themselves, the developing literacy should be utilized in seeking the goals of a comprehensive adult education programme: health, economic improvement, better family life, etc. Alumni associations of newly literates should be organized for neighbourhood service.

(See Bibliography, pp. 202-3.)

LITERATURE

Commonly linked with discussion of literacy is consideration of Christian literature. This is proper, for a pressing need in literacy campaigns is for appropriate reading matter for the newly-literate. The problem is larger than that, however, for the printed page is a powerful mode of expression under all conditions.

In Western countries, the rural press has been a very powerful tool of rural development. Magazines catering to the whole family have found their way into most rural homes—agricultural articles for father, home-making hints for mother, stories for the children, and entertainment for all. Before the radio was developed, thousands of farmers in America followed the grain and livestock markets in daily newspapers. These media, in addition to books and pamphlets, need to be developed for rural people everywhere. How eagerly a good rural periodical will be accepted is demonstrated by the phenomenal growth of *The Christian Farmer* in China in recent years.

Fundamental Emphases in Literature

1. New simple literature must be created for the hundreds of millions of newly literate people: short sentences, familiar words, large type, every word meeting a real need. It must:
   a. Be designed to meet specific needs

b. Be simple in language but adult in thought
c. Proceed from the known to the unknown
d. Be illustrated whenever possible
e. Be supplied in many fields: devotional materials, stories, biography, knowledge of home and farm and social problems, current events

2. Research must be conducted in each language area to discover:
a. Basic word lists
b. The most deeply felt needs of the people
c. The possibility of a common written language for people speaking related dialects
d. The advisability of using a *lingua franca* in meeting certain literature needs

3. Christian literature must be produced to meet the advancing needs of Christians who have learned to read:
a. To deepen understanding of the Christian message and of its implications
b. To interpret rural life—its values, its problems, its opportunities
c. To guide rural Christian programmes
d. To entertain rural readers wholesomely
e. To broaden the horizons of rural people, leading to contact with, and understanding of, regional and world problems, movements, achievements.

4. Christian groups must cooperate in the production and distribution of Christian literature.
a. The need is too great for small agencies to meet
b. Cooperation leads to more economical use of resources and personnel and to a broader understanding of needs and resources

(See Bibliography, pp. 202-3.)

CITIZENSHIP EDUCATION

In many countries, citizenship rights are just now being achieved by millions of rural people. Civic participation is new to them, and it behooves every group which believes in popular government to help prepare people for this step.

Moreover, in other countries which have enjoyed universal suffrage for many years, there is often gross neglect of the rights and duties of citizenship, and seldom is there a sound understanding among Christians of the role of civic participation in Christian discipleship, of the opportunities for constructive influence which it offers when understood and utilized, and of the proper attitude of Christians toward government. That some of our most profound Christian scholars are not in agreement on this last does not change the importance of the question.

We are all part of the body politic, and citizenship is a tool to be understood, appreciated, and utilized.

Fundamental Emphases in Citizenship Education

1. Citizenship education should recognize that civic participation may be a powerful tool of Christian discipleship.
2. Christians should be led to realize that they share with all other citizens responsibility for civic policy and therefore responsibility for shaping it.
3. The Christian should be led to see that his primary loyalty is to God; government is only a tool, albeit a necessary tool, to organize and give effect to the will of the social group.
4. Only when virtual unanimity exists among the members of a Christian organization should the organization take an official stand on a civic issue, but individuals should inform themselves on neighbourhood, regional, and world issues and participate actively in political discussion and decision.
5. In civic participation, Christians should have particular concern for the welfare of the unfortunate, the inarticulate, and the crippled in body, mind, or spirit.
6. Organized groups of Christians should attain fully democratic standards of participation and decision in the activities of their own groups.

ART ACTIVITIES

As farmers participate in the life of God by cooperating in the creative processes of agriculture, so also does the artisan who conceives and fashions a chair to beautify his home; likewise the basket-maker who binds reeds into a lovely form to hold the grain of the field; and so too does the village musician who weaves a web of melody at eventide. For as the God they adore created and still creates, so they must create. Rural people do not live exclusively by farming; they have also a rich heritage of manual arts, crafts, and fine arts.

Among the values these arts may have for Christian living are the following:

They provide a means whereby people can give expression to that creative impulse, that esthetic sense within them which is so intimately related to religious emotion, and which in turn may stimulate another person to worship.

They provide a splendid technique for maintaining mental health.

They provide a valuable means of raising the level of people's living, enriching their lives with objects of beauty and utility.

They provide a constructive use of leisure time.

They provide an effective means of developing a sense of the dignity of working with one's hands.

The arts are broad in scope, varying from the manual arts of the machinist or the carpenter, through the craft of the basket-maker, the wood-carver, the block printer, or the potter, to the fine art of the painter, dramatist, sculptor, and musician. In the following fundamental emphases the word "arts" is intended to cover this whole field of creative endeavor.

Fundamental Emphases in the Arts Activities

1. People should be led to become aware of the religious implications of the arts.
2. Tools and materials should be those of the local neighbourhood, or those which are within the economic reach of the people.
3. The starting point should be indigenous arts, to which new techniques may be added where possible. Other arts may be introduced when a "felt need" arises.
4. The primary emphasis should be upon the enrichment of home and community life, rather than upon production for sale.
5. Creative expression in planning and executing should be fostered in manual arts and crafts as well as in the so-called "fine" arts.
6. Leaders should become aware of the characteristic modes of expression of the people among whom they live and of their indigenous ideas of beauty.
7. People may be led to feel a kinship with other people through an acquaintance with folk art the world over.

METHODS OF ADULT EDUCATION

Many of the foregoing activities involve working with adults. To do this successfully requires the use of techniques somewhat different from those employed with children. Even a cursory survey of the literature of the past decade on the Christian mission among rural people will reveal how important these techniques are felt to be, as indicated by the attention they have received.

Fundamental Emphases in Adult Education

1. Use every avenue of approach—eye, ear, hands, imagination, sense of humour—in combination for the greatest impression.
2. Get action. People learn through doing. Make the action co-operative wherever possible. Do not attempt to teach that which you cannot do yourself.
3. An ounce of demonstration is worth a pound of explanation, particularly when the demonstration is by the people themselves.
4. Work intensively in a small area until methods are tested, then expand the work to a larger area.
5. Put as much fun into the process as possible.
6. Proceed from the familiar to the unfamiliar.
7. In discussion, try to agree and modify, rather than disagree and argue.
8. Seek development of the present culture of the neighbourhood, rather than attempt radical substitution.
9. Give major attention to meeting the problems of the neighbourhood as a whole.

RURAL RESEARCH

Research, investigation, and study are indispensable in a task the magnitude of which we are only beginning to comprehend, and in a world which is always changing. Every activity we discuss here, every opportunity we perceive, involves problems far beyond our present understanding. In addition, even if we had solutions to all of our present problems, our world is dynamic, conditions are always changing; and new studies, new investigations are continually necessary in order to discern the implications of the Christian spirit for new problems, and for new situations.

The best insurance that these studies be pertinent to the immediate problems of Christian discipleship is intimate association between scholars and practitioners. The best insurance that they really arrive at Christian conclusions is thorough acquaintance with the Christian tradition on the part of those conducting the studies. As part of the Christian programme, research must itself be conducted in a manner befitting a Christian activity.

Fundamental Emphases in Rural Research

1. The problems to be examined should be set by the actual conditions which exist and by the urgent difficulties to be overcome.
2. Research workers should be intimately related to the application of the results of their studies (a) by rural people, (b) by professional rural specialists, and (c) by pastors.
3. Research should be conducted in a Christian manner. It should be dedicated to the glory of God, and it should respect as children of God all of those connected with the enterprise.

SUMMARY

At the risk of repetition, it is well to point out again that we have been discussing in this chapter the variety of activities necessary to present the Christian gospel in its fulness, in a rural neighbourhood. Each of these activities has a contribution to make to the whole enterprise. Each may be, at the same time, a means of achieving Christian discipleship within the participating group, and a witness to Christian faith in God by the participating group.

Let it be repeated, further, that whether or not all of these activities should be administered by the church depends upon many local factors. In many instances health activities, rural schools, agricultural education, and other programmes may be carried on by other agencies, in which individual Christians may or may not be active. To the degree that these activities, even when not administered by the church, are interpreted and influenced by the Christian group, they may be made parts of the comprehensive Christian programme in rural areas. The unique role of the church in the neighbourhood is discussed in Chapter VII.

6.

Leadership of the Christian Programme In Rural Areas

THREE factors must enter into the leadership of the Christian programme:

First, most of the responsibility for the programme must be in the hands of laymen; they must carry it out and they must participate in formulating it. The Christian fellowship must be a serving fellowship and it can be that only when it is essentially a lay movement.

Second, to be most effective, the Christian community needs trained pastoral assistance for its task.

Third, because of the technical intricacy of many phases of Christian discipleship, the Christian community needs the consecrated assistance of experts in many fields in order to fulfill its tasks.

These three requirements for leadership will be considered in the form of three principles.[1]

I.

The Christian programme must be carried on preponderantly by volunteer workers. All Christians should participate in the programme and all should be trained for their responsibilities.[1a]

This principle might be recast to state that most *rural* programmes, whether Christian or not, must depend on volunteer leadership, for it is not possible for the variety of activities needed in a rural neighbourhood to be conducted by professional workers. The cost would be too high. Even where there are many doctors in private practice, many of the health activities of the neighbourhood must be carried on by parents and

1 Principle I appears on page 87 in Chapter V.

1a This is Fundamental Principle II, see page 85.

other interested individuals. Even where there are many professional teachers, much of the actual teaching is done, often very informally, by people who do not earn their livelihood thereby. The same is true of youth clubs, cooperative organizations, social recreation, etc. The same must be true of that part of the neighbourhood conducted by the church.[2]

But there is a deeper necessity demanding that the Christian movement be predominantly a lay movement. The character of Christianity itself requires it.[3] "Be ye doers of the word" expresses the conviction that every Christian has a part to play in the task of Christian living. To be sure, most of the discipleship of each Christian will be expressed in his own farming, in her own home-making, in the personal contacts and problems of each. But all are part of the neighbourhood and of the Christian community and are called to corporate discipleship as well. The activities of the church are the cooperative activities of its members. In these days of the growing importance of group activities, the church must become a fellowship of people who are participating fully in its activities.

Christ's commands to love, to share, to teach, and to witness, are addressed to every Christian. Growth in Christian living does not take place in a vacuum; it requires social responsibility and participation. It is that in which people actively participate which moulds them, and thus total participation matures the participants while accomplishing the task which the group has undertaken.

This participating by laymen must not be a scheme for running errands and performing the menial tasks in a minister-centered church. It needs to pervade the whole fellowship. There are today, in Africa, many Christian congregations so fully cooperative that the pastor can be away for weeks and the laymen will carry on, conducting the full programme, including the regular worship services. The same is true of many churches in Korea, of some in China, and of a very few in the United States.

[2] "The outstanding churches in Asia are those which make the widest use of their lay members and in this way multiply the services of their paid staff and extend the influence of Christianity in their neighbourhood." Davis, J. Merle, *The Economic and Social Environment of the Younger Churches*. New York: International Missionary Council.

[3] *Liberating the Lay Forces of Christianity*, by John R. Mott, remains the classic exposition of the role of laymen in the Christian movement.

Thus the role of volunteer leadership is not that of carrying out plans made by the pastor or other local leader, or by any outside authority. The programme ought to be drawn up by the entire group, discussed by the entire group, and initiated only when it has the support of the group or of a "cell," a congenial smaller fellowship within the group, behind it. Volunteers do not retain enthusiasm for an imposed programme, but they will persevere in the face of difficult obstacles in one which they have themselves wrought out to meet a need which they feel keenly.

In order that this total participation of the Christian community may be effective, the church must provide adequate training for it. Participation is itself a training ground; it should be directed consciously toward training for all types of responsibilities: in worship services, in health activities, in care of the physical plant of the church, in administration and integration of the church programme, in personal evangelism, and in neighbourhood service activities. This training for lay participation is discussed on pages 159-163.

Two special problems arise because of the fact, noted in Chapter VII (p. 123), that the Christian programme in a neighbourhood may actually be much broader than that administered by the church. Very often individuals who are not themselves avowed Christians are in sympathy with a particular phase of the Christian programme and are eager to participate in it. Most Christian workers are agreed that such cooperation should be encouraged.[4] A similar problem arises where a secular agency is administering what is (or might be) really part of the comprehensive Christian programme. In such cases the church must help the Christians who participate to recognize the values and limitations involved, and must prepare them fully to exert their Christian influence.

Some people possess qualities which automatically make them leaders in the groups of which they are a part. In this connection, let us call attention to a passage in an article found later in this volume:

How are we to find the men and women for key positions in the service of the church and neighbourhood? To secure the needed leadership it is best not to stress leadership at all. What we want is

[4] See Dr. Hatch's emphasis on "socialization" in *Further Upward In Rural India,* p. 18.

the enlistment of all laymen in active discipleship. If such a spirit gets root in the local church, laymen all serving to the best of their several abilities, leadership will emerge. There need be no arbitrary choosing. There must, however, be some competent steering, for there may emerge those with selfish ambitions, wanting to take the lead for the sake of prestige or esteem. And there may be those naturally too diffident and backward to assume any prominent place, who yet have the potentialities of mind and heart for the greatest contribution to the cause.[5]

Christian leadership makes its talent available without seeking to dominate the group.

II.

A pastor or other trained leader is needed, exemplifying the Christian life, enlisting and guiding the people of a neighbourhood in their Christian living, helping to interpret and inter-relate Christian activities, and connecting the local Christian group with the world-wide church.[5a]

The limitation on a Christian community which is *exclusively* a lay fellowship is imposed by the necessity of each member's having to earn his own livelihood. For the community to achieve its full stature, it needs the constant attention of some one of its number. It needs someone who can devote his full attention to pondering its message, caring for the state of its health, weighing its emerging opportunities against its present abilities, keeping its devotion bright, keeping the machinery of its democracy working smoothly, and to maintaining its relationship with the larger neighbourhood.

Most Christian groups have felt that the best way to provide for this important and difficult role is to train some of their members who possess qualities of Christian leadership for it, and then to provide the livelihood of the families of these men and women so that they may devote their full time to the welfare and tasks of the church. This is the Christian ministry. It is not a substitute for, but a means of achieving, full and effective lay participation.

What are the tasks of this pastoral leadership?

1. To enlist, inspire, train, and guide the men, women, and children of each parish, opening up new vistas and areas of service.

[5] Page 159.

[5a] This is Fundamental Principle III, see page 85.

2. To deepen its own experience of God, so that it may lead others to this same experience.

3. To study and ponder the Christian revelation, the history of the Christian tradition, and the outreach of the Christian spirit; and then to bring the fruits of this study to the people of the parish.

4. To make itself intimately a part of the neighbourhood and keenly aware of the trials and compensations, the worries and the faith of rural living, in order to know the problems and the aspirations of the people.

5. To become skilled in the techniques of its craft: competent in the priestly duties of the ministry—especially worship—, effective in preaching, skilled in personal counselling, capable in organizing the community for fellowship and for action.

6. To use the time which the Christian community affords it, through supporting its families, to facilitate productive fellowship and service of the Christian group, giving unstintingly of its talents and sympathy, while refraining from dominating the policy or planning of the group.

7. To participate as a layman among laymen, in the life of the neighbourhood and in the programmes of service which the Christian group undertakes.

8. To become familiar with the function, potential contributions, and actual and potential dangers of neighbourhood activity, whether conducted by the church or not, in order to seek to integrate all of those forces in the neighbourhood which can contribute to Christian goals, while focussing attention in judgment on the ills of the neighbourhood.

9. To bring to each parish, through its contacts with other Christian communities, and with other ministers, through its reading, and through wide civic interests, the realization of the interdependence of all men everywhere, and of the necessity for fellowship and sharing of resources among Christians of all lands.

10. To understand the need for, and to seek to achieve in itself, integration of all of the phases of Christian discipleship. To recognize the importance and contribution of each facet of Christian living.

In other words, the function of trained pastoral leadership is to do what every layman and laywoman ought to do, and must do to some extent, but to do it more thoroughly because of the additional training and time for it. Thus, the Christian movement can be a lay movement, yet have the advantages of trained, full-time leadership.

As a matter of fact thousands of congregations do, and must for many years, get along without full-time pastoral leadership. Some of the strongest groups, particularly in Africa and Asia, arrange for intensified training of selected laymen who serve as they can, without remuneration, within their groups. Another common practice is that of "lay preaching," in which laymen, often untrained, perform certain ministerial duties.[6] Still another is the custom, in some communions, of having trained pastors who earn part of their livelihood by farming or another occupation, but have some of their income provided by the congregation.

In a few places, a type of group ministry is being introduced into rural parishes. This provides for full-time employment of several ministers, each with specialized training in one or two phases of the minister's task. One may be interested and trained in religious education, another in worship programmes, a third in personal counselling, and a fourth in the preaching ministry. Such a plan is within the reach of those rural neighbourhoods which are large, or where several adjoining neighbourhoods cooperate by having the minister in each make his specialized talents available to the others.

That so many rural churches have become "preacher-centered," with the preacher expected primarily to preach and to carry alone the activities of all laymen, does not change the fact that such a state of affairs is not capable of producing sound, vital, Christian rural churches. The church forfeits its genius when it ceases to be primarily a participating, serving fellowship. To repeat, the function of pastoral leadership is to inspire, to remind, to integrate, to encourage, to caution, to befriend, but not to dictate.

III.

Advisory and training specialists, fully aware of the breadth of the gospel and in intimate contact with rural life, are needed for leadership in specialized fields and for training and assisting volunteer workers.[6a]

[6] See Felton, Ralph A., *The Rural Church in the Far East,* New York: Foreign Missions Conference, 1938.

[6a] This is Fundamental Principle IV, see page 85.

In Chapter IV we discussed the fact that presenting the Christian gospel in its entirety requires a variety of activities, because the Christian message has implications for every phase of life, and because each activity of men is at the same time a method of achieving their purposes and a witness to the character of the purpose they pursue. Thus, health activities, schools, cooperative organizations, and all of the other activities discussed in Chapter IV have a place in the comprehensive Christian programme in rural areas, whether they are administered by the church or not.

Obviously, many of these activities require specialized, professional leadership. The fields of knowledge involved are too broad, the skills required are too intricate, and the need of any one neighbourhood for each one of them is too great, for more than a few fields to be mastered by any one person. Specialization in agriculture, in health, in education, in worship, in church school education, and in other phases of neighbourhood welfare is essential.

Two situations predominate in rural areas. In some parts of the earth, leadership in these specialized fields is almost entirely lacking in rural areas. Doctors tend to congregate in the cities. Villages have no schools. Agricultural extension programmes are non-existent. It is under such circumstances that the Christian movement feels impelled to introduce these services, and in order to do so it must enlist, train, and support qualified leaders.

The second common situation is that there are experts in these fields present in the countryside, but their professional training has been almost entirely secular, and they, therefore, are not in a position either to assess the contribution of their service to the Christian programme, or to perform their service in a way which will yield maximum results to that programme. If a rural doctor is fully aware of the breadth and depth of the Christian gospel, and committed to it, he can interpret the role of health in Christian discipleship; and he can so conduct his medical practice that he is as fully an instrument of the Christian rural mission as though he were employed as a missionary doctor. An agent of a government department of agricultural extension, if he becomes a thorough student of the role of agricultural improvement in Christian discipleship, can be the full equivalent of an agricultural missionary in his service to the neighbourhood and to the church of which he is a member. A trained teacher in the public schools, if he or she takes the trouble to learn and to understand the place of teaching in the comprehensive Christian programme, can serve as an advisory and training specialist to the Christian programme in this capacity. The tragedy is that so few laymen look on their professions as distinctively Christian callings and so devoutly apply themselves, first, to the full application of the Christian spirit in their professions and, second, to assessing and interpreting the specific contributions of their professional activities to the mission of the world Christian community.

As the Christian Community faces the task of presenting the Christian message to a secularized world and of translating this message in terms of concrete action, it finds itself seriously handicapped by the lack of a Christian "intelligentsia" within its ranks. The problem is not merely that the number of highly educated men and women who are active members of the churches is relatively small. It is rather that those of its members who are qualified to become pioneers of Christian thought and life in their respective professions and occupations are unaware of their particular calling as Christian intellectuals, or, if they are aware of it, are unable to implement this calling and to establish a connection between their Christian convictions and their daily task. We have many doctors and lawyers and politicians who are faithful members of the Christian Church and who are loyally attempting to live as Christians in their private life; but we have almost no Christian doctors or lawyers or politicians who have thought through the implications of their faith for their profession and act accordingly.

In saying this I do not wish to infer that Christian laymen in the liberal professions have low standards of professional ethics. The issue goes much deeper than that. A Christian psychiatrist may have a most idealistic conception of his task and a strong Christian faith but he may at the same time be a complete pagan in his conception of psychiatry. The same holds true in the spheres of law, politics, economics and many others. The point is that the general departmentalizing of life, together with the influence of modern individualism, has led to a situation in which it has become exceedingly difficult, if not impossible, for a Christian intellectual to relate his Christianity to his intellectual activities. And thus the intellectuals within the Christian fold, instead of contributing to the integration of Christian life and helping to work out a coherent framework of Christian thought and ethics, are today most often divided beings whose hearts are Christian, whose heads are pagan, and whose actions are therefore semi-Christian and semi-pagan.[7]

Thus, almost universally, the Christian movement faces a problem of developing qualified leadership for many of the activities which must be part of its programme.

At one extreme, where professional specialists in these fields are already part of the rural environment (and where many of them are church members) the problem is one of helping these specialists to interpret their services in the light of their Christian commitment, so that their professional contribution can be an integrated phase of the comprehensive Christian programme.

At the other end of the scale, in situations where the church needs to carry on a comprehensive programme itself, due to the lack of other qualified specialists in the neighbourhood, the administration of such a programme—to be carried chiefly by volunteer workers—necessitates the utilization of advisory and training specialists in each of the fields involved. In such neighbourhoods, the Christian farmer and his pastor need expert help in all phases of living: public health, education, literature, economic activities, agricultural extension, church organization, recreation, and village development. They need help in training volunteer workers for all of these activities.

Inherent in the utilization of specialists is the danger of secularization and of segmentation of the life and thought of the church. In order to avoid this, *each specialist participating in the Christian programme should be fully aware of the breadth of the gospel and of the way in which his specialty may be integrated into and contribute to the complete range of its activities.* In order that his contribution may be germane to rural life, *the specialist needs intimate association with a particular rural neighbourhood and with the total Christian programme in that vicinity.* He needs to be part of a *rural neighbourhood* in order that its problems may be his problems and its experiences his experiences, and he needs to be intimately acquainted with the *whole Christian programme* in that neighbourhood in order that he may be able so to conduct his activities that they fill their place and keep their place in the total programme.

It is well to point out again at this place that the function of the specialist is not to dictate but to counsel. The decisions in

[7] Visser 't Hooft, *op. cit.*, p. 122.

programme formation need to be in the hands of the people and the lay volunteers themselves, acting democratically (see page 159). It is the role of the specialist to put the resource of his training and understanding at the disposal of the democratic local group. (See article on Training Specialists, p. 171.)

SUMMARY

Thus there must be three elements in the leadership of the comprehensive Christian programme in rural areas:

I. Total participation by all members of the Christian community, in a programme democratically adopted and administered; with each person trained in the activities in which he participates; with outsiders who are interested in a particular phase of the programme invited to share in it; and with members who, as individuals, belong in other groups in the neighbourhood, competent to make the activities of that group part of the Christian programme.

II. Trained pastoral leadership, to undergird and encourage the life of this lay movement, trained in the Christian tradition, in techniques of achieving the purposes of corporate Christian living, and in integration of the life of a neighbourhood around this central loyalty to God in Christ.

III. Specialists who are competent in the techniques of their field, who understand the role of their specialty in Christian discipleship, and who are eager to be part of the comprehensive Christian programme.

7.

The Rural Church

WHEN the Madras Conference sought to state the nature of the church, it found it necessary to resort to paradox.[1] In this there is the recognition that the church is called both to be and to do something.

But here, again, the genius of the Christian tradition, rediscovered for the rural church in recent years, is that these are not two tasks but one task which is insufficiently understood unless both things are said of it. It is only in *being* a *serving, self-forgetful fellowship*[2] that the church becomes itself. It is only through realization of itself as a *human and human-divine fellowship* that the church becomes capable of the peculiar service to which it is called.

These two streams are well brought together by Dr. Visser 't Hooft:

> It is true that the church, like its Lord, is in the world to serve. But it is not in the world to serve the world as the world wants to be served. In other words, its service to its Lord and its service to the world are not two different tasks. Both mean obedience to God, and thus serving the world consists in giving to the world what it needs according to God and not according to itself. . . .[3]

The key to the function of the church in the rural neighbourhood is to be found in two facts already pointed out. These

1 "The Church on the one hand is built on the foundation of the apostles and prophets, one and undivided, perfect and holy, and, taught by the Holy Spirit, is the teacher of truth and right-living. As such it is an object of faith. On the other hand, as a human attempt to realize God's will, it is incomplete and sinful: it shares in the limitations and imperfections of human nature; and because of its worldliness and divisions, it is often a hindrance to the coming of the Kingdom of God, i.e., the rule of God over all." *Madras Conference Report,* Vol. 2, p. 279.

2 See Smathers, Eugene, "A Rural Church Program that Makes Religion the Qualifying Factor in Every Experience of Life." *Christian Rural Fellowship Bulletin,* No. 66.

3 Visser 't Hooft, *op. cit.* p. 75.

are: (1) the nature of the neighbourhood church as the Christian community, the group of people bound together by a common loyalty and seeking to approximate the kind of life to which God calls all men;[4] and (2) the fact that of the many organized activities which contribute to achieving Christian discipleship in a neighbourhood, some are often administered by bodies other than the church.[5]

Out of these two facts flow four principles relative to the rural church, which take their places with the four already given[6] as the fundamental principles of the comprehensive Christian programme in rural areas.

I.

The Christian community, the church, is the Body of Christ in the rural neighbourhood, and therefore responsible for mediating the Christian programme (recognizing that its message is life as revealed in Jesus Christ, and that the method of propagating this life, as well as of achieving it, is Christian faith and Christian living).[6a]

It is the living of the Christian community: working, being friendly, cooperating, health building, studying, teaching, recreating, worshipping, and preaching, which—together with the Bible and the Holy Spirit—brings the voice of God to rural people. Part of this living is individual, by members of the group; part of it is corporate, in activities in which they join together.

No better description of the Christian community can be found than that hallowed by tradition: it is the Body of Christ. As such (coming back to our recognition of the paradoxical nature of the church[7]) it must seek to be the kind of fellowship for which Jesus prayed for his disciples; it must seek to serve its neighbourhood and its world as Christ would serve them. A healthy body responds obediently to the willing of its mind (its head). In this literal sense, Christ must be the head of each church. It is the task of the Christian community to let Christ be its mind, to make his will its own, through prayer and conse-

[4] Discussed in the final section of Chapter IV, pp. 81-84.

[5] Discussed in introduction and conclusion of Chapter V, pp. 87, 88, 110.

[6] Pages 87, 111, 114, 116.

[6a] This is Fundamental Principle V, see page 85.

[7] P. 121.

crated study. It is the task of the Christian community in a rural neighbourhood to be the serving instrument of God's loving will for that neighbourhood.

It is as the Body of Christ that the Christian community must assume responsibility for mediating the comprehensive Christian programme. Its task is not to vitalize or to spiritualize a secular programme of rural improvement. Its task is to achieve and to exemplify the loving, sympathetic, suffering participation of God throughout the whole range of the problems, perils, and potentialities of the neighbourhood.

II.

The church should seek to integrate all neighbourhood activities essential to achieving the implications of the life and teachings of Jesus for rural people, itself providing for those activities not carried on by other agencies.

It has been recognized that some activities of the comprehensive Christian programme may be carried on by organizations other than the church. To the degree that this is true, the function of the church will be to judge these activities, to assess their contributions, to interpret their significance, and to suggest ways of integrating them into the life of the neighbourhood.

This task is the social counterpart of a function of Christian discipleship for the individual. Allegiance to God can pull the life of the individual together, resulting in an integrated personality. It is a task of the rural church to seek a similar integration of the activities of the neighbourhood by referring all of them to the same ultimate reality. Lacking such integration, a variety of activities may make the life of a neighbourhood hectic and conflicting, rather than abundant and meaningful.

1. *Integration in the task of Christian discipleship distinguishes the Christian programme in rural areas from secular programmes for rural development.* In the Christian programme, agricultural improvement is not an end in itself but a phase of more efficient trusteeship of God-given resources. Health development is not an end in itself but is another phase of trusteeship. Education is never an isolated attainment but

is always a training for competence in Christian service. Cooperative societies are not allowed to be considered a panacea, but remain that which they really are, a tool. No phase of the programme is allowed to become an end in itself; it is (or ought to be) always related to other phases of a way of life which loves God and which sees the implications of the Good News of Christ for all phases of rural life.

If only the church would accept this role of integration in neighbourhood life, it would be in a sound position to recognize, utilize, and cooperate with many splendid neighbourhood programmes now conducted under other auspices.

It is a good time to suggest that from now on we more seriously attempt to assess and understand the very great contributions to the Kingdom of God which are being made by many of the so-called secular agencies, especially those that are related to agriculture, the home, health and other community interests. And, furthermore, that we go as far as we can in cooperating with them and, in turn, get their cooperation in the service of the church. To my mind, one of the greatest weaknesses of organized religion, and therefore of loss of it, today, is that we have no adequate way to recognize and utilize the tremendous spiritual, ethical and moral values which undergird the services of these secular agencies referred to above. Thousands of their personnel are members of our churches, but because we have no ecclesiastical or administrative relation to or control over them, we naively assume they are none of our concern. Here and there, and increasingly so, there are exceptions, but, by and large, we have supinely acquiesced in the process by which great areas of life—agriculture, the home, the school, health, recreation—have been secularized and commercialized. But God is in them all and we must proclaim his Lordship over them. To do otherwise is to continue to promote secularism and to deny that God is in all and over all.[8]

We are driven back to this position: that rural reconstruction, although primarily a Christian duty, is too comprehensive and too complicated to be accomplished by any single agency, even though that agency be the Christian Church. Cooperation offers the one sovereign remedy, and for its effective application we must not grudge decades of patient endeavour.[9]

Religion is never so grand as when it is so closely connected with our everyday activities as to be indistinguishable from them, except

[8] John H. Reisner in Christian Rural Fellowship News Letter, Jan. 18, 1944.

[9] Hodge, J. Z., "The Missionary and the *Ryat*," *International Review of Missions,* 18:522.2

for the more glorious color it gives to the whole picture. Perhaps a modern version of that great vision in Revelation 21, of the city without a temple, might be a society which, in itself, is an all-encompassing Temple.[10]

There is evidence that the church is not quite so backward in this role as we have often judged it to be. But while the church has been an integrating force in many neighbourhoods, it has scarcely dreamed of the tremendous role it could play, were it thoroughly and critically to acquaint itself with the various threads of group life in its neighbourhood, and to set itself the task of weaving these threads together.

A rural church is particularly well situated to achieve this integration of the neighbourhood (provided it is not badly split along sectarian lines), because the same people who are associated in the work of the week are often associated in the congregation. There is a possibility of the rural neighbourhood and the Christian community becoming co-extensive to a degree not possible in the city.

> Church unity builds the community in spirit. This is true because the lay leaders of community agencies in the country are usually the same persons who lead the lodges, school and farm organizations. When the church is effective these laymen will take their Sunday religion over into their weekly activities. The church becomes a shepherd of community agencies. It leavens all the secular agencies with the spirit of service. The church demonstrates the adage that "the whole is greater than the sum of its parts" when it labours to put itself into the community rather than striving to get the community into the church.[11]

This task of integration is an administrative problem where the church itself carries on the full neighbourhood programme. To the degree that other resources are not available to meet the needs of the neighbourhood, the church will seek to equip itself, both by skill and by organization, to meet those needs. Under all circumstances, the church will develop whatever programme is needed for the nurture, development, and extension of the Christian group itself. Organization for the activities of worship, of witnessing, of church school education, are thus characteristic of all churches in all types of cultural environment.

10 Robert Hargreaves in Christian Rural Fellowship News Letter, Jan. 18, 1944.
11 Wyker, James D., "A Village Is My Parish," *Motive*, April, 1943, p. 23.

2. *The Christian community has a responsibility to make its prophecy, its interpretation, its judgment as broad as all activities of the neighbourhood, by whomever administered, and to make the programme it administers as broad as the needs of its neighbourhood not otherwise met.*[12]

Two types of integration have been found necessary where the church itself administers a broad programme, as it does in parts of the so-called "mission lands."

One of these types of integration is that of assuring that the different phases of the programme reach the same people. Typical of many mission stations was one in North China. "Our station was departmentalized so that we were educating some, healing others, evangelizing still others and scattering bits of agricultural knowledge, famine relief, and cooperative organization to other groups. The best results were apparent when the full programme touched the same individual."[12a]

The second type of integration called for is integration of the different phases of the programme within the leadership itself.

The comprehensive programme of the Christian rural mission is not different from other comprehensive programmes simply in its motive; it is an entirely different programme. When applied to a secular programme the word "comprehensive" means all-inclusive, all-around, ministering to the "whole man," to the "whole community." When it is applied to the programme of the Christian rural mission, it must be interpreted to mean complete, or whole, in the sense that the programme presents the "whole Gospel," the whole implication of the will of God for people living on the land, implications respecting the relationship between man and God, between man and man, between man and ideas, between man and material things.

Accurately to determine many of these implications, and to develop in people the tools of Christian discipleship, demand a division of labour between specialists in many fields. . . .

But that programme which we subdivide for analysis, we must re-assemble before it leaves our hands. At the point at which the Christian rural programme touches the countryside it must be one programme, an integrated programme, a religious programme, and it must be transmitted through a specialist in integration, perhaps the local pastor, perhaps a trained layman, who may not know as much Greek, and monetary science, and animal genetics, and edu-

[12] This is Fundamental Principle VI, see page 85.

[12a] Agricultural Missions, Inc., New York, Mimeograph Series No. 75.

cational theory, and liturgical history, as some of those who have helped to formulate the programme, but who, like the people with whom he lives, has had to integrate all of these into a unified outlook. He must be one who has learned to see what a certain change in one field will involve in other phases of our complex, interdependent common life, one who has combined the metals of many specialties into the fine alloy of effective discipleship.

The specialization within the Christian rural programme must be deep inside of it. It must be the arteries, the nerves, the muscles of the programme, not the face and hands and bearing. The face must be the face of the Christ it serves, its hands must be those of the servant, its bearing must be that of the majesty and eternity of God.[13]

Under all circumstances, the church should seek to produce individuals in whom all aspects of the implications of the gospel are integrated. It should seek as well to integrate all of its activities and those of other agencies which contribute to the development of Christian living,[14] so that the life of the neighbourhood shall be whole.

III.

The field of the comprehensive Christian programme is the entire neighbourhood, including its regional and world interrelationships.[14a]

The distinction between the Christian community and the geographical neighbourhood in which it is located is sound. At the same time, the two are inseparable. Disease may pass among all in the neighbourhood. Uusally there is a high degree of economic interdependence. Just as the Christian community influences the moral tone of the neighbourhood, so the moral tone of the neighbourhood influences the Christian community. Moreover, while there may be a valid distinction between "brother" (within the family of believers) and "neighbour" (outside this family) in the New Testament, Jesus was quite

13 Mosher, Arthur T., "The Spiritual Basis of a Comprehensive or 'Larger Parish' Program," *Christian Rural Fellowship Bulletin*, No. 75.

14 Where the services of numerous specialists are available it is often necessary to integrate these, prior to their introduction into the neighbourhood. All the specialist services available to a neighbourhood may well be integrated into a suggestive programme by regional councils (in consultation with specialists and local leaders), and executive officers of these councils may give continuous aid in integration and application of these services.

14a This is Fundamental Principle VII, see page 86.

explicit that all who are in need are to be treated as neighbours, and it was the inclusive term "thy neighbour" which he used in stating the New Commandment: "Thou shalt love thy neighbour as thyself."

Increasingly, we are coming to see that the *field* of the local church must be the whole neighbourhood: that health, both physical and spiritual, is indivisible; that in economic well-being most of a neighbourhood is interdependent; that "community (fellowship) is to be desired embracing the whole neighbourhood, shared in by Christian and non-Christian alike."

It is especially desirable that, in establishing new churches, sectarian divisions be avoided and the church led to develop as a true neighbourhood church. In rural areas the church can best serve if its parish is co-extensive with the neighbourhood, for then unity of spirit may pervade the economic, social, and spiritual life of the region and a true community may develop. Where the Christians are divided, jealousies between groups can make the church a divisive force, and there is little hope that any one of the disagreeing can fulfill its Christian function.

The Christian community, with all of its members participating, should set up its programme of activities for the whole neighbourhood, cooperating with non-Christians in the programme the latter may set up for neighbourhood welfare in so far as these do not prejudice the Christian spirit, and accepting their cooperation in the enterprises of the church.

In many instances, maintaining its essential Christian witness will cause its members to be shut out of neighbourhood participation whether or no. But such exclusiveness should not characterize the programme of the church. That programme should recognize both the fact of social solidarity and the fact of the responsibility of the church to maintain its distinctive witness, seeking to make the whole neighbourhood the field of its activity, with all of its members a part of the working force.[15]

It must be remembered that each rural neighbourhood is itself an interdependent part of its region and of the whole

[15] "The Church, the Christian group, which reaches out into the community in friendship and service and which influences ideals of reconstruction by its own faith and spirit, becomes stronger, not weaker. It finds new friends, it expresses Christian love. It is more of a leaven in community life. It becomes more deeply rooted in village society. Evangelism, religious education and community service can go hand in hand." Frank W. Price.

earth. Rural-urban relationships, the role of the farmer as a world citizen, his membership in the ecumenical church, and his relationship with other races are thus all a part of the fabric of the rural neighbourhood.

The church exists not for itself but to bring the holy and loving purposes of God to bear upon all the relationships and affairs of the community-family. As Carl C. Taylor has well said: "No social institution is an end in itself. Every item in the program of the church and every purpose it seeks to promote should be not for itself but for the community. The chief fault of the rural church of the past has been, and the abiding one of the sectarian church still is, that it looks upon the community as territory and population to be worked for the sake of building up the church rather than looking at the church as a working agency in the life of the community." Unless the rural church has this larger conception of its program, it will be a divisive influence and a hindrance to the realization of the community. . . . It is my faith that in the long run the rural church itself will grow in proportion to the degree in which it loses itself in service to its community. Someone has said that the church should not only provide "services" for its people but also a channel of "service." I stress this point because the conception of the rural church as the "serving" center of its community is the keystone in any program which would make religion effective in all of life.[16]

IV.

The organizational form of the church must vary from region to region with the social culture and economic resources of the people who are its members.[16a]

The whole Christian movement has been strengthened and enriched by the penetrating studies made under the leadership of Mr. J. Merle Davis which have established the importance of this principle.[17] Practice does not yet conform to the principle, but progress is being made.

The need for recognising this principle is most clearly evident in the lands of the younger churches. Missionaries going from one culture to another inevitably clothe the Good News

16 Smathers, Eugene, *op. cit.*

16a This is Fundamental Principle VIII, see page 86.

17 See *The Social and Economic Environment of the Younger Churches,* and *New Buildings on Old Foundations,* both by J. Merle Davis, New York and London: International Missionary Council.

at least partially in the forms of the culture from which they go. The means of achieving Christian discipleship in the rural neighbourhood which missionaries seek to develop are always coloured by the organizational patterns which similar means assume in their homelands. Eager to see the Body of Christ established in the new land, missionaries (and many national leaders) too easily assume that this means virtual adoption of the organizational form of the church in the "sending country."

It happens that in recent centuries the sending churches have been chiefly those of Europe and North America. All of these churches live in Occidental cultures. Increasingly, these cultures are dominated by urban-industrial patterns and ideals. To a very great extent they are influenced by secular and materialistic forces. These dominant forces have had great influence on the organizational form of the church in Europe and in North America. To expect the Body of Christ to assume similar organizational forms in Oriental and African cultures, among preponderantly rural peoples, is to ask the impossible and to encourage that which is unhealthful.

The rural churches of Asia and Africa must achieve organizational forms consonant with their own social cultures and with the economic resources of their own members. They cannot become indigenous so long as they try to reproduce Occidental patterns. Among the specific features of church organization which must be subject to such regional variation are the degree to which the church relies on professional personnel, the method of support of this personnel, type of church government, type of congregational organization, extent and type of church buildings and equipment, etc.

Every rural minister and missionary should become well acquainted with the studies growing out of the investigation of this problem and should be alert for opportunities to bring practice into conformity with the principle, to the end that the religious organization he aids in establishing may become, in reality, the church.

This Principle is discussed at greater length in Part II of this Report. See page 186 ff.

V.

Permeating all of the activities of the church should be an attitude of love—sympathetic and forgiving, yet persevering and unswerving—like that manifested by Jesus in all of his living and in his death on the cross. The Christian community should maintain this attitude at any cost.[17a]

An impelling, understanding, forgiving love permeated every day of Jesus' life. It was the intimate love of fellowship and the radical love of unswerving loyalty to God.

Whether well received or opposed, with steadfast devotion Jesus went forward with his ministry. With no avoidance nor complaint he accepted the costs, whether the misunderstanding that turned followers away from him, the stubbornness of self-centred lives, the passive inertia that could be overcome only by love, the questions meant to trap him, open ridicule and taunts, the cowardly plots against him, or the false accusations, farcical trials, and ignominious execution at last forced upon him.

But has the church realized sufficiently that, in its corporate life, it is called to this same high quality of living? It sings its praise of Jesus' atoning sacrifice. In memory it honours its outstanding martyrs from Stephen to those of our day. But what about the church's record of life and witness in the social order? Has it not sinned by turning prosecutor? Has it not compromised on moral issues? Has it not been weak and cowardly in watching great wrongs perpetrated without hindrance? In the modern tensions between tenants and landlords, employer and employee, minority and majority groups, white and colored races, has the church taken the stand that Jesus would have taken? Has it wrestled in agony of spirit with the wanton sin of war, insisting that competent organs can be established and upheld to serve the peoples of the world for amicable settlements to meet every legitimate need and solve every vital problem without resort to war?

To be sure, the church can point to notable instances of persecution and hardship endured for its faith. We cannot forget the patience and perseverance of the early church in the catacombs. The Pilgrims underwent the hardships of migration to preserve religious freedom. All over the world, new Christians have been ostracized by their friends and often by their families. The Armenian Christians suffered mass deportation for their faith. Scores of German pastors have suffered the restrictions and privations of internment because they and their churches would

[17a] This is Fundamental Principle IX, see page 86.

not bow to dictation. These are but a few of many instances of churches paying heavy costs, even unto martyrdom of members, for their faith, and in each instance with no small measure of Christ-like forgiving spirit.

However, we tend to look on these as the exceptional, unfortunate occurrences rather than to recognize them as dramatic instances of what must be the everyday portion of a church which is living up to its faith. God's method of redemption is always the cross. To be the Body of Christ in a rural community is to live as a group such a steadfast life of loving service to the neighbourhood as must necessarily, ever and again, bring down the retribution of the neighbourhood upon it. Thus do men in their self-centredness ever react to the loving importunity of God, until the moment when they see the light and yield their wills to their Father.

In very few instances do the Christians comprise all of a given neighbourhood. More typically, they are a minority group. The majority may be adherents of non-Christian religions, or they may be "nominal Christians" or "non-church people." While there is some difference between these, the problem posed for the earnest Christian is about the same.

As a minority, what is the place of the church in the neighbourhood? It has five tasks:

a. To be a truly Christian community.
b. To call men into discipleship to Jesus Christ.
c. To provide Christian nurture for individuals, families, and groups.
d. To serve all those who are in need, physically, socially, mentally, spiritually, as far as it can, out of its compassion for all the sons of men.
e. To evaluate all neighbourhood activities and to seek to integrate the life of the neighbourhood.

In attempting these tasks the church may or may not find congenial atmosphere and friendly response. It may be misunderstood and opposed by the government, by adherents of other religions, or by unenlightened and unredeemed society. Its very loyalty to truth and right may be the factor that brings it most into controversy. For government may be biased and bigoted and given to unethical practices; the practices of established cults and religions may be deeply entrenched; business interests in the countryside may be given to exploitation; gambling and immorality may have deep rootage and be backed by vested interests.

Happy the church with such moral strength and fibre within its own body, and with such degree of sympathetic support from outside, that it can face opposition and evil in all these fields with conquering virility!

Too often the witness which might be given by the activities of a local Christian community is destroyed by the unloving attitudes within the group. Not only in early Hebrew and pagan practices were hymns of hate and egotism and prayers for revenge to be found; Christian worship today is not always free from them. Worship is too often self-satisfied consolation rather than the evidence of a seeking love. Preaching has contained embittered polemics against others and has at times descended to petty bickering. Groups have carried on worthy activities in the name of the church while certain members of them were "not speaking" to one another. There have been leaders who have competed with one another for places of authority and who have led by dominance rather than by the persuasion of love. From Paul's time on there have been sects and divisions in the Christian community, whether within one organization or among different ones. No love is lost between them, nor is any used. One sect of Christian farmers can even seriously ask whether or not they should share their agricultural machinery with Christians of another denomination! The spirit of love is lacking.

No matter how many or how few activities may be carried on in the Christian rural programme, it is only when Christians love one another and all people that the world receives the Good News through the testimony of their lives. What the Christian community now needs is to make this spirit the norm of all its working and witnessing and enduring, for the undergirding of its common and continuing tasks in its own parish and neighbourhood, for the clarifying of its vision for participation in the wider complex affairs of mankind, and for its strengthening to meet all puzzlement and all opposition. "Love suffereth long and is kind; love envieth not; love vaunteth not itself, is not puffed up. Doth not behave itself unseemly, seeketh not her own, is not easily provoked, thinketh no evil; rejoiceth not in iniquity, but rejoiceth in the truth; beareth all things, believeth all things, hopeth all things, endureth all things. Love never faileth."

POSTSCRIPT

THERE are those who have said of this report that it describes the kind of impact rural Christians and the rural church might aspire to in maturity, but that it does not grapple with the problems of the first approach to non-Christians or with that of the new Christian group.

It is true that a complex, multiform programme is not often the advisable first step. Our study convinces us, however, that, *from the very first,* leadership of the Christian mission among rural people must:

1. Be appreciative of the peculiar advantage of rural life.
2. Be personally happy in rural surroundings.
3. Realize what it is that the Christian revelation brings to rural people and how this has implications for every phase of rural life.
4. Realize that every activity of life either contributes to or detracts from (a) achieving Christian discipleship and (b) witnessing to faith in God; and that these two are inseparable.
5. Understand the central importance of the family and the significance of the local Christian community.
6. Recognize that no one activity can mirror fully the Good News, but that this can be done only through a variety of activities, however elemental these may be, carried on by the growing Christian group itself.

While specialization is found necessary among the personnel of an advanced programme, it is not essential to the kind of outreach we have tried to describe. Some of the most realistic Christian programmes have flowed from the life-wide interests of single individuals. Similarly no Christian programme is valid simply because it is inclusive. If there is a variety of activities, consecrated integration of these is imperative.

For this reason, we are inclined to insist that the Christian programme must be "comprehending" rather than "comprehensive." It is not an omnibus of all good rural programmes, but it is a programme which results from comprehending the full Christian gospel, and from comprehending the people and problems of the countryside.

PART II

Expansion of Phases of the Report

A.

Implications of the Life and Teachings of Jesus for Rural Living

THE central ceremony of a Hindu wedding lasts from two to four hours. Most of this time is consumed in an alternating recital, by the two officiating priests, of the duties in marriage of the husband and wife respectively. This recital goes into minute detail, covering all of the everyday, concrete problems with which the couple will have to deal, from the moment when they are joined in marriage until death separates them.

Such a ceremony may become very tiring to the guests and to the bride and groom, since the dialogue is in Sanskrit, which few common people understand. Its great merit is that it brings principles down to problems, it translates general ideals into specific duties.

A discerning rural pastor three years ago pointed out our great need for such a process in rural living. We glibly assert that Christian discipleship has implications for all of life, then proceed to make "for all of life" a vague password, itself not translated into specific attitudes and duties. Too seldom do we follow general Christian attitudes through to explicit duties. Too seldom do we sit down before a diagram which charts these implications (many of them well-known, but oftentimes neglected because so long established) in building a Christian rural programme, a preaching programme, or a church school schedule.

It is in an attempt to make this concrete application, therefore, that we set down here the consensus of opinion of Christian leaders as to the detailed implications of the life and teachings of Jesus for rural people. These are not a marginal outgrowth of a central gospel. They are the gospel itself translated into the vernacular of rural life today.

I. IMPLICATIONS FOR SOCIAL RELATIONSHIPS

Whether it be within the family, within the neighbourhood, or within the broad brotherhood of men across the earth, the implications of the life and teachings of Jesus for relationships among men are those flowing from recognition of all men as equals in the sight of God, regardless of position, ability, caste or class, sex, race, or attainments.

1. *Implications for Relationships Within the Family*

In the United States, the typical family is thought of as composed of father, mother, and children. In India and China, a family typically includes all of the living sons and their families, as well as the father and mother. In the Congo and other sections of Africa, the clan is the important group.

We use the word "family" here to include the living members of the "larger family": grandparents, parents and children, cousins, aunts, and uncles. The implications as to fundamental attitudes and relationships among these would seem to be the same whether they live in the same home or in several homes, in the same town or in different places.

The family group is particularly strong in the countryside. Whether it be the "larger" family of the Orient and of Africa, or the restricted family of European countries, it is bound together by common interests much more in the countryside than in the cities. Farm tasks which even the children and the aged grandparents can help perform bind the family together in a way not common in an urban setting. Where families live in scattered farmsteads, the isolation from other people strengthens the family group. Whether they live in separated farmsteads or in villages, their constant intimacy, their shared tasks, and their common concern over variation in family income as crops and prices vary, result in a feeling of family solidarity which may be lost when the joint income is regular and stable. For those reasons, the opportunities for strong family development are great among rural people.[1]

a. *The older generation.* In the family, as in all social relationships, the Christian ideal is respect for each individual as an end in himself, having his own peculiar and unique contribution to make, as a child of God. In one's attitude toward family-members of an older generation, (parents, grandparents, uncles, and aunts), this implies honour and love for each individual and respect for the guidance of the older person, based on love and on confidence in his desire to be helpful. It implies the expression of gratitude, by means of conduct and through courtesy, for support, security, and affection. It means acceptance of responsibility for family duties and care and support of parents when and if necessary. It means sympathy with the attitudes and folkways of older generations even after these have been generally abandoned by one's contemporaries. And it means loving memory, but not worship, of those of the family who have made their contribution and have passed on.[2]

[1] See Sorokin, Zimmerman, Galpin, *A Systematic Source Book in Rural Sociology*, University of Minnesota Press, 1931, Vol. II, Ch. X "The Family As the Basic Institution and Familism as the Fundamental Relationship of Rural Social Organization."

[2] "The teachings of Christ appear in the nature of a high explosive laid at the foundations of Asiatic society. To place love and honor of parents as of secondary importance to love of God is to the Chinese a shocking impiety, for

b. *The younger generation.* Whereas the attitude of children towards their parents is based on respect, gratitude, and sympathy for those to whom the child owes his early nurture and training, the attitude of the parent toward the child is that of one who has assumed responsibility for bringing the child into the world and for starting him on his way through life. This involves, first of all, providing physical care and security for the child as long as it is to the child's advantage. It means intelligent affection without favoritism. It implies treating the child from the first as an individual in his own right, carefully avoiding any emotional or economic exploitation to satisfy a desire of the parent at the expense of the child. It means an earnest endeavour to develop the character and personality of the child, based on sharing the Christian message with him as rapidly as he can understand it; so that the child may himself become heir to the spirit which Christ brought to earth, and may himself grow into that discipleship which will quicken him and transform him into a son of the Father.

The Christian parent will realize that his own example in conduct, attitudes, and ideals, family fellowship and mutual loyalty, training in good habits and in skills, specific religious education, and general education, all have their part in this process.

c. *The same generation.* Among brothers, sisters, and cousins these Christian principles ought to express themselves in love and mutual service, in cooperation in family enterprises, in respect for the individuality and right to freedom from exploitation of each person, regardless of age or sex, in an attempt to understand sympathetically each others' points of view, and in an endeavour mutually to assist in the development of each.

d. *Christian marriage.* Unique among relationships within the family, at least to Christians, is that between husband and wife. The Christian concept of marriage is a paradox. It insists on recognition of the fact that in marriage "the two become one" and it therefore looks on marriage as permanent and insists on loyalty to monogamy. This is at the same time a recognition of the role of the home in the rearing and training of children through a long period of dependence, and of the sacredness of the procreative process, symbolizing the devotion of the husband and wife to each other and to their common responsibility. Therefore the Christian

it undermines their most sacred life obligation and with it the corner stone on which the solidity and security of society rest . . . the injunction to chastity and the guarding of the sanctity of marriage may run counter to the obligation of every family to provide a male issue to insure an unbroken family line. The security and continuity of the family takes precedence over every personal consideration." Madras Conference Report Vol. V. "Economic Basis of the Church," p. 50.

pledge of marriage is "for better or for worse, for richer, for poorer, in sickness and in health, till death us do part," recognizing that in their role as parents, husband and wife have become one, both in their children and in their responsibility for their children. Consequently, one of the cardinal implications of the Christian gospel for the relationship between husband and wife is faithfulness in permanent, monogamous marriage.

The other aspect of the paradox in the Christian concept of marriage is that even while "the two shall become one," each retains his own individuality. The fact that they have in a real sense become one person does not alter the fact that each is still a person in his own right. Within the Christian tradition there cannot be the type of slavery and exploitation which regards the wife as the property of the husband, nor can there be sanctioned the domination of the wife by her husband, or of the husband by his wife. Husband and wife are complementary, each bringing to marriage the equally important but distinctive qualities of his sex. They are to share their family responsibilities according to temperament and abilities, with no sense of superiority of one over the other, and with no difference in their degrees of authority over the children.

These two aspects of the paradox of Christian marriage come together in the attempt at Christian discipleship of the husband and wife in trusteeship of their respective abilities.[3] The Christian marriage, like the Christian individual, looks outward and reaches outward to the common life of mankind. As an individual each has peculiar abilities and talents, of which he and his partner in marriage are trustees. Some of these are best utilized within the home; others make their greatest contribution outside of the home. The Christian husband and wife assist each other as they can in the development of these abilities, and seek so to arrange their life together that the abilities of each may be dedicated to the welfare of others, to the extent that is consistent with the welfare of the family.

The above discussion assumes that both husband and wife are devoted disciples of the Master. One of the most difficult problems of discipleship arises when this is not the case. Where one has been drawn to Christ, after marriage, while the other has not, or where it is discovered that the two do not share compatible opinions as to what Christian discipleship involves for them, the problem is acute. Participation in the corporate life of the Christian community, to the extent that the less enthusiastic partner is readily willing, may ease the difficulty. Jesus stated in no uncertain terms that loyalty

[3] Discussed on page 152.

to the spiritual family of God must take precedence over human family ties and responsibilities. "If any man come to me, and hate not his father, and mother, and wife, and children, and brethren, and sisters, yea, and his own life also, he cannot be my disciple." But he did not mean by this to condone abandoning family responsibilities.[4] Christian discipleship seldom suggests running away from problems, slipping out from under responsibilities voluntarily assumed. It demands rather the facing of problems and the shouldering of responsibilities.

e. *The family and the neighbourhood.* With families, as with Christian individuals, the primary allegiance and relationship outside themselves is to God the Father. This allegiance becomes the controlling one for the life of members of a family and for their outreach into the community. To the end of realizing God's presence in the home and in the affairs of the neighbourhood, family worship and Bible study are needed. In family worship, the family feels itself knit into a unit with common commitment to the Christtian life. On farms where there are employed workers and their families, it is desirable that arrangements be made to include these in the family worship. There is no better opportunity for inspiring equitable and sympathetic relationships among those thus intimately associated in the life of the farm.

A local church congregation is a family of families. Congregations are strong when they are composed of steadfast Christian families. It is desirable, in so far as possible, that Christians participate as families in the life of the local congregation. Social contacts between families of the church as families add appreciably to the understanding and sympathy which are the bases of Christian fellowship.

2. *Social Relationships*

a. *Between individuals.* Since the family is the analogy which Jesus continually used in setting forth God's will for relationships among men, the implications of the Christian gospel for relationships between individuals within a neighbourhood are simply the Christian attitudes among members of a family extended to everyone in the locality.

b. *Individuals and groups.* One of the groups to which individuals are related in the neighbourhood is the local church. The Christian will recognize the church as the family of God. He will seek a welding together of the members of the church in worship, in fellowship, in service, and in cooperative and constructive living. He will give the church his whole-hearted but discriminating

[4] Mark 7:10-13.

loyalty, recognizing that, while the church is the earthly expression of the fellowship of believers, it is dependent upon the loyal criticism of its members for correction and interpretation. For this reason he will maintain a spirit of sympathetic appraisal of the life and activities of the church. He will participate in determining the attitudes and decisions of the church, expressing his personal convictions courageously but without seeking to dominate the group. He will participate actively in the life of the church, along lines of his interest and abilities. He will help to enlist others in the Christian fellowship.

As for groups other than the church, the Christian ought to participate in a limited number of those which are most helpful to the neighbourhood and for which he is best qualified. He participates in the group because of what it can contribute to the neighbourhood; and because its contribution is in a direction indicated by the Christian outlook. With Christian love and tolerance he courageously sponsors righteous causes and opposes evil practices. In doing so he must maintain his loyalty to his Christian commitment since it is much broader and deeper than the interest of any one secular group. He will be alert to recognize emerging needs of the neighbourhood which can be met only by group cooperation.

c. *Group with group.* In most rural sections there are comparatively few organized groups of people within each local community. But in a few regions there are many, and then Christians find it necessary not only to define their relationships as individuals to the groups of which they are members, but also to help define and mould the policies of groups with respect to each other. In many rural neighbourhoods there are other religious groups in addition to the church. Some of these are Christian; some of them are non-Christian. There may be political organizations, lodges, recreational organizations, farmers' organizations, cooperatives, and others.

There are three principles which Christians should continually strive to uphold in dealings between groups. These apply equally to local, to national, and to international situations:

First: In group as in individual contacts, Christian motives and the Christian ethic should prevail.

Second: Each organized group ought to recognize the valid functions of other groups and ought to cooperate with them where desirable and possible, rather than duplicate their contributions.

Third: Christians ought to insist on freedom of conscience and belief in and between groups of which they are members.[5]

[5] "Determination to practice, and by all Christian means to defend, religious freedom." Recommendation 43, Church Conference on African Affairs, *Christian Action in Africa,* p. 167.

3. *Implications for Relationships within the Larger Social Order*

To turn to the question of the implications of the life and teachings of Jesus for social relationships within the larger social order is to recognize again the interaction of rural and urban people and to enter into a problem which is perhaps the most crucial, so far as the witness of the church is concerned, and the most controversial, so far as thought about it is concerned, of all of the issues facing the Christian community today. But that cannot release us from the necessity of recognizing the problem of the will of God for farmers within the context of the whole social order.

When Jesus lived in Galilee the dominant ethical issues concerned the relationships between individuals. He was considerably widening the horizons of those among whom he lived when he included the Samaritans, the Gentiles, and the publicans within his fellowship. As communications and transportation have improved and as the present complex world order has emerged, sensitive Christians have striven to read the mind of Christ with respect to the ethical issues involved in modern citizenship, production, and commerce. Many of these issues impinge on farming and on farmers.

a. *Realization of interdependence.* We have come far enough in our realization of this problem in rural neighbourhoods to understand and accept the interdependence of men across the earth: the dependence of the welfare of each neighbourhood on the decisions, customs, and habits of people halfway around the world. The sugar planter of Cuba knows the influence of Javanese policy. The beef farmer of America recognizes the influence of decisions in Argentina. The indigo farmer of India learned the power of distant chemical research to replace a whole agricultural industry. These lessons have not been pressed home to rural people in Asia and Africa as thoroughly as they have to those in more industrialized agricultural regions. But even on those continents the influence of distant events and decisions is sometimes keenly realized. In 1938 groups of farmers in the Ganges Valley were asked to name their greatest economic needs. In one village after another, after naming ten or twelve specific needs such as irrigation water or better milch cows, some farmers would say, "What we really need is another World War. Then the price of wheat would rise and we would all be prosperous." The entire group would nod agreement.[6]

Farmers are learning the principle of interdependence but few have accepted specific responsibilities with respect to it. Not until they take it upon themselves to know what other farmers produce,

[6] Reported by A. T. Mosher.

what effect policies of production, of tariffs, and of trade have on other farmers, and what is the effect of farm prices on consumers of food and clothing, will they be in a position to follow Christ, with respect to their brothers around the earth. Far too often they see the Christian implications for urban industrial problems, and extol the reality of the interdependence of all people, without critically examining the effects of their own agricultural policies on far-away peoples and without continually making the costly readjustments necessary in the interests of their distant brothers.

b. *Individual involvement in social policy.* While we are well on the way to realizing the extent of our interdependence, we have gone only a step toward realizing the individual-social paradox in each person which is at the heart of much of this problem. In face-to-face contacts of individual with individual each has control over one-half of the contact. Given sufficient grace and sufficient knowledge he can make at least half of the contact what he wants it to be. But where policies of groups of which we are inescapably a part impinge on the welfare of other groups, we do not have this control.[7] We may have the privilege, within our group, of influencing policy while it is being formed, but once the policy has been decided, perhaps along lines which we feel are un-Christian, what are we to do? This is the dilemma which modern interdependence, coupled with democratic participation in the life of society, forces upon us.

The last few years have seen a few excursions into this important field of rural discipleship. While many official Protestant agencies have taken stands with respect to certain rural problems, such as conditions of land ownership and tenancy, development of cooperative marketing facilities, and have urged fuller understanding between rural and urban groups,[8] few of these have included explanations as to how the approved attitude was to be achieved. Few have challenged national policy with respect to foreign trade and international opportunity. Notable exceptions are the Malvern and, more recently, the Delaware Conference, which broke ground in coming to grips with specific problems and making definite proposals in this field.

An attempt to state the problem of farmers' relationships in the larger social order, and a suggested approach to it, are contained in *The Spiritual Basis of a Comprehensive or Larger Parish Program* by Arthur T. Mosher. The question which Mr. Mosher raises is

[7] See Niebuhr, Reinhold, *Moral Man and Immoral Society,* New York: Charles Scribner's Sons, 1932, p. 277.

[8] *The Social Ideals of the Churches for Agriculture and Rural Life,* Christian Rural Fellowship Bulletin No. 73, June 1942.

whether or not it is possible to develop an individual technique, in accord with the Christian spirit, for meeting issues of group morality.

> Is it not true that the need of our generation is for clarification of a Christian ethic which may be applied effectively by *individuals* living in a *groupistic* society? . . . A farmer in North India, wishing to be a Christian, must realize the moral issue involved in raising sugar cane, for which India is poorly endowed by nature, with high tariff protection, while his neighbors in Java and Cuba suffer because of a glutted market. But he must be equipped with a technique which he can himself employ without having first to change the tariff policy of the Government of India.[9]

It may be that there are instances where the action of an individual can at least demonstrate disagreement with a group policy. Repeatedly throughout history, some Christians have stood out from or in the group, living by standards in the economic and social world quite different from those called for by convention or by general practice. We need to be looking for such opportunities in corporate rural life today. However, in many, if not in most, such issues, the individual is inextricably involved and quite unable to dissociate himself from the action of the group. The late Archbishop of Canterbury in his little book, *Christianity and the Social Order,* has probably gone as far toward stating this problem fairly and toward setting sign-posts for its solution as any Christian thinker.

> It is not only individuals who must, if Christianity is the truth, guide their policy or career by the principles of service; all groupings of men must do the same. The rule here should be *that we use our wider loyalties to check the narrower.*[10] A man is a member of his family, of his nation, and of mankind. It is very seldom that any one can render a service directly to mankind as a whole. We serve mankind by serving those parts of it with which we are closely connected. And our narrower loyalties are likely to be more intense than the wider, and therefore call out more devotion and more strenuous effort. But we can and should check these keener, narrow loyalties by recognizing the prior claim of the wider. So a man rightly does his best for the welfare of his own family, but must never serve his family in ways that injure the nation. A man rightly does his best for his country, but must never serve his country in ways that injure mankind.[11]

Less commonly recognized, though no less pressing, is another problem arising from the relationships of the individual with the group. In areas like Africa, China, India, and Burma as well as

9 Mosher, A. T., *The Spiritual Basis of a Comprehensive or Larger Parish Program,* Christian Rural Fellowship Bulletin No. 75, p. 4.

10 Italics not in the original.

11 Temple, William, *Christianity and the Social Order,* p. 53.6.

certain parts of the western world, it is one of maintaining the values of group living in the face of a rising tide of rugged individualism. The disruptive force of an industrial system which considers only the individual challenges the traditional group life of the clan in Bantu Africa. Amish farmers of Pennsylvania find it difficult to maintain their mores when faced by a school system the whole emphasis of which is to educate individuals.

In the western world, this becomes a problem of rediscovering these values of group living. The whole Christian community is frequently faced with critical difficulty in fostering that group solidarity which was in the mind of Christ in his prayer for unity. This is by no means simply an urban problem: no group cherishes its tradition of independence and individualism, born of rugged pioneer life and the isolation of frontier existence, more devotedly than the American farmer. Cooperation, mutual service, and fellowship are frequently the most pressing need and the most difficult to develop, even among the members of a single denomination in a rural neighbourhood.

c. *Political participation as a tool of discipleship.* The rural follower of Christ must recognize that, to the degree that he is free to participate in civic life, he is responsible for the policies of his civic group, and partner in its achievements and its sins. He will use any opportunities for participation he has, to try to make Christian principles basic in political decisions. Christians can implement their discipleship by banding together with other people in political action, in order to promote health in the village, to provide facilities for education, to secure an equitable distribution of the tax burden, and to eliminate certain social evils by legislation. Many individuals whose primary allegiance is not to Christ are interested in civic improvement, and Christians should realize that whole-hearted cooperation with such people in these interests is a splendid way to further their own discipleship.

The trusteeship of certain resources can be satisfactorily accomplished only through civic action. For example, the conservation of forests, of mineral deposits, and, to a degree, of soils, requires legislation. Christians should feel much greater responsibility to promote such laws than they have demonstrated in the past.[12]

d. *Participation in the world Christian fellowship.* Today the individual Christian farmer, tilling his land in one small community, can feel himself a participant in the broader life of the

[12] See Madras Conference Report, The World Mission of the Church, Ch. XIII, XIV, XV: "The Church and the State," "The Church and the Changing Social and Economic Order," "The Church and the International Order."

earth through his membership in the world Christian fellowship. Now that there are Christians in nearly every country, and that Christian bodies are drawing closer together in cooperative action, this World Church is more and more an effective reality.

Such participation involves, first, the acceptance of responsibility by each local congregation *to be* the world fellowship within its community, to make its atmosphere one of global discipleship and its field of interest the whole earth, and to represent worthily the world fellowship of believers. Obviously, any denominational division within a small neighbourhood weakens the witness of the church in this regard. Yet this division is the actual situation in thousands of communities. Local units will not get together within neighbourhoods, and state and national denominational organizations are unwilling to give up any measurable amount of sovereignty in the interests of larger unity. Even while they call upon nations to resign elements of sovereignty to make possible a practicable world federation for the peaceful solution of international difficulties, they remain unwilling to federate themselves in a practical unification of the activities of Christians. Denominations are not ready to follow the Christian principles of losing life in order to gain it. Until Christians rise above local jealousies and the pettiness of denominational prerogatives, rural Christians are hamstrung in their attempts to be full participants in, and representatives of, the world Christian fellowship.

Participation in the ecumenical fellowship involves, second, acceptance of responsibility for participation in its corporate activities. There are many tasks of discipleship which can be performed only by many congregations working cooperatively. The resources of congregations often are not proportionate to the problems and opportunities in their vicinity. This calls for re-allocation of resources within the church across the earth. Churches in the "lands of the younger churches" are rapidly achieving autonomy. Therefore, both "foreign" and "home" missions are rapidly becoming phases of this re-allocation of resources that must be made in order that the church may meet strategic opportunities in any part of the world. For such wise cooperation to be effective, each Christian should urge that the local congregation of which he is a member participate fully in these wider activities.

Third, in the worship experiences in the local congregation, every attempt should be made to help each worshipper to realize that he is a member of the great family of those who meet God through Christ in every section of the globe, who together dedicate their resources to him, who are baptized into one name. In worship, each should learn to unite with others in spite of differences, and each should thus obtain emotional rootage for the growing ideal of ecumenicity.

Fourth, Christians need increasing opportunity for mutual enrichment of their common life through the contributions of Christians of different racial and cultural backgrounds. The emerging World Church is teaching us this: that we are all provincial, and that the truth of God is interpreted more fully when it is interpreted by men and women from many lands and many backgrounds, joining together in discipleship of the Master. Especially do the white races need this lesson.[13]

II. IMPLICATIONS FOR TRUSTEESHIP OF RESOURCES

> "And man shall have dominion over the fish of the sea, and over the birds of the heavens, and over the cattle, and over all the earth, and over every creeping thing that creepeth upon the earth."

Each of us stands in a great succession, born upon an earth and into a culture developed before his time and needed by his children and by his children's children. Each of us, therefore, is a trustee, administering for the common good of all people resources which he has had little or no hand in creating, and therefore little or no right to control in pursuit of his own advantage.

Each person has responsibility for trusteeship over (1) material resources, (2) abilities and skills, (3) cultural resources, (4) the human body, (5) time, and (6) income.

1. *Material Resources*

Jesus was never more explicit in his teaching than when he was talking about a man's attitude toward material things. He was concerned about the danger of absorption in things. This he recognized as a danger both for those who have much and for those who have little. It was to those who had much that he spoke about the difficulty of a rich man entering the Kingdom. It was to the rich ruler who inquired about the Law that he said, "Go, sell all you have to feed the poor, and come and follow me." But he was equally concerned about the preoccupation of the poor with the things they did not have. "Consider the lilies of the field . . . " he said, and do not pay too much attention to how tomorrow's needs will be met. Thus Jesus' primary teaching about material things is that man is greater than they, and is not to become absorbed in possession of or in desire for them.

[13] See Fleming, Daniel J., *The Ecumenical Series,* Harper and Brothers. 1. *Heritage of Beauty.* 2. *Each With His Own Brush.* 3. *Christian Symbols in a World Community.* 4. *The World At One In Prayer.*

But Jesus did not belittle material goods. He emphasized that they are gifts of God to men, and that God is concerned that men shall have what they need. "Your heavenly Father knoweth that ye have need of these things."

Jesus emphasized the attitude of trusteeship, of stewardship, toward all material things. The parable of the talents, the parable of the slothful servant, the gathering of fragments after the multitude had eaten, all attest to Jesus' principle of careful trusteeship of material things for the common good.

Foremost among the material resources of rural life is the land itself. Perhaps no phase of trusteeship has received greater attention in recent years that this. In many cultures, the importance of the land is recognized, but all too often recognition of its importance has not led to intelligent understanding and utilization. Thorough study of the soil in recent years has been helping to overcome this weakness, and the nature of the problem of soil management is beginning to be understood.

"Most of our difficulty with the earth lies in the effort to do what perhaps ought not to be done. Not even all the land is fit to be farmed. A good part of agriculture is to learn how to adapt one's work to nature, to fit the crop-scheme to the climate and to the soil and the facilities. To live in right relation with his natural conditions is one of the first lessons that a wise farmer or any other wise man learns. We are at pains to stress the importance of conduct: very well: conduct toward the earth is an essential part of it."[14]

Production is cooperation with God. Few of the material things of earth meet human needs on the spot and in the form in which they naturally occur. Even wild fruits must be gathered. So even in the simplest economy the utilization of the material things of the earth requires a degree of cooperation between men and God. Some products of the earth need only to be gathered: native fruits in season, fish along streams and seacoasts, firewood from the forests. Some are greatly multiplied by cultivation. Corn in the corn field, and rice in the rice field, produce more food than similar plants growing wild. Other materials make their contribution to human welfare only after being processed and refined. Ores must be smelted, gems cut, and petroleum refined. Still others need to be combined with each other: carbon and iron into steel and steel with various elements to suit it for particular uses, linseed oil and lead oxide into paints, leather and fabric and nails into shoes. But no matter how complicated the manufacturing process may become, the real nature

[14] Bailey, Liberty Hyde, *The Holy Earth,* New York: Christian Rural Fellowship, 1943, p. 9.

of "production" remains the same: it is one of cooperation between man and God. It is one of the advantages of rural life for the development of Christian discipleship that constant contact with plants and animals and the weather emphasizes this partnership.

Many materials are concentrated in certain parts of the world, although the contribution they could make is potential for all the earth. Only the delta of the Ganges and the Brahmaputra can support large quantities of the jute plant, but the industrial countries of Europe and America need millions of gunny bags and millions of yards of burlap made from jute fibre. Most of our cocoa must be transported from West Africa and most of our tea from Ceylon, Assam, and China.

Thus all production is cooperation between men and God. God furnishes the raw materials. Men, in cooperation with God, gather these materials, refine them, process them, transport them, combine them, store them until needed. Men sort out the processes of God: setting one useful plant in one field to the exclusion of others, practising selective breeding of plants and animals in order to secure desired results. Men cooperate in minutely-specialized capacities to achieve the efficient manufacture of finished goods. In all of these they are increasing the utility to man of God-given resources by the application of divinely-created processes.

Here is the basis of the fundamental dignity of all labor. On the one hand, all worthy labor is cooperation in creative processes; on the other, it fulfills the needs of men for food, clothing, shelter, medicine, books, and other requirements of existence. Thus the Christian attitude is not one of disrespect for labor, nor is it the Old Testament idea of work having been laid on man as a curse. *The Christian attitude is the simple statement of Jesus of a transforming partnership: "My Father worketh even until now, and I work."*

Trusteeship of material resources involves (1) utilization, and (2) conservation. Jesus condemned unequivocally the servant who hid his talent in the ground. Resources are for use, not for storage. But they are for *use through a period of time.* The farmer who is conscious of his membership in a family of many generations, each in turn cultivating the same farm, has a wholesome regard for the effect of his cultivation on the land itself which the tenant-at-will can hardly be expected to have. A good illustration of the roles of conservation and of utilization of material resources is to be found in the attitude of the Chinese farmer. He has a strong sense of family. His dominant religious tradition has been to worship his ancestors and his great passion has been for sons to carry on after his death. Therefore, he feels his responsibility for maintaining the productive capacity of his land. But, at the same time, the members of his immediate family need the produce of the land. They live in a land of many people, with comparatively few industries, with great pressure of population on the soil, so that farms are small and fields must be cultivated intensively. The greatest possible current production would diminish the productive power of the soil. Maximum conservation would reduce current production. The point of optimum trusteeship is somewhere in between, with both objectives of utilization and conservation always in mind.[15]

In some regions where technical knowledge of farming methods is most advanced, there still is conspicuous lack of a sense of obligation to conserve and to improve the soil for the sake of future generations.

To the end of this wise trusteeship, the Christian farmer will utilize the knowledge systematized in the agricultural sciences: descriptions of the ways by which God works in agriculture. Jesus' call to trusteeship of resources means that, for the farmer, scientific techniques of agricultural production are instruments of Christian discipleship. It means that, for the Christian, the function of the sciences of crop production, of soil chemistry, and of animal husbandry is to contribute to Christian trusteeship of resources; and the function of the art and science of farm management is to aid in the integration of the trusteeship a particular farmer exercises over the various agricultural resources under his control.

Maintenance of the dominance of personality over things. Important as is trusteeship over material things, to the Christian things always remain less important than the people who handle them. "Is not the life more than the food, and the body than the raiment?" The employee is more important than his product.

And life is broader than production. "Man shall not live by bread alone." No matter how fine a trustee of material resources a man may be, he is not fully Christian if he allows management of things to crowd out of his life worship, fellowship, and leisure enough for full expression of a friendly life. Nor may he allow these to be crowded out of the lives of his employees and their families by the duties which he assigns. Therefore, the Christian farmer must not accept the trusteeship ("control" or "ownership") of too

[15] The determination of this point in farming is one of the problems of agricultural economics, which is the study of optima in agricultural production. This point is one of the optima which the manager of each farm ought to seek. Only very rarely will it be one at which the productive capacity of soil is decreasing. It may be that at which soil fertility remains constant, or it may be at a point at which fertility increases.

many resources.[16] Society, on the other hand, should respect its duty to see that each person has resources to utilize, but should refrain from loading any one individual too heavily with responsibilities. Trusteeship of material resources is a part of Christian living, but Christian living is broader than trusteeship of material resources.

2. *The Resource of Abilities and Skills*

The attitude of giving, of contributing all that one can to enrich the lives of other people, demands a sensitive trusteeship of one's skills and abilities. Just as every Christian is eager to utilize effectively the days given him to live on earth, so he must be eager to develop his latent abilities in order that he may possess as tools a mind trained for clear and incisive thinking, fingers and shoulders and feet agile for manipulating the resources of earth.

To this end, the Christian is committed, first, to discovering what his own peculiar aptitudes and skills are. To a degree, this is accomplished through self-examination; to a degree, through the counsels of parents and friends. He then makes these aptitudes and skills the basis for his own contribution to the common life of his neighbourhood and of mankind. Some of these skills and abilities, fully developed, will become the basis of his vocation. Others will result in avocations, furnishing recreational relaxation and enjoyment for himself and for his friends, enriching the programme and life of his church, and flavouring the quality of his incidental contacts and of his unconsciously spoken words which are so great a factor in human influence.

Knowledge of one's own abilities often does not solve the problem of vocational choice. "Is it not true," writes George Carpenter, "that God has placed in the world the same extravagant fecundity of human potentialities as of germinative power in seed; so that limiting factors external to the person must be taken into account? Furthermore, people generally have extremely great powers of adaptation and adjustment, so that vocation is not chiefly a question of personal capacities but of the balance of social needs and the discovery of a niche which will afford resources and facilities for some kind of productive work within the range of personal capacity. . . ."[17]

Martin Luther stated well the spirit in which a Christian undertakes his vocation:

> Lo, thus from faith flow forth love and joy in the Lord, and from love a joyful, willing and free mind that serves one's neighbors willingly

[16] This applies to other than material resources as well: to too many irons in the fire, too many hobbies, too many committees, too many activities.

[17] Criticism of a preliminary draft of this section.

and takes no account of gratitude or ingratitude, of praise or blame, of gain or loss. For a man does not serve that he may put men under obligations, he does not distinguish between friends and enemies, nor does he anticipate their thankfulness or unthankfulness; but most freely and most willingly he spends himself and all that he has, whether he waste all on the thankless or whether he gain a reward.[18]

A man does not live for himself alone in this mortal body, so as to work for it alone, but he lives also for all men on earth, nay rather, he lives only for others and not for himself. And to this end he brings his body into subjection, that he may the more sincerely and freely serve others, as Paul says in Romans 14, "No man lives to himself, and no man dies to himself. For he that liveth, liveth unto the Lord, and he that dieth, dieth unto the Lord." Therefore it is impossible that he should ever in his life be idle and without works toward his neighbors.[19]

And it was Martin Luther who vigorously fought the idea that there is any qualitative difference between the services performed by clergymen and laymen:

It is pure invention that pope, bishops, priests, and monks are to be called the "spiritual estate"; princes, lords, artizans, and farmers the "temporal estate." . . .[20]

A cobbler, a smith, a farmer, each has the work and office of his trade, and yet they are all alike consecrated priests and bishops, and every one by means of his own office must benefit and serve every other, that in this way many kinds of work may be done for the bodily and spiritual welfare of the community, even as all the members of the body serve one another.[21]

Aptitudes and skills are resources capable, if developed, of contributing to the common life. Since people themselves ought never to be resources to be managed by others, each person must be the trustee of his own abilities.

3. *Cultural Resources*

The implications of the Christian gospel for trusteeship of cultural resources may be deduced from the attitude of Jesus to the Old Testament. How much at home he was in it! The Psalms and the words of the prophets came to his lips with the ease of long familiarity. He recognized the richness of his inheritance and evidently began early to appropriate it for his own. Amos, Isaiah,

18 "A Treatise on Christian Liberty," *Works of Martin Luther,* Philadelphia: A. J. Holman Co., 1916, II, 338.

19 Ibid., p. 335.

20 Martin Luther, "An Open Letter to the Christian Nobility," 1520, *Works,* II, 66.

21 Ibid., p. 69.

Hosea, David, Moses, and the long tradition of the Jewish people were parts of the cultural resources which were his to utilize. Whatever was good, true, inspiring, and beautiful he took to use and thereby to perpetuate.

But he held it in no sacrosanct reverence. It was not to him valid just because it was old, or because it was Jewish. "Ye have heard it said by them of old times . . . but I say unto you . . . !" Whatever was harmful, outmoded, or outgrown, he vigorously eliminated from further influence in so far as he was able, regardless of its age or of its origin.

Today his spirit lives in the hearts of men of many backgrounds, many cultures, many inheritances. And his attitude toward men's cultural inheritances—religious experience, customs, literature, architecture, sculpture, music, folklore, painting, and drama—still guides us. Whatever is fine, uplifting, and life-giving in the heritage of a people is to be preserved by being utilized and is to be made available to all. Whatever is tawdry, stifling, misleading, and outmoded is to be discarded. Festivals and customs which can be given creative meaning are so to be transformed. The cultural values of rural life are to be discovered, enjoyed, and enriched. Beauty is to be cultivated and developed in all of its constructive forms, utilized in recreation, and dedicated to the enrichment of homes, of church buildings and furnishings, and of forms of worship.

Foremost among the cultural resources of every Christian is the Bible. Its record of the trials and insights and struggles of the people of Israel, its portrayal of the life and teachings of Jesus the Christ, and its record of the spirit and sufferings and triumphs of the early church are the matchless heritage of Christians everywhere and in each generation. It is so important that translation of the Scriptures into the local language is always an early item in missionary endeavour, and the spread of literacy is deemed essential, if only to enable Christians to read the Bible.

4. *The Resource of the Human Body*

His own body is each man's fundamental material instrument in life. Only while it functions can he maintain his contact with his family, his farm, and his friends. Trusteeship over every other resource, and the creation of brotherliness among his fellows all hang on this: the development and conservation of his own body to express his will. His body is the temple of the living God only to the degree that his spirit reflects the spirit of the Christ. But the most thoroughly Christian spirit is handicapped, so far as earth is concerned, unless it is enshrined in a body through which it can adequately express itself to the world. The maintenance of optimum health, therefore, becomes a cardinal implication of the Christian gospel for every man.

However, health is not the "highest good" to a Christian. It is a *resource,* and, like other resources, it is to be utilized. Under ordinary circumstances, it is to be conserved. There are times, however, when the Christian deliberately expends health for a greater good. For it is more important to maintain and to express the spirit of Christ than to retain physical life in a human body. When a conflict arises between maintenance of health and expression of the Christian spirit, the follower of Christ sacrifices health.

5. *The Resource of Time*

"The Christian uses time under a sense of the eternal." Here is the touchstone in the trusteeship of time. When the Christian attains his objective in any given circumstance, his spirit and its expression in action are timeless. The Christian attitude toward time is that of "the man who lives in Eternity, now"; he lives timelessly in the midst of time.

Time is a resource which may be utilized or squandered, consecrated or desecrated. Each man's days are finite, to be used or abused. In them he must normally make provision for seven activities if he is to grow in discipleship. He must set aside adequate time for home and family life, for his economic vocation, for recreative relaxation, for gifts of economic and of spiritual services, for worship, for cultural growth, and for rest. As to the proportion to be devoted to each of these, the judgment of Christians differs considerably. The Occidental emphasis tends to be on getting things done. People of African and Asiatic countries have a higher appreciation of leisureliness in the wise economy of time.

For Christians of all cultures the issue of constructive use or of waste of time is an important one. The occasional North Indian farmer who spends hours in idleness while weeds steal the moisture from his fields, the occasional Chinese cultivator who fritters away time in the winter when he might be procuring and preparing fertilizer, the occasional American farmer who toasts his toes by the fire when he might be repairing machinery preparatory to the rush of spring work, are being lax in their trusteeship of a valuable resource no less than the man who allows the rains to wash an unnecessary amount of soil from his fields. On the other hand, those Korean Christians who use the slack times of the year for training for volunteer service in the church are improving their trusteeship of time.

As the discussion of trusteeship of material resources has made clear, the Christian farmer should not accept trusteeship over more agricultural resources than he can utilize fully and still leave time for other important activities. The capable farmer, be he ever so efficient a trustee of land and livestock, is a poor trustee of time if he tries to manage so much land and livestock that he has insufficient time for his family, for worship, for cultural growth, or for rest.

The Christian seeks the ageless values. But as a man he seeks these *in time,* and the days it is given to him to live among men are resources of which he has been made trustee, days in which to live eternally, in work, in worship, in friendliness, and in rest.

6. *The Resource of Income*

Today, families are not self-sufficient with respect to goods and services. Different families and members of families produce different goods and services for general consumption. They exchange these for other goods and services or for money which becomes their claim, through purchase, to the goods and services of others.

This general claim to the goods and services of society is an additional resource at the disposal of the Christian family. It seems strange that so much of the discussion of stewardship (trusteeship) should have been concerned with the utilization of income, for the foregoing sections make it clear that *the fundamental resources are not income but are* (1) *material resources,* (2) *abilities and skills,* (3) *cultural resources,* (4) *the human body,* (5) *time.* It is these, first of all, of which men are to be trustees. Where they are free to choose, men are to choose their vocations on the basis of the way in which their aptitudes and skills can make the greatest contribution to the common good. This means that they will seek to assume trusteeship over such available resources as will help them to make that contribution. The amount of "income" which each receives as the result of this trusteeship depends upon the economic institutions of the society in which he happens to live. This income will bear little relationship to his contribution to the common good. But whatever it is, it does itself constitute an additional resource.

The repeated and numerous references to trusteeship of income have been unfortunate only in so far as they have diverted attention from the necessity for trusteeship of the more fundamental resources. For income, too, calls for trusteeship.

Uses of income. There are four primary uses to which the Christian puts his income: (1) family or personal living, (2) the church, (3) sharing with others, and (4) joint expenditure through taxation and assessments. The fact that one of these is the church must not be interpreted to mean that only part of one's income ought to be devoted to Christian activities.

Render unto God, not a tenth, not a third, not a half, but all that is God's, be it more or less; by employing all on yourself, your household, the household of faith, and all mankind in such manner that you may give a good account of your stewardship.[22]

Sharing. To achieve the implications of the life and teachings of Jesus for rural people requires a great many activities which Christians can carry on only through cooperation. The benevolence boards of the various church bodies: Christian education, missions, social action, and others, are avenues of that cooperation. These depend upon voluntary financial participation by Christian families. By participating in them Christians become participants in the world Christian movement, extending the influence of their discipleship around the world and throughout the non-Christian life surrounding them. This ought to be achieved through each family's designating a given portion of its income for the activities of its local congregation; for every local congregation true to its Lord must make adequate provision for these cooperative tasks a regular feature of its budget.

Along the life-path of almost every family are less fortunate people who, perhaps because of illness or of accident or of undependable providers, are in need of help. In order to furnish the helpfulness called for by such need, some of the family income ought to be so designated. With increasing social organization, many of these needs can be met more equitably by organizations than by individuals. This entails contributions from family incomes for such organizations.

Joint expenditures in taxes and assessments. It is important to keep in mind the function of payments made in the form of taxes and assessments. These are, in reality, joint expenditures made by the community to achieve tasks on which there is substantial agreement and for which there is widespread support in public opinion. Certain of these expenditures are of direct benefit to most taxpayers, such as the provision of schools, roads, and fire and police protection. Some are in the nature of organized sharing, to meet the needs of particular sections of the population. As part of the family income goes into these joint activities, it is well to recognize them for what they are, and to seek to make them ever more effective through vigilant civic participation.

Techniques of sharing income. Among the techniques of sharing income with the church, the one most peculiar to rural communities has been founded upon the principle of the first fruits. Sanctioned early in Old Testament times, partly as a source of income

22 John Wesley, Sermon on *The Use of Money*, quoted by Scaff, op. cit., p. 76.1.

for the tabernacle but also to symbolize the divine source of the good things of life, this practice has been revived at various times within the history of the Christian church. It has increased in popularity again within recent years, together with such practices as that of the Lord's Acre plan, and still retains the values which it had in old Judea. Where people have low cash incomes, such plans are particularly valuable since they make it easier for all to participate in the support of the Christian movement. Often, too, gifts in kind and of services are an integral part of non-Christian cultures. Hence, carrying these practices over into Christian discipleship conserves a value out of the old and incorporates it into the new.

The other technique of ancient sanction is that of tithing cash income. "And of all that thou shalt give me, I shall surely give the tenth to thee." To designate a given proportion of one's income for the work of the church is not to repudiate the previous principle that all of one's income is a trust to be used by the Christian "to the glory of God." Systematized giving is essential, and the tithing practice of setting aside one-tenth for the cooperative activities of Christians in the church persists in many places because, where it is followed, churches do not lack funds, yet it is a practicable arrangement for most people of modest means.

Ethical significance of decisions in spending. In any economy of producers, those goods and services are produced for which purchasers are ready to pay. This lays an ethical responsibility upon the purchaser each time he makes a purchase, for by his purchase he confers approval on the product and, implicitly, upon the process, the working conditions, the financial arrangements by which it was produced. Obviously, in a complex economy no purchaser can investigate personally each product which he purchases, but this does not change the fact that his purchase involves him in the righteousness or the sinfulness of the process by which the product was prepared. One of the advantages urged for the consumers cooperative movement is that it makes possible adequate investigation of the conditions under which goods are produced.

Spending requires a quality of trusteeship no less exacting than that required in giving.

B.

Training Leadership for the Christian Rural Programme

I. TRAINING VOLUNTEER LEADERSHIP

It is easy to theorize about an elaborate programme of lay training which, if carried out, would convey men far along the road to professional preparation. And, thinking of the needs in the villages more than of the potentialities of the laymen, it is easy to talk of using lay leaders for far more service than they can reasonably be expected to give. We must constantly remind ourselves of the poverty of the masses and the necessity for men to work at making a living. And we must expect, as a rule, that the finest lay leadership will come from among the busiest of the people.

Yet, while these are busy people, they are also the ones who want to be taught how to serve. It is the experience of the church everywhere that men and women who, with undaunted spirit, carry heavy household and vocational burdens of their own are the ones who become pillars of the church and who serve best in her activities.

But in most areas of the world there are "slack seasons" of the year when the tillers of the soil, or the lumbermen in the forests, or the fishermen by the seaside are less busy. Periods of intensive training, to supplement apprenticeship, are thus practicable as well as highly desirable.

To train leadership it is best not to stress leadership at all.[1] The goal should be the enlistment of all laymen in active discipleship. If such a spirit gets root in the local church, laymen all serving to the best of their several abilities, leadership will emerge. There need be no arbitrary choosing. There must, however, be some competent steering, for there may emerge those with selfish ambitions, wanting to take the lead for the sake of prestige or esteem. And there may be those naturally too diffident and backward to assume any prominent place, who yet have the potentialities of mind and heart for the largest contribution to the cause. It should be the responsibility of the pastor and the more seasoned leaders or officers of the church to help give the intelligent and tactful guidance that will recognize and bring forward those with inherent abilities and with the Christlike graces that count most in Christian service.

[1] "You cannot teach men to lead; you can only teach them to serve." E. Stanley Jones.

The service which laymen may render is not limited to any one type. Practically every activity in the full Christian programme can be conducted by volunteer leadership: worship, youth projects, financial management of the church, health activities, agricultural improvement, preaching, etc.

In any of these lines of service willing laymen can begin to learn simply by taking hold and helping. They can learn from pastors who will take time to demonstrate some first steps and to give concrete instructions or advice. They can learn from fellow laymen who have already worked in the same field or who are willing to unite with them in effort. Leadership will emerge as a by-product of earnest devotion to service.

But, to be of greatest value, it must be intelligently directed. With some who are eager for service there may be the need of curbing them from launching into too many projects, and so dissipating their efforts. Each should undertake only a reasonable amount and then concentrate on making his help count as richly as possible. The craft shop that takes on apprentices has a master workman who works with the new recruits, demonstrates the use of tools, lays out the work to be done, gives instructions, and watches to prevent or correct mistakes and to reiterate instructions. The church has much to learn from the handicraft shop. Especially do new converts and maturing young people need just that careful supervision and personal encouragement that a foreman in a shop can give his apprentices.

But just learning "on the job" is not all that the lay recruit needs. While there may be locally those who can help him, yet adequate expert training cannot always be looked for in the usual parish. The layman needs backgrounds for understanding his type of project, and orientation to appreciate its relation to other projects and to the larger ongoing movements of the church and of society. And he needs fuller and more expert knowledge brought in from outside, where experiments have been made, where there is progress to report, and where enthusiasm runs high. This outside help can be brought in to supplement learning by doing. A weekly conference period between members of a small group with like interest can be of great profit. They can exchange experience, discuss problems, study any literature that may be available in their special field, or carry on correspondence with agencies that can help them. If their pastor or a more experienced layman[2] can give their projects special study and preparation and meet with them as leader or advisor, they will gain further profit.

[2] See discussion, pp. 117-120, on utilization of laymen of the congregation who are expert in their own fields.

A proved method of utilizing expert advisory and training personnel from outside the congregation is the short intensive local training class or conference, with leadership partly or wholly from outside. Those specialists invited in should be informed very concretely of the interests of those who are to be enrolled, of their experience and attainments, and of the situations that they locally face. If the leaders can, then, for a period of a week, two weeks or a month, address themselves very concretely, out of their wider experience and more specialized knowledge, to the giving of wider and deeper insights into the type of work under consideration, and the sense of comradeship with those making like endeavour elsewhere, and the encouragement of knowing that success can come, they will have prepared the recruits for greatly improved service.

A more fruitful plan for training laymen right in their own localities, where the staff for it can be found and supported, is the plan for a small well-selected staff to settle in a limited field, such as a large parish, for several months or a year, and enter into the full life of the church, to guide, to inspire, and to train.[3] If this staff is good at placing primary responsibility upon the laymen, and then acting as helpers of the laymen, they can leave behind when they move on a very active church with a well-rounded program of love-inspired service.

The same general principles should guide in more advanced classes, or centralized classes for larger areas. From the point of view of the church it is more ideal to have the inspiring specialists come in and conduct classes locally, so that laymen may attend with minimum sacrifice of time and expense, and gaps in attendance need be few. But training class leaders will be too few to reach every parish for such needed classes at frequent intervals. Hence, there must be regional classes to be attended, so far as possible, by really key men and women from all the localities. These may be in the nature of winter folk schools[4] with a variety of courses to serve both men and women in various lines of service, or they may be institutes specializing strictly in one type of service, or they may be just brief conferences or retreats, intended more for inspiration than for technical training.

There may be persons of exceptional promise and of consecrated life and ambition for whom advanced training should be offered. The planning for any such training courses should be based on accurate knowledge of the field to be served and survey of needs.

[3] Such a programme developed over tweny years is described in detail in *Training and Guiding Lay Leadership in the Village Church,* by Alice E. Murphy, Mimeograph Series No. 157, Agricultural Missions, Inc.

[4] Helpfully described in *The Winter Folk School,* by James A. Hunter, Mimeograph Series No. 155, Agricultural Missions, Inc.

The most practical plan for these may be the "slack season" school of one to three months, perhaps offering integrated courses running two, three, or even four years, and leading to a certificate of recognition. Or there may be call for a course of six months or a year, especially if the layman is preparing for some line of technical social service such as better farming or stock raising, or community health and sanitation.

Always, since it is volunteer service that is here discussed, the advantages of a long period of training must be balanced against such disadvantages as loss of time and income from regular vocation and necessity of leaving family or other burdens on other people.

Perhaps the most complete system of such training institutes, well integrated as to length and continuity, is that which has been developed by the church in Korea.

To a large extent the rural church in Korea is made up of low-income farmers and their families, and yet the church has made remarkable progress and has amazing staying power and vitality. Where cash income has been low the systematic stewardship of time has resulted in a great expansion of the church through the use of lay leaders. In the early days of the church the individual Christian pledged so many days of service for the evangelization of his community. He also put his spare time, in the slack season on his farm, to good account. From countless rural villages thousands of men and women all over Korea streamed into the central station Bible Institutes to spend the "off weeks" in the study of the Bible. "Back again in their rural church community they could contribute little or no money but they gave days of service. This experience developed them and from the first the missions sought to build up an indigenous church independent of financial aid so far as its local work went."[5]

The Korean church took advantage of the season when farming operations were at a standstill and used the hours previously spent in "pass-time" recreations of an unprofitable if not harmful nature. The conclusion was early reached that stewardship of time might become as potent a factor in building up the Korean church as stewardship of money or possessions. Training Institutes were provided in the stations for both men and women.

A course of intensive and systematic Bible study is provided. There is a thorough-goingness about the programme that is noteworthy. Buildings, staff, and heat are provided but the students bring or provide their own food. When the men have had their turn, the women who can be spared come in to attend a similar Institute for

[5] Jerusalem Meeting Report, International Missionary Council, Vol. 6, Brunner on "Rural Korea," pp. 139-140.

women and to study a curriculum in which they, too, are required to pass terminal examinations in all the subjects set for the different years—four, and, in some cases, five years in all. Year after year women young and old gather in from the rural communities. Sometimes it is the old mother or mother-in-law who attends the Institute. Sometimes it is the mother-in-law who remains at home to care for the children while the younger women of the household set out the ten, twenty, or thirty miles to the Station Institute. Here they settle in happily for a month or four weeks of intensive Bible study, hygiene, and singing. If the following year they must remain at home, then they will take turns until the course has been completed.

What has been accomplished in Bible study can be accomplished by selecting "key men and women" to be trained as voluntary workers in the larger Christian programme. If the stewardship of time coupled with consecrated purpose can accomplish so vital an objective in one area of Christian thought and experience, it can accomplish the equally vital purpose of training men and women in every activity that brings to the villager an enlarged vision of what Christianity really means. Even a low-income church, if it has the vision, the consecration, and the help of specialized workers, can develop within its own membership the ability to carry through a comprehensive programme that will meet the outstanding needs of the rural community in which it is placed.

II. TRAINING RURAL MINISTERS

The same paradox which characterizes the church is true of the Christian pastor. On the one hand, he is a "speaker for God," seeking to reveal the will of God for the life and problems and opportunities of a particular congregation of Christians. On the other hand, he is the human leader of a group of disciples (himself a disciple among them) seeking to inspire and guide them in their work, to point out problems and possibilities calling for application of the Christian spirit, to integrate the efforts of the group and the thinking of its members.

He must fill both of these roles.

There are, therefore, special difficulties involved in discussing the training of rural ministers. For one thing, the idea of "training" a "man of God" is itself most difficult. For a second, increasing awareness of the distinctive problems and distinctive opportunities of the rural church has made its leaders more and more dissatisfied with the types of training most rural ministers are receiving. For a third, the fact recognized in the last chapter that many types of church programmes are the church's answer to the needs of its neighbourhood in different parts of the world under different conditions of secular institutional development means that there may be necessary differences in ministerial training parallel to these differences in church programme.

Preliminary Observations

1. Let it be emphasized at the outset that no amount of training (provided it be properly balanced) can be too much for a Christian minister, for the riches of God and the implications of his love for the multiform life of each neighbourhood are boundless, ever revealing new insights to him who diligently seeks. On the other hand, it is not true that years of formal training are indispensable in the development of a splendid minister. For above all, it is important for a minister to combine personal experience of the God of Jesus Christ with a feeling for fellowship, for service, for community within his neighbourhood. These can be had at different levels of formal training and sometimes without it. "I have sought and found the shepherd's heart"[6]—this is achievement for a Christian minister.

2. Let it be noted next that training for the ministry is not a matter for two, three, or four years set apart from the stream of life. It must be a continuous process, beginning with general early Christian nurture and enduring throughout life in habits of personal devotion, of purposive contemplation, and of social discipleship, supplemented by short "refresher" courses, by periods of spiritual "retreat," and by frequent intimate contact with other ministers and with training centres. Even the years of seminary training must be as little as possible apart from the stream of life. These experiences of deepening faith, of broadening horizons, of developing competence in the tasks of the church need to come while one is actively engaged in "this great task of being a Christian." Increasingly, methods are being worked out for combining study with practice in the functions of the minister. Sometimes these take the form of alternation of fairly long periods of apprenticeship with periods of study in the training centre. Another method is to include supervised pastoral activities through a long week-end each week as part of ministerial training. Still another is to concentrate training into one-month periods at intervals of six months to one year extending through many years of active ministry.

Quite apart from formal training, the minister's library should be his constant silent teacher. In many areas circulating library arrangements have been concluded for making more books available to ministers than they could afford to purchase alone. And his field must be his laboratory in which he learns how to minister.

[6] Truett, George, Autobiography.

The problems and insights of his people, and the guiding of the spirit of prayer and meditation are part of his constant preparation for his high calling.

Elements in Ministerial Training

Every minister is first of all a Christian, and as such, in most instances, he has grown up subject to the usual training in the faith which the church provides for its young people. But now he is to undertake peculiarly important responsibilities. Henceforth he is to try to speak for God to a group of believers. He is to lead them in their group expressions of their faith which they give their children. For this difficult task he must have special preparation. (1) He must seek the deepening of his own faith, that his spirit may be adequate to the heavier demands to be laid upon him. (2) He must maintain his sense of identity with his people, his deep appreciation of rural culture, so that he may know their thoughts, their reactions, their needs, their temptations, their exultations. (3) He must study the Christian revelation in order that the riches of God's speaking in the Bible, in Jesus Christ, in the tradition of the church, may be available to his ministry. (4) He must develop competence in the activities of the church: in proclamation, interpretation, in expression, in integration.

Deepening of Experience of God

The minister who is to shepherd wisely and lovingly must have a continuous deepening of the experience of God in his life, so that his "cup runneth over" to refresh his fellow wayfarers. Brother Lawrence said that "we should establish ourselves in a sense of God's presence by continually conversing with Him. . . . That we should feed and nourish our souls with high notions of God." He wrote to a friend, "We must . . . always work at it, because not to advance in spiritual life is to go back. But those who have the gale of the Holy Spirit go forward even in sleep."[7]

Fulfilling this experience of God through continual communion with him, the minister will have a growing knowledge of God, as he will through having tried and proved him in the hard experiences of his daily life. Muriel Lester tells of the Chinese preacher who returned to his Shanghai congregation physically worn from an extended experience in the war zone but with "tears of joy" running unnoticed down his cheeks "as with radiant face he tried to convey to his hearers how real God had been. . . . The thing they had believed in theory, that they expressed in hymns and psalms and prayers, they now knew to be real. It worked. It hap-

[7] Brother Lawrence, *The Practice of the Presence of God.* New York: Fleming H. Revell, 1895, p. 8.

pened. God was adequate."[8] Thus must experience of God deepen the minister's heart, and thus he be able to lead his people on to that deepening, enlivening experience.

This deepening of faith is peculiarly difficult for any training school to impart. Candidates for the ministry are more apt to experience disappointment in this than in any other phase of their training. They are apt to expect that a study of religious subjects will automatically deepen faith. But study, even of religion, brings mental fatigue; it often necessitates detailed analysis, whereas religious quickening comes best from synthesizing and harmonizing thoughts and feelings.

No academic training as such can be relied upon to deepen the spiritual life. Any impartation of it is elusive. The atmosphere of the school as a whole will have far more to do with success or failure than will any classroom teaching. Success will depend mainly on two factors: first, right mental and emotional attitudes on the part of the student; second, the personal contagion of teachers who live intimately with the God whom they teach.

To make possible a growth in the experience of God and of his brooding presence, it should be the concern of the whole body of faculty and students together to live on a plane of friendly sharing in study and ministry. As they open up freely to one another their inmost thoughts, whether of doubt or assurance, of joy or pain, of baffling problems or of triumphs accomplished, as children of one Father, there will be nurture of the deeper spiritual springs of life for each.

Appreciation of Rural Culture

To lead men and women of the countryside into the Christian experience and discipleship described in these pages, the rural minister must have a genuine appreciation of rural life. This must be more than an academic recognition of the potential values of rural life, more than an academic acquaintance with outstanding rural problems. It must include an eager participation and personal gladness in the life of rural people. There is a rhythm of the seasons which, through the years, becomes a dominant though unconscious factor in the lives of rural people. The rural minister needs to have in his marrow this same rhythm. He must be a country-man at heart and by choice. Ministerial training has as its purpose not the transformation *from a country-man* into a minister but the training *of* a country-man in the calling of a minister.

Although this appreciation of rural life must be more than academic, it is vitally important that the rural minister be trained

[8] *The Christian Century,* quoted by Kirby Page, *Living Prayerfully,* p. 340.

in analysis of rural culture, made aware of the critical studies which have examined it, and schooled to become himself a critical student of rural life. In most countries there are now universities and government agencies making critical studies of rural problems: of agricultural production, of social institutions, of economic activities, of civic problems. He who is to become a rural minister needs to be aware of these resources, to know the possible contributions (and the limitations) of each of these fields of study to the realization of the Kingdom of God among men. In most countries, there are government facilities for agricultural extension, for public health work, and, in some countries, for extension in home economics. The rural minister needs to know about these, their scope and function, and to become acquainted with the representatives of these services in his vicinity.[9]

Various schemes have been tried in the attempt to achieve this understanding of rural life in ministerial training. One procedure has been the provision of short courses in rural life for seminary students.[10] Another has been efforts at cooperation between the seminaries and agricultural colleges of a given region.[11] A third has been the creation of a chair of rural life, or of rural sociology, or of rural church, in a seminary.[12] Perhaps the most favourable circumstances for a happy solution of this problem are found where a college of agriculture and a theological seminary are located near each other, as at the University of Nanking, China. Such an arrangement allows full interchange of library, laboratory, and faculty facilities.[13]

Where practically all of the churches into which graduates of a training institution go are rural churches, the ideal situation would be one in which each member of the faculty, whatever be his special field of study, would have the fundamental "feeling for the soil," the basic rhythm, the essential attitude of the country-man, so that

9 See, in this connection, *The Significance to Rural Religion and the Rural Church of So-called Secular Agencies Related to Agriculture, the Home, and Rural Life,* by J. Robert Hargreaves, Christian Rural Fellowship Bulletin 72, May, 1942.

10 Such an arrangement is in effect between Leonard Theological College, Jubbulpore, India, and the Allahabad Agricultural Institute, Allahabad, India.

11 Being tried in the Midwest of the United States of America.

12 Some seminaries not yet providing a full department of rural work are inviting specialists to give courses of lectures. The list of seminaries providing such studies is too long to give here. Denominational headquarters can supply information.

13 Students majoring in Rural Church at Nanking Seminary take one year of their training in the College of Agriculture of the University of Nanking. A somewhat similar plan is in operation at the Foochow (China) Union Theological Seminary in cooperation with the Union (Vocational) High School.

he might make his contribution within that atmosphere.[14] The one caution to be observed in such an instance would be that while appreciation of the life of the countryside is essential in order to reach the lives of rural people and to guide them into effective discipleship, there are broader relationships of rural to urban people and to people of other lands which must not be ignored.

Where some graduates of an institution enter the rural, and some the urban, ministry, provision needs to be made for deepening the understanding of rural life of those to be ministers there, while seeking to maintain, through alternate periods of study and field work, or through long week-end ministries, the rhythm of rural living and the essential spirit of the country-man.

"The often heard plea not to draw a distinction between the rural and urban aspects of the ministerial office is contradicting the facts. It is true, there was a time when the above mentioned claims were not crying out loud as they do now, but that time is passed. The changes through which the world has passed during the last generation imply a myriad of adjustments. The church cannot stand alone trusting that she can escape making provision for adapting her methods and thinking to the various needs of her different groups, among which the farmer and the small community, without which the city church would starve, occupy a strategic place."[15]

Study of the Christian Revelation

"The essential task of the Church is to be the ambassador of Christ, proclaiming His kingdom."[16] The prospective minister must, therefore, learn as much as he can about the Word of God which bears this message to man: (1) about the Bible, with its matchless history of a people seeking, and being sought by, God, (2) about Him who came to earth and walked the lands of Galilee and Judea for a while, revealing the heart of the Father in Himself, (3) about the continuous witness of the Spirit through the Christian church

[14] "If I were to become a rural minister, I would hope that I could attend a rural theological seminary—that is, a seminary established especially, if not exclusively, for persons intending to enter the rural ministry. I would be assured, in that case, of having teachers sympathetic with farm and village life. I would also expect to find a group of young men there who had picked out the rural ministry as a life work. I would hope also that this theological seminary would be situated in close contact with one of our agricultural colleges, so that I could mingle with the young rural students and attend some of the agricultural college courses." From *If I Were a Rural Minister,* by Charles J. Galpin, Christian Rural Fellowship Bulletin 55, p. 3, October, 1940.

[15] Schroeder, Martin, *The Country Church is Different,* Christian Rural Fellowship Bulletin 55, p. 2-4, Oct., 1940.

[16] Madras Conference Report, Vol. 2, p. 277.5.

down through the centuries, (4) about the world-wide fellowship and life-wide witness of Christians across the world today.

It cannot be too strongly urged that the necessity for rural ministers to be well-trained in analysis of rural life grows not only out of the need for full application of the Christian spirit to all of life, but out of the contribution this training makes to understanding and appreciating the Christian revelation, as well. For the Word of God reaches the heart of man through human words to the degree that those words, those creedal statements, those liturgies, those sermons are cast in the thought forms with which people are familiar, and address themselves to the burning contemporary problems of people. The theologian, if his craft is to aid in revealing God, must be himself a pilgrim, a *participating* pilgrim, on the Christian way. The professor of church history will understand far better the role of laymen, and the spirit of the martyrs, and the problems of the scholars if he is himself a pilgrim, participant in the full life of a neighbourhood. And if these be pilgrims of the field and the forest, of agricultural production and of rural organization, their witness will be doubly valuable for rural ministers.[17]

Developing Competence in the Activities of the Church

Out of the fullness of his own religious experience, with his understanding of his people and of the Christian revelation deepened by study, the minister is to serve his neighbourhood. The congregation of which he is a part normally carries on four activities in the pursuance of its task, and in each of these the minister needs to be competent. He must be aware of the avenues by which the church *proclaims* its message. He needs to learn the art of preaching, the technique of individual witness, the organization of lay evangelistic efforts. He must be skilled in the *interpretation* of the Word of God to men, the translation of eternal principles into the thought and problem vernacular of his people. He must be aware of the ways by which the Christian community *expresses* its faith, competent in the design and conduct of public worship, in the organization of Christians for group action on problems facing the neighbourhood, in inspiring individuals to the expression of particular insights they may have, or to meet problems of the neighbourhood which they sense particularly keenly. He must be skilled in *integrating* in the lives of his people the insights of Christian faith and in contributing to the integration of the life of the neighbourhood by interpreting the role of the different neighbourhood institutions, seeking to cooperate with them, urging laymen to participate fully in those which make large contributions to the life of the community.

[17] See: Mackay, John A., *A Preface to Christian Theology*, pp. 22.5-26.5.

The elements of the Christian rural programme are comprised of these basic activities in different combinations and patterns. It is important that the rural minister be at the same time (1) adept at guiding each of these elements of the programme and (2) aware of the basic activities and processes involved in each. Thus he needs to be (1) trained in the practice of pastoral work and personal evangelism, (2) aware of the elements of proclamation, interpretation, expression, and integration present in it, and (3) alive to the contributions it makes to the realization of each of the manifold implications of the Christian gospel for rural people. He will not, of course, keep all of these in mind as he makes his rounds, but his training should analyze these functions of the minister and school him to lifelong critical review and appraisal of his own work.

The Christian ministry demands craftsmanship of a high order. All of these activities involve special skills and understanding. One of the phases of ministerial training must be to develop these skills and achieve this understanding. There has grown up a sound experience in the craft; this must be put at the disposal of each new minister.

Balance in the Training of the Minister

We have discussed four elements in the training of the rural minister: (1) deepening of religious experience, (2) appreciation of rural culture, (3) study of the Christian revelation, (4) developing competence in the activities of the church. It remains to be stressed that *all* of these are *essential* in the training of *all* rural ministers. Because of the present low economic standards among rural folk around the world and because of lack of appreciation of the values of advanced training, it may be that for many years the rural church in many lands will have to draw its ministers from among men and women of comparatively little general education. The growing conviction is that all grades of ministerial training need to be well balanced with respect to these four elements. None of them is a luxury. No matter what the period of training, every minister needs to be capable of outstanding Christian leadership in his neighbourhood. Well-rounded training, no matter how much or how little there be of it, is imperative.

Opportunity for Specialization

While every candidate for the rural ministry should have a well-rounded training, preparing him for the full life of the church ministry, this need not wholly exclude the cultivation of special interests. One man may have special aptitude for preaching, another may love children and want to mingle with and inspire them; another may have ability to inspire and guide youth. Along with general training there should be room for developing any such special talents.

Apprenticeship

There is no doubt that the general practice of church bodies establishing training schools for the express purpose of preparing men and women for the ministry is sound. There is, to be sure, an alternative. This is apprenticeship, whereby a young recruit of promise is made the assistant of an experienced servant of the church. By helping such a pastor, observing him at his work, studying and serving under his direction, the recruit develops his own talents. This is a method not to be despised. It may be especially fruitful for a young woman to work with a devoted and experienced woman leader in the neighbourly service of a parish. For this to be effective, either the older woman must be skilled in interpretation and in pointing out values, or else the apprentice must be particularly alert and have enough intellectual background to see the values in what she observes.

Apprenticeship has resulted in the preparation of many worthy leaders, some of whom proved outstanding in service. It was by such a method that Jesus trained his disciples, sharing with them his ministry and the intimate living of his busy days. Supplemental to schooling (as in a plan for internship or a directed year of work under supervision) such shared discipleship should still have a large place in the training program.

III. TRAINING SPECIALISTS

1. *Rural Medical Workers*

The importance, if Christians are rightly to follow their Master, of the ministry of healing and of the maintenance of health has been pointed out.[18] And it has been noted that in many of the rural areas of the world, the lack of other adequate medical facilities forces the church to include this in its own programme. It is important that those who carry on this specialized ministry in the name of the church should have the best preparation possible, both of mind and of heart.

There is no need to dwell on the elements essential to a sound medical education as such. What does concern us here is the peculiar preparation needed for rural health workers if they are to serve in a Christ-like manner and to give the type and quality of help needed by the mass of country people.

If the health worker is to minister to people in a Christian way,

18 "Churches and missions are under the same obligation to train doctors and nurses as teachers and preachers," from "Christian Ministry of Health and Healing," *Madras Conference Report,* p. 80.

he must have that attitude of dependence upon God and that loving concern for human kind which Jesus had. He must know that every tendency toward healing in the body is of God's creation. He must know that every discovery and advance of science has been just learning how to work with God, using God-given materials and abilities. Ideally, the words spoken in memory of George Washington Carver, "His faith was co-extensive with all his acts and his plans," should be true of every health worker.[19] With his knowledge and skill, he should be impelled by an overmastering compassion for men, so that he will want to lessen their suffering.

The worker in rural areas needs, in addition, to learn to feel quite at home in rural surroundings,[20] to know the common thought patterns of country folk, their prejudices and superstitions, and any techniques of the "medicine man" or of the "motherly soul" that may have real virtue, for some of the herbs and oils of any locality may have certain kinds and degrees of efficacy.

The health worker should not only be at home with rural attitudes and interests in general but should seek intimate knowledge of the particular locality in which he is to work.[21] Some of the rural-mindedness he needs can and should be gained as part of his advanced training.[22] Much of it, if he has learned the right approach and sensitivity, he will gain for himself while practising in his field.

It needs here to be pointed out that any rural health staff, far more than urban, must be composed of "general practitioners." This should be held as a guiding principle in all of their training, since in most rural areas, for years to come, there is no hope of such adequate staffing as to permit any high degree of specialization.

Whatever may be true for the urban field, it is preeminently true in the rural world that the broader aspects of public health stand out as of prime importance.[23] Maintenance of health rather than

19 Poteat, Edwin McNeill, at Memorial Service, Cleveland, February, 1943.

20 "The Council's Statement," *Jerusalem Conference Report,* Vol. VI, p. 251.

21 Welch, "Medical Missionary Training," *International Review of Missions,* Vol. 29, p. 269.

22 ". . . all catechists, rural pastors, rural doctors . . . should be provided with a training that will acquaint him in a direct and personal way with the diverse conditions of rural life (and a) . . . knowledge of resources whence he could draw for solving its problems, alleviating its suffering or preventing its evils." From "The Council's Statement" of the Jerusalem Meeting of the International Missionary Council, 1928, Vol. VI, p. 25.

23 Dr. Hugh Cabot writes, "I am inclined to suggest that modern education . . . has tended to neglect the very larger social implications essential to the highest type of medical care. The modern physician is extraordinarily well trained in science but often sadly ignorant of the economic and social setting in which his work will have to be done if he is to . . . (be effective)" "The Place of Nursing in Health Service," *Public Health Nursing,* April, 1943, p. 182.

restoration of health is primary. And a clear recognition of this fact should be an underlying principle in all training of doctors, nurses, midwives, and other health workers.[24]

In the training of what types of health-workers should Christian agencies today be particularly interested? Naturally, there should be no lessening of interest in well-trained physicians and nurses—shall we say those with full professional preparation. But the plain fact is that, in most rural areas of the world, there is not the slightest hope, even with strong government effort, in addition to that of Christian and other agencies, of supplying an adequate staff, in our generation, of such professionals, nor of their being supported if available.[25] In China, for example, we are told that, at the present rate of graduating doctors, it would take 226 years to supply enough for one to 10,000 persons. The same reporter states that by Western standards the correct ratio is considered to be one doctor to every 2000 persons.[26]

The training of auxiliary workers seems, then, the only answer to the problems of insufficient numbers of fully-trained medical workers and of the financial inability of rural areas to support such workers in any way commensurate with the cost of their education.[27] [28] [29] In this field Christian agencies are peculiarly fitted to lead or to take large share.

Some Christian hospitals have undertaken the training of several

24 "Modern thinking regards health service as including not only the diagnosis and treatment of disease but the fullest application of our enormously increased resources in preventive medicine, including sound hygienic and nutritional habits. This shift in our thinking requires a shift in our educational offerings." "The Place of Nursing in Health Service," *Public Health Nursing,* April, 1943, p. 181.

25 "Were there one qualified doctor for every three villages . . . more than ten times the number of qualified doctors to be found in all of India would be needed there." *The Ministry of Healing in India,* Wesleyan Mission Press, Mysore, 1932, p. 11.

26 Shih, Margaret, "The Church and Rural Health," *Chinese Recorder,* Vol. 68, 1937, p. 40. Using Dr. Faber's Report of 1934 published in the Chinese Public Health Monthly, V. 1, November 1940.

27 Lerrigo, P. H. J., M.D., D.D., "The Next Steps in Medical Missions," *International Review of Missions,* Vol. 21, 1938, p. 432.

28 Ibid. "Practical nurses, being people with less prolonged and elaborate training . . . can yet do a great deal of the work, essential and time consuming, now done by more highly trained people . . . These should be trained at least a year and a half under hospital. As a matter of fact such an education offering would add much to the richness of the formal education of almost any woman in the world." p. 184, and Miss Hubbard (op. cit.) adds, "The recognition of the existing need (in U.S.A.) for these workers no one active in P. H. nursing doubts."

29 " (Health nurses need) . . . a training broader and deeper than we ordinarily think of as required for trained nurses." Cabot, *op. cit.,* p. 181.

types of these workers, who, under supervision of fully-trained workers usually with a central hospital as base, are of much more value than poorly but supposedly fully-trained workers "on their own." Several mission hospitals train in a five year course "infirmers" who receive government diplomas and some in a shorter course train "aid-infirmers." The mission hospital at Yakusu in Belgian Congo is an example. This hospital supervises those of its partially trained workers who are stationed in its own outlying districts. However, since these workers receive government diplomas they may practise where they do not receive such careful supervision. When thus removed from Christian supervision and companionship, they may lose their ideals of service.[30]

Ralph Felton tells of a similar method used by Dr. McClure in China. There the partially-trained workers receive no government diploma. They take the course with the sole idea of being placed in an outlying station which will have the supervision and the name of the central hospital.[31]

Shorter courses, such as those for the "aid-infirmers" already mentioned, can prepare workers for still smaller stations and to aid qualified doctors, nurses, midwives and the partially-trained medical practitioners.

In large areas, midwives who have been thoroughly trained and rigidly tested are an essential part of a programme of health. Particularly in rural areas they should be responsible for maternal and child health. This service is particularly appreciated by country people. Through it, confidence of families and communities can be gained and the maternal and infant mortality rate can be appreciably lowered. Many rural communities cannot, however, support a fully qualified midwife even though she has not had the desirable but more expensive nurse's training. Nor is the number of these midwives adequate. Shorter courses[32] given by hospitals or in maternity health stations by nurse-midwives can train workers to use clean methods in simple maternity cases and to assist fully-trained workers. More nurse-midwives are needed to train and supervise such workers.

In addition to its responsibility to its patients, the Christian hospital should train various types of subsidiary or auxiliary workers, where needed, to extend the services of larger health centres to unreached rural areas. It has a still greater responsibility

[30] Chesterman, C. C., "Medical Missions in Belgian Congo," *International Review of Missions,* Vol. 26, 1937, p. 282.

[31] Felton, Ralph A., *The Rural Church in the Far East,* Dept. of Social and Industrial Research, International Missionary Council (Baptist Mission Press, Calcutta, 1932), p. 213.

[32] See Papers, p. 206.

for imbuing all of its medical workers with ideals of Christian service.[33] Many medical and nursing schools should provide refresher courses for various types of medical workers.[34]

Whether health workers receive their training in Christian institutions or not, the church has a responsibility for providing a training in Christian discipleship which will equip medical workers (working alone as they often must in rural areas) to impart the full Christian message to those among whom they work. "A missionary should be able to impart and interpret his religious experience to others. For after all, the missionary in any kind of service is a 'servant of the Lord'."[35]

2. *Rural Teachers*

The rural teacher has an intimate relationship to the total Christian programme for rural life. That relationship exists in ascending scale of cooperation. The teacher may be antagonistic to the Christian church and work to destroy its influence. But even then the teaching that he does has its function in the realization of the implications of the gospel through the giving of knowledge, skills, and attitudes to the members of the community. The teacher may be indifferent to the church and do nothing consciously either for or against it. Yet the education which he directs does have its function. The teacher may be in the employ of the government or the community and still be a very strong member of the church and aid in its activities. Still closer in relationship is the teacher who realizes that his teaching opportunities are avenues for complementing the work of the church in the development of the people in the community. In many countries a larger number of the teachers are workers in the church programme. For example, eighty percent of the education in Africa is carried on by the church. Such workers naturally consider the work of the school and community education as an element in the service of the church to the area. In some countries it is possible for the teacher to be a part of an integral programme of education in which the church school and the public school have one single, unified curriculum. At the top of this ladder of ascending intimacy is the situation which exists in many villages of the world where the teacher and the pastor are the same person and his work as an educator and as a minister are but facets of his single task.

This union of pastor and teacher in one has been a solution of

33 Chapman, O. H., "The Functions of Christian Medical Work in Modern China," *Chinese Recorder,* Vol. 18, October 1937, Reprint, p. 5.

34 See Papers, pp. 206-7.

35 Butterfield, K. L., "The Christian Mission in Rural India," International Missionary Council, New York and London, 1930.

the difficulties of financing two leaders for a small group with inadequate resources. There may be disadvantages in the plan, but advantages outweigh them.[36]

All along this line the Christian programme has an interest in the training of the teachers. And where the schools are in the hands of the Christian church it has the major if not complete responsibility for that training. In the last case, that of pastor-teachers, the training for teachers must be combined with that for ministers. There are many training schools in which there is such a unified pastor-teacher course.

This relationship and our principle of integration require that the teacher in common with all other Christian workers should be conscious of the fullness of the Christian life and the way in which his work as a teacher may make its contribution to the total programme. He should have contact with the work of the church, clubs, cooperatives, government extension agencies, etc. and, if possible, experience in some of them, that he may have as broad a view of his task as possible. Above all, if the teacher is married, he or she should have a clear conception of how the teacher's home may be an educational centre for the whole village in better ways of living. Both husband and wife should be given definite training in this field so that their home and their children may give a genuine inspiration and example to the whole village.

The discussion which follows attempts to outline the principles which should be kept in mind in the selection and training of rural teachers who will be related to the comprehensive programme for community life.

"He who knows can teach." For years this has been the basis of teacher training, and even to this day for the greater part of the world little beyond this factual knowledge is given the prospective teacher. This is especially true in rural areas, and doubly unfortunate, for there, if anywhere, competent skilled teachers are needed.

Really competent teachers are needed because the rural elementary teacher is not only the first, but often the only teacher for many students. He or she furnishes the only contact for many rural communities with the outside world. The task, too, is far wider than that of the teacher in the urban school. The teacher may be

[36] This might very well be a way out for a great many communities in America. A well trained man could find a challenging opportunity, together with adequate support, as a pastor in a community and a teacher in its school system. It would be a load to carry, but certainly no greater one than when a minister tries to be pastor in from three to eight communities at the same time in order to build a supporting constituency large enough to carry the financial burden. Such pastor-teachers might be separate units, or possibly assistants in a larger parish with a full time director.

the only educated person in the village and as a result people go to him for every situation involving anything outside their own limited experience. The whole community is his field for teaching. And to bear this load there is little help given. The teacher is peculiarly alone.[37]

Teaching is an art and like all other arts depends upon a certain amount of natural ability. But natural ability is simply a sound foundation for proper technical training. Both are needed if a teacher is to be rightly prepared to teach. Hence both the selection of desirable candidates and their suitable training are of great importance.

What are the qualities that make a desirable candidate? A good body and a clear mind are certainly a minimum essential. Mental health is especially important, for the task is one to try nerves. A teacher should have a love for children, a real interest in their progress, a love for rural life, a feeling for the rhythm of the land and the seasons, faith in the ability of adults to learn, a sense of community, and a desire to help improve communal living. Without these there can be no joy in the service, and without joy there is little efficiency. He ought also to have patience, tact, and sympathy to enable him to get along well with people, and with these a sense of humour.

How shall we enlist the young man or woman with such virtues in so humble a calling? From the church's standpoint the best method is that of personal work of pastors, teachers, and intelligent parents. Observing young folks at work and play they can note the "lad of parts" and follow the good example of the old school master of Drumtochty by sending him along for higher education and training. These primary rewards of leadership,[38] usefulness to others, a sense of achievement of something worthwhile, and that inner glow of character in service, should be presented rather than following Moses' initial mistake with Jethro's son, promising what would be done for him.[39]

[37] Mason, Olcott, "Better Village Schools", pp. 155-6. "The village teacher is usually sent to a lonely outpost where he has very little contact with educated people. The only person to visit him from outside during the year may be the school inspector and a few officials. He may be the only literate man in the neighborhood, but in any case heavier responsibilities for village affairs are thrown upon him than would be placed upon the town teacher. One danger is that he will keep his standards but become lonely and stay in the village as little as possible. An opposite danger is that he will get his standards from the residents, sink to their level and make no effort to raise it."

[38] Cf. Dwight Sanderson, "Leadership for Rural Life" 1940, Association Press, New York. The chapter on the *Rewards of Leadership*. Cf also p. 55. Usefulness rather than leadership should be the motivation in training potential leaders.

[39] Numbers 10:29-32.

The Training Needed. When suitable candidates offer, how and what shall they be taught? The how is just as important as the what. For after all these teachers are going to teach as they are taught. You cannot teach the way of creative education to students entirely by the lecture method! They must be taught as you want them to teach. In the training school there must be the utilization of available resources, the following of interests, the solving of problems, the development of projects, the use of pupil ability, the learning by doing, the relation to community needs in practical life, the close link with the land and its cultivation, that are wanted in the village schools which are to be conducted by the teachers after they are trained.

> If the function of the teacher is to guide the child through a series of carefully chosen and educative experiences that will bring him not only personal self-realization, but a knowledge of and a skill in the use of the techniques of living, then the program for the education of teachers should be planned accordingly.[40]

> The curriculum for the professional education of teachers should consist of a carefully selected series of teaching experiences out of which, as a natural outgrowth, should come a philosophy of education, an understanding of the psychology of the child and of the learning process, and all those techniques, attitudes, capacities and skills that constitute the equipment of a good teacher.[41]

As they are taught it should be remembered that they are being trained as leaders of community education. "They would need to develop the attitudes and skills and to obtain the knowledge which would make them valued advisors of community groups which were facing the problems of village life. They can do this best by actually working with such groups in solving the problems of communities."[42]

In developing this "how" of training rural teachers, the author just quoted gives four stages in the preparation of prospective teachers and the maintenance of their training and efficiency in actual work. "The first stage in the training of community teachers under the experience plan should be in meeting the problems of their own school community through activities, conferences and individual initiative . . . (p. 200) with particular emphasis upon the ideal and methods of cooperation." "The second stage in the preparation would be to carry on enterprises in community education in one, two or three villages near the school . . . with daily seminar meetings." (p. 205) "The preparation should be furthered by a graded series of teaching trips (and experiences): One day

40 Frank E. Baker, Educating Teachers by the Experience Method, *Childhood Education,* Dec. 1936, p. 101.

41 Ibid, p. 104.

42 *Teaching a Bantu Community,* Newell S. Booth, 1936, p. 196.

visits with the teacher . . . in order to meet some one specific need; . . . student group in different villages; . . . go by two's and three's for a week's time; . . . vacation enterprises in community education . . . from two weeks to two months in length; . . . each graduating student should be placed in sole charge of a two-month enterprise in community education . . . under supervision." (pp. 224-226) The final stage is supervision. (pp. 228-241) The plan for supervision carries through all the work of teaching and makes training a continual process.[43]

When we consider what the content of the training should be, we find the following basis:

1. *As broad a general education as possible.* Economic circumstances in many countries will inevitably limit nearly all to the secondary school level or even below. But they should get the fullest, and best balanced training possible at whatever level can be attained.

2. *Knowledge of the nature of the rural community* and the contribution that education can make to its life in integral relationship to other agencies. There is need for a study of these other agencies and the functions in the community.

3. *Introduction to the problems and methods of agriculture,* sufficient to lead to intelligent personal participation in such projects as diversification of food crops, soil conservation, improvement of seed, cooperative marketing; also to the elementary teaching of such things in the school and experimentation in school gardens; and particularly to the necessary knowledge as to the specialists and services available when need for help is manifested.

The training course for a rural teacher or pastor-teacher should aim to produce a person willing to live close to the soil and close to people and capable of helping the people of the soil grow in their ability to meet their problems of living.

4. *Knowledge of and skill in the use of the materials and methods of community education.* This involves a knowledge of the way the child or the adult learns, as well as the materials and the way to teach to each such things as, the tool subjects, the scientific approach to life around, hygiene and public health, the land and its use, methods of utilizing resources at hand for the betterment of livelihood, socially helpful ways of living together in family and community, the development of character, creative use of time, the story of the wider world of which the community is a part, religion as an integral part of living, and in general cooperation in making

43 See *The Jeanes Visiting Teachers* by Jackson Davis, The Carnegie Corporation, New York, 1936. Also the report of the Inter-territorial Jeanes Conference, Salisbury, Southern Rhodesia, Lovedale, South Africa, Lovedale Press, 1936.

life personally, economically, and socially adequate. The aim of preparation of prospective teachers should be to make it possible for them to help each pupil in their schools to be growing along these lines in accord with the level of development each has attained, and also to help all in the community to develop in these ways.

This implies a knowledge of the theory of education, psychology, principles of teaching, school and class-room management, community extension, etc. But these should not be taught as unrelated lecture courses, but should be based on the discussion and solution of actual problems in the practice school and community.

5. *Knowledge of people and the development of right attitudes* towards them and their learning. It is essential to know how to do something, but it is of still greater importance to know how to do it with someone. Teaching is cooperation between teacher and student. Therefore the teacher must know those with whom he works as he teaches. He must be helped to form the right attitudes towards them and their ways of learning.[44] This is particularly true in regard to the adults in the community.[45]

3. *Industrial Experts*

There are three primary requirements in training those who are to contribute skill and experience in industry to the Christian rural programme. (The most important industry to be represented in any rural planning is agriculture, but increasingly the other industries of the agricultural village demand special attention.)

The first requirement is technical competence. This has long been recognized in the fields of medicine and of teaching. The need is equal in social and industrial activities. Too often those who were to serve as experts have been trained barely beyond the level to which they were to encourage others. Sound and understanding technical competence is indispensable.

The second requirement is that the industrial training be pertinent to the actual problems of the people to be helped. In the past, too many "industrial schools" have fitted boys to use equip-

[44] "While the future teacher must reach a certain standard of general education and some skill in a variety of crafts, the most vital element in his training is the general attitude of mind." Memorandum on the Education of African Communities, Colonial No. 103, London 1933, p. 12.

[45] Ibid. p. 14. "While the education of adults must in the main be the work of other agencies, the school can cooperate with these and where they do not yet exist in some measure fill the gap. Excessive as may seem the demands on the village teacher and his wife, not a few African teachers have in fact succeeded in making the school a centre of inspiration for the whole community."

ment and to make products quite foreign to the markets available to them. This requirement, too, is being increasingly fulfilled.

The third requirement is a thorough understanding of the Christian gospel and of the relationship of one's own industrial training to the whole Christian programme. Only by such understanding can secularization be avoided and the contribution of industrial experts fully utilized.

It will be noted here, as in the training of other experts, that this is one of the major functions of the Christian college. In agriculture, for example, the agricultural college should produce:

a) teachers of agriculture
b) agricultural research workers
c) agricultural extension agents
d) managers of large agricultural enterprises

Considerable confusion has been caused in the past by misunderstanding the role of college teaching in agriculture. It is only in regions of extensive agriculture where industrial farms become large business enterprises that any number of college-trained men themselves become farmers. Even in such regions, the great contributions to the training of farmers have been made by agricultural schools and by agricultural extension. For the most part, agricultural college graduates become teachers, research workers, extension agents, and managers of large agricultural enterprises.

No greater challenge faces the Christian church today than the problem of college and university training. Advanced study in any field increases the danger of secularization, of narrowing appreciations, of segmented outlook. Continued and concentrated attention to the processes of nature tends to push realization of the ultimate initiative and sustaining power of God further and further out of mind. Yet specialized study plays an essential role in Christian discipleship in identifying and solving new problems, in mastering difficult techniques necessary to efficient trusteeship of material resources, to development of health, to creative relationships with people. Constant study of the contribution of one's special knowledge to the whole Christian programme is the best insurance of balanced development.

4. *Home and Family Life Experts*

In the training of home and family life personnel attitudes that are truly Christlike must be developed if the work is to succeed. Reverence for human life, respect for individual personality, a deep desire to help the underprivileged and sympathy for those who are perplexed by the tangle of family relationship and problems, will be developed concurrently with skills of a more material kind and techniques of a specialized or practical nature. The acquiring of factual knowledge, of scientific techniques and disciplines is important but not so important as the development of right attitudes and a sympathetic approach to the problems and needs of others. The example set by Jesus in his training of the twelve disciples—a sympathetic approach to the needs of men and a deep understanding of their human weaknesses and failures geared to a great concern that the Kingdom of God might be established in their hearts; that the substance of life might not be dissipated or squandered but used for the building up of that Kingdom—might well be emulated by home counselors and by those responsible for the training of personnel and for the "set-up" of training institutions and courses.

Sincerity of purpose, a willingness to sacrifice for the welfare of others, a determination to be used "as fuel for God's flame" in helping those who are in spiritual, physical, or economic need, should be part of the candidates' equipment and must be stressed in the training of all those who seek to qualify as home and family counselors.

Another major requirement is that there shall be provided comprehensive courses in the rural philosophy of life, in rural sociology, and in the patterns of rural social organization prevailing in the region where the counselor is to work, particularly as these culture patterns affect the life of the home and rural Christian community.

Systematic observation, accurate tabulation of significant and essential data, skill in diagnosing factors and influences that tend to create unfavourable reactions and relationships between individuals and contribute to the break-down of family life, must be developed as tools in all home-counseling work. Adequate training will include factual knowledge and techniques for dealing with social evils existing in the rural community—such as poor housing, child labor, poverty, extravagance, debt, intemperance, insecurity, and the resultant delinquency and undesirable behaviour patterns.

In the training of workers the psychological factors that make or destroy character must be stressed. A knowledge of the way in which emotional tension or emotional unbalance between parents reacts unfavourably in the life of the home; the value of sound emotional states in early childhood; the profound reactions throughout adult life of adolescent emotions unless guided into right channels, and the psychological interaction of individual upon individual, is a necessary part of the training of home experts or counselors.

Parent education in personality development particularly in relation to character building must be given a prominent place in the curriculum. How to help parents in the training of their own children to realize that the character development and socialization of the child is of great significance in the building up of the rural Christian community, and that at the very heart of character training there must be a sincere concern for the rights and the general welfare of others must be looked upon as fundamental knowledge in the training of workers.

Developing a sense of neighbourhood responsibility in dealing with the rural family and its problems is of peculiar importance in the training of home counselors. Service to the neighbourhood and to the larger community, of which the family is an integral part, and not the selfish interests or ambitions of the individual family must be the goal. The family must be helped to see its problems in the light of the needs of other families, and the well-equipped counselor must be taught how to give direction in this regard. Tools must be provided that will enable him to give sound leadership in the building up of this essential attitude.

Care must be taken that there is a clear understanding of the way in which Christian principles are to be applied in family relationships, the extent to which the rural Christian family is responsible for the uplift of the neighbourhood and community environment, and ways of maintaining Christian family life in the face of non-Christian standards in a non-Christian culture.

Courses in mental hygiene, the biological beginning of plant, animal, and human life, and the premarital counseling in preparation for marriage and Christian home-making are all "musts" of a well-planned and adequate training.

It is essential that all counselors have a clear understanding of the distinction between the regional tabus of a changing culture and the moral code founded upon the principles of Jesus.[46]

Standards of rural home economy—budgeting and marketing—child-care, home nursing, sanitation, suitable recreation, the nutritional needs of the family and the relation of health and thrift to character must all receive attention in any adequate programme of training. It must always be borne in mind, however, that it is the

[46] "Tabus will change, for conventions are always changing, and of course the law may be changed. All of them do no more than reflect the assumptions of society, the ideals and needs of culture, in the day when they were made. But with *morals* there is a difference. (We are here concerned with Christian morals; but this difference is true in some degree, of every moral system.) It is not that moral *codes* don't change at all—they do. But their purpose doesn't change. There is always a fixed intention; the kind of life designed by God, for the men whom he has made. Christians have an authority for their moral standards which is independent of human judgments and scientific evidence, though not unrelated to these, and indeed supported by them." *Sex and Society,* by Gilbert Russell in *Religion and Life,* p. 920.

development of Christian character and personality that counts in a summing up of ultimate values. Better standards of living have a large bearing on the growth of Christian character and it will be part of the home counselor's work to help in raising the standard of physical and economic life in the rural home, but it must be remembered that in his training the making of better men is the ultimate goal and the criterion by which success is measured. One of the leading educators in China, Mr. James Yen, has stated:

"Not better schools, better farms, better bodies as integrated ends, but better men are to be the irreducible minimum for the new order of society."[47]

It will be of great value to the rural homes expert that complete mastery of the technique of two or three cottage or village industries of a practical nature be achieved during student days. These may help in the solution of an urgent financial problem in the home or rural neighbourhood when field responsibilities are undertaken. The wise educator will plan carefully that this mechanical or technical knowledge be made available for the candidate under his care. Practical work in some neighbouring rural village or district should also be provided for the individual students or for students in groups, that theories acquired in the class-room may be put to practical test in the rural home, and that cooperation may be developed.

It is of vital importance that all candidates be taught the importance of integrating this work with that of other phases of the comprehensive Christian programme, and that the inter-relation of church and home be clearly understood. The homes worker must be able to coordinate and work smoothly with others for the attainment of all objectives, that there may be neither uncoordinated effort nor overlapping of certain phases of work. He must seek to supplement the work of others or to build up new work independently where there are no other agencies mediating essential home and rural neighbourhood services. To bring the home and church into closer union must be a constant objective, that in this important work of developing Christian personality home and church may supplement one another.

Finally, all workers must be trained in the Bible as the living word of God, and in worship techniques. Guiding the family in its worship experiences and leading the family group into deeper fellowship with God through faith in Jesus Christ, and into an ever increasing sense of unity with other Christians will present a challenge to the worker which he must be equipped to face.

[47] *The Common People's University,* by William H. Gleysteen in *A Symposium on the Tinghsien Rural Institute—China,* p. 9.

There are roughly speaking two classes for whom training in home and family life and parent education should be provided:

a) Those who intend to become experts in the general field of home and family life and to make this a life-work.

b) Rural pastors and teachers who desire to master disciplines and skills in home and parent counseling, and who must of necessity give only a portion of their time to this work.

For the first group academic training supplemented by a broad range of practical courses must be provided. Special emphasis must be laid upon personal discipleship and consecration to Jesus Christ. Understanding of the comprehensive task must be developed.

For the second group previous academic training and pastoral or other experience will have provided the necessary foundation for the building up of further knowledge of a specific and technical kind. For this important group the required techniques and specialized knowledge must be provided. Such training should be made available through courses in colleges, theological seminaries, and Bible schools, and through district classes for ministers where the services of thoroughly trained and widely experienced leaders have been secured.

C

The Rural Church

1. *Principles of Organization of the Rural Church*

a. *The Principle of Inclusiveness.* One principle of church organization in any locality should be acknowledgment of close relation to the parent or generating body and the use of every opportunity to knit the local group closely into the richly-patterned fabric of the Church Universal. Protestantism has brought shame and weakness upon itself by division and separation. We now live in a time when this is widely recognized and deplored. Forces are at work bringing about many projects of united effort and many steps toward vital union. The time has fully come when, in every rural neighbourhood where there is new planting and growth of the church, there should be planned avoidance of divisive denominational mind-sets or fixity of practices. Every effort should be made to secure united action and spirit in the Christian community of a neighbourhood where there are different denominational groups. The welfare of the people should outweigh the exigencies of denominational control.

A church should be a community even while individuals differ in temperament and in disposition. It should be able to hold in fellowship the more emotional and the more rational, the mystical and the speculative and the utilitarian, the ritualistic and the informal. This volume will have failed seriously if it does not encourage those interested in the spread of the gospel in rural areas to visualize and work for a church which can unite all of the Christians of a neighbourhood into one inclusive fellowship.

b. *The Principle of Conservation of Native Traditions and Genius.* Jesus prepared no creedal statement for his church, no one pattern for its organization, no particular mode of worship, no list of functions. But he did promise the Comforter, whom he repeatedly called the "Spirit of truth," and of whom he said, "When he, the Spirit of truth, is come, he shall guide you into all the truth." It is for Christ's disciples so to live among rural peoples as to make this "Spirit of truth" known to them, and then to trust them to find and follow his guidance. Different peoples have their own music and song patterns. They have their genius for art, expressing itself in carvings and sculpture, in drawings and pictures, in their architecture, their literature and their proverbs. The guidance of Christ's Spirit should bring fresh inspiration to this genius and lead it into

Christian symbolism and expression entirely native to each people.

Peoples have their economic and social habits, to meet the problems of livelihood and to provide friendly intercourse and fellowship. Let the Spirit of truth teach all that is meant by Christian trusteeship and there will be modifications of old ways, but not necessarily any fundamental displacement. In short, the church becomes indigenous in its corporate life and religious expression by just such reshaping of native ways and interests of a people as seems necessary to embody the new content and the new outlook of truth that are found in Christ Jesus, not by any adoption of outward trappings brought from other parts of the world.[1]

c. *The Principle of Balance of Democratic Liberty with Corporate Life and Control and the Acceptance of Leadership.* Jesus came to liberate the human spirit from all external bondage whatsoever. In his words the very charter of human liberty is, "If ye abide in my word, then are ye my disciples; and ye shall know the truth, and the truth shall make you free." (John 8:31, 32.) Men are called individually to repent and to commit their ways to the Lord. They are accountable as individuals before God. They are willingly to accept no authority counter to God's authority of truth.

Yet the liberty of the Christian should never have in it the element of personal license nor of individual wilfulness. It should be a dedicated liberty, subject to the "law of liberty," using James' expression (James 1:25; 2:12), a liberty contributing to the freeing of others round about. Related to the church this means acceptance of leadership and a cooperative share in its corporate life and activities. It also means acceptance of needed overhead control and participation in widely inclusive organization and government. In the church there should be full scope for the use of individual abilities, for Paul's "diversities of gifts," his "diversities of ministrations," and other diversities. The "body of Christ" that Paul went on to describe was to recognize a head and such organs as those of sight, hearing, and touch. But "God tempered the body together." So the

[1] The Church Conference on African Affairs (Westerville) pleaded for the nurture of an "Africanate edition of Christianity" (p. 24). It stated: "Our particular American or European forms of Christianity are shaped according to the racial genius and culture of the Western world—in accordance with our biological and social heritage. To impose those forms upon other peoples would be a kind of spiritual imperialism that is contrary to the due respect for humanity which is inherent in our Christian faith. Each nation, we believe, has its own contribution to make to the universal Christian fellowship of the future." (p. 23). "We have before our vision a Church in Africa that is self-propagating, self-governing, self-supporting—and fundamentally African: indigenous, not foreign: rooted in the soil of the African ethos; a spiritual home for the Africans." (p. 48).

church is a body tempered together, with free and equal but directed participation by all of its members.

2. *Provision of a Tangible Rallying Center: the Church Building*

There are thousands of Christian congregations across the earth which have no buildings at all. Some of them meet in the homes of their members, perhaps in a room set apart, but very often in the open courtyard or in one of the living rooms of the family. As a congregation grows, however, it usually wants a place set aside for its corporate worship and, as its activities expand, rooms where these can be planned and some of them carried on.

At first, this place of worship may be a room set apart in one of the homes, or it may be simply an area of ground in the shade of a tree, marked by a cross and simple boundaries, as in many villages of India, or it may be a building much like the dwellings but designated "for the glory of God." This place of worship soon takes on sanctity as the meeting-place of Christians. Therefore from the beginning an effort should be made, at least in decoration and furnishings, to make it seem a place of worship. Such a place of meeting, whether the humblest room where ten or a dozen worshippers may meet familiarly together or a great church to seat a thousand, should be so in keeping with the rural scene and so accommodated to local ways that it will seem "the church home" to the family of believers, in which none will feel strange nor out of place. In rural areas, there ought to be houses of worship which are themselves a glory to God, inviting to worship, with dignity of design not foreign to local traditions of architecture and religious aspiration, yet with distinctly Christian symbolism of universal meaning and appeal.

The countryside is rich in sites where worshipful churches may be located in inspiring surroundings. One thinks of the tiny village chapel in Japan, set high on a hill overlooking the village and the sea, with a great window in the chancel framing the distant view of Mt. Fuji. And of the lovely building of Christ Church at Alpine, Tennessee, set on a prominent knoll in the center of the valley which is its parish, built of native stone by members of the congregation, with pews and pulpit of valley-grown timber, carved by one of the worshippers, and all in a style of simplicity and serenity. They are springing up around the earth today, churches rich in rural tradition and in Christian symbolism which utilizes the familiar scenes and tasks of field and forest and home.

With the broadening of the programme of the church to render various services to the neighbourhood and to centre the lives of the Christians in the church, church buildings are increasingly being designed to accommodate church schools, social gatherings, and sometimes health clinics and agricultural classes, in quarters apart from the sanctuary reserved for worship.

A church building is not indispensable to a congregation, but it can enrich worship, provide for an expanding discipleship, and stand itself in the heart of a neighbourhood as a rugged and sensitive monument to the Christian faith of those who worship in it, and to the ever living presence of the Father.

3. *Financial Support*

It is generally agreed that the goal should be a church free from the necessity for subsidy. The problems in achieving this arise both in the decision as to when "self-support" has been achieved[2] and in the decision as to how rapidly outside help should be withdrawn. These problems vary so with traditional types of denominational organization and with different countries that few generalized statements are possible.

There is one universal principle. That is that high spiritual vitality is indispensable, being of far more value than any technique of securing financial support. *It is our conviction that the greatest contribution to financial support of the rural church will be made by the church understanding its message to rural people and the means by which that message may be transmitted effectively, through the development of deep Christian faith and full discipleship.* Millions of toilers on the soil, in vineyards and forests, and with fishing-nets, accumulate little or no cash surplus. Any expense beyond family livelihood constitutes a real burden. Great numbers are normally in debt. Under such circumstances, there is no path to "self-support" short of devotion which results in very sacrificial giving. Such devotion, however, can work miracles. People can plan ahead for the church if they will. Sometimes the penniless can contribute time that will save pennies and dimes. They can contribute sweat and toil on buildings and grounds. Perhaps they can unite with others to farm or garden a plot of ground for the church. Those with property of their own can enlist in some sort of "Lord's Acre" project. The fisherman may dedicate a certain proportion of his catch. It is a well-known fact that many non-Christians, living in great poverty, spend in the aggregate great sums in connection with temples and shrines, in elaborate clan and family celebrations, on wedding and funeral rites, for the support of all sorts of magicians, scorcerers, and witch-doctors. As such people enter the

[2] Davis, J. Merle, *The Economic and Social Environment of the Younger Churches,* 1939, see pp. 187-189.

church, some of this outflow should be diverted to the church, just as much of it should be used in family discipleship.[3]

After a passionate Christian devotion which impels giving, the most important aid to church support in many lands is improvement of the economic conditions of members of the church. In many places this needs to be an important part of the church's programme.

One of the pressing reasons for church union, even in those rural areas in which farmers have quite adequate individual incomes, is the necessity for adequately undergirding the church financially. Entirely too many small agricultural neighbourhoods are trying to support four or five churches which could be united into one congregation with adequate resources for carrying on a programme of full discipleship.

[3] Where non-Christians resort to borrowing to meet such obligations, this transfer obviously cannot be made, for no one would suggest borrowing in order to contribute to the support of the church.

PART III

The Rural Bookshelf

Bibliographies

Papers Related to Chapters V-VII

Index

The Rural Bookshelf

As a result of its study, the Work Committee wishes to draw attention to the books which, in its opinion, should form the core of the library of every serious student of the Christian mission among rural people.

The Christian Mission in Rural India, by Kenyon L. Butterfield, published by the International Missionary Council, 156 Fifth Avenue, New York City, 1930. This is the best of the reports by Dr. Butterfield.

The Economic and Social Environment of the Younger Churches, by J. Merle Davis, published by the International Missionary Council, 156 Fifth Avenue, New York City, 1938.

The Rural Church in the Far East, by Ralph A. Felton, published by the Baptist Mission Press, Calcutta, 1938.

Come Over Into Macedonia, by Harold F. Allen, published by Rutgers University Press, New Brunswick, N. J., 1943.

Further Upward in Rural India, by D. Spencer Hatch, published by Oxford University Press, 1938. One of the best discussions of rural development policy and program by one with long experience in the villages.

A Book of Worship for Village Churches, by Edward K. Ziegler, published by Agricultural Missions, Inc., 156 Fifth Avenue, New York City, 1939.

Rural People at Worship, by Edward K. Ziegler, published by Agricultural Missions, Inc., 156 Fifth Avenue, New York City, 1943.

The Holy Earth, by Liberty H. Bailey, published by Agricultural Missions, Inc., 156 Fifth Avenue, New York City, 1942.

Christian Rural Fellowship Bulletins, complete file, Christian Rural Fellowship, 156 Fifth Avenue, New York City.

The House of the People, by Katherine M. Cook, U. S. Government Printing Press, Washington, D. C., 1932.

The Ministry of Healing in India, Handbook of the Christian Medical Association of India. Mysore Wesleyan Mission Press, 1932.

The Family and Its Christian Fulfilment, a joint study, published by the Foreign Missions Conference of North America, 156 Fifth Avenue, New York, 1945.

Source Book on Home and Family Life, by Irma Highbaugh, published by Agricultural Missions, Inc., 156 Fifth Avenue, New York, 1947.

The Story of John Frederic Oberlin, by Augustus Field Beard, published by The Christian Rural Fellowship, 156 Fifth Avenue, New York, 1946.

Bibliographies

Chapter I. THE BACKGROUND OF RURAL LIFE

Bailey, L. H. *The Holy Earth,* new edition. New York: Agricultural Missions, Inc., 1942.

Baker, O. E. "Rural and Urban Philosophies," *Christian Rural Fellowship Bulletin No. 10,* March, 1936.

Bonsack, Charles D. "Nature Speaks of God," *Christian Rural Fellowship Bulletin No. 36,* November, 1938.

Brightman, E. S. "A Christian View of Nature," in *Christian Bases of World Order.* The Merrick Lectures. New York: Abingdon-Cokesbury Press, 1943.

Brightman, E. S. *The Spiritual Life.* New York and Nashville: Abingdon-Cokesbury Press, 1942.

Butterfield, K. L. "Rural Work and Mission Policy," *International Review of Missions,* XXI (1932), 412-422.

Drake, F. S. "Heritage of the North China Peasant," *International Review of Missions,* XXVII (1938), 174-182.

"Enduring Values in Rural Life," *Christian Rural Fellowship Bulletin No. 46,* November, 1939.

Hodge, J. Z. "The Missionary and the *Ryat,*" *International Review of Missions,* XVIII (1929), 518-528.

Horning, Emma. "Values in Rural Chinese Religion," *Chinese Recorder,* LXI (1930), 299-307.

Huss, Bernard. "Agriculture Amongst the Natives of South Africa," *International Review of Missions,* XI (1922), 260-269.

Lindstrom, D. E. "Preserving Rural Values," *Christian Rural Fellowship Bulletin No. 64,* September, 1941.

McConnell, C. M. *The Rural Billion.* New York: Friendship Press, 1931.

Murray, A. V. "Christianity and Rural Civilization," *International Review of Missions,* XIX, 388-397.

Sanders, E. T., and Spicer, T. W. "The Social and Religious Significance of the Rural Neighborhood," *Christian Rural Fellowship Bulletin No. 65,* October, 1941.

Symposium, "Agriculture as a Way of Life," *Christian Rural Fellowship Bulletin No. 27,* December, 1937.

Wilson, Warren H. "The Faith Man Shares with Beast and Tree," *Christian Rural Fellowship Bulletin No. 7,* December, 1935.

Ziegler, E. K. "A Christian Rural Life Philosophy," *Christian Rural Fellowship Bulletin No. 67,* December, 1941.

Chapter II. THE CHRISTIAN MESSAGE: FOR THE WHOLE OF LIFE

A. THE CORE OF THE CHRISTIAN REVELATION

Berdyaev, Nicolas. *The Destiny of Man.* New York: Charles Scribner's Sons, 1937.

Brunner, Emil. *Our Faith.* New York: Charles Scribner's Sons, 1936. Pp. 1-6.

Kagawa, T. *Love the Law of Life,* Philadelphia: John C. Winston Co., 1929.

Mackay, John A. *A Preface to Christian Theology.* New York: The Macmillan Company, 1941.

McConnell, F. J. *Human Needs and World Christianity.* New York: Friendship Press, 1939.

Visser't Hooft, W. A. *None Other Gods.* New York: Harper and Brothers, 1937.

B. IMPLICATIONS FOR SOCIAL RELATIONSHIPS

"African Family Life," Report of General Missionary Conference, Pretoria, June, 1940. Obtainable from Christian Council of South Africa, 152 Nicholson Street, Brooklyn, Pretoria. 2s. 9d.

Chandler, Robert E. "A Social Aim for a Chinese Christian," *International Review of Missions,* IX (1920), 106-115.

Church Conference on African Affairs, *Christian Action in Africa.* New York: Foreign Missions Conference, 1942.

Landis, Benson Y. "The Social Ideals of the Churches for Agriculture and Rural Life," *Christian Rural Fellowship Bulletin No. 73,* June, 1942.

Matthews, Shailer. "Missions and the Social Gospel," *International Review of Missions,* III (1914), 432-446.

Mosher, A. T. "The Kingdom of God and Rural Reconstruction," *Christian Rural Fellowship Bulletin No. 56,* October, 1940.

Rapking, Aaron H. *Building the Kingdom of God in the Countryside.* New York: Methodist Book Concern, 1938.

Skinner, Stanley E. "The Characteristics of a Christian Rural Community," *Christian Rural Fellowship Bulletin No. 59,* February, 1941.

Smathers, Eugene. "The Characteristics of a Christian Rural Community," *Christian Rural Fellowship Bulletin No. 61,* April, 1941.

Temple, William. *Christianity and the Social Order.* New York: Penguin Books, Inc., 1942.

The World Mission of the Church. New York: International Missionary Council, 1939.

Taylor, Henry C. "Rural People and World Peace," *Christian Rural Fellowship Bulletin No. 60,* March, 1941.

Wiser, William H. and Charlotte V. *For All of Life.* New York: Friendship Press, 1943.

C. IMPLICATIONS FOR TRUSTEESHIP OF RESOURCES

Calhoun, R. L. *God and the Common Life.* New York: Charles Scribner's Sons. 1935.

Hays, Brooks. "The Christian's Relation to Land," *Christian Rural Fellowship Bulletin No. 68,* January, 1942.

Higginbottom, Sam. "Christianity and Agriculture in India," *International Review of Missions,* IX (1920), 252-259.

Kester, Howard, and Kester, Alice. "Ceremony of the Soil—A Service of Worship," *Christian Rural Fellowship Bulletin No. 69,* February, 1942.

Lacy, Mary G. "Religious Significance in Rural Handicrafts," *Christian Rural Fellowship Bulletin No. 30,* March, 1938.

Landis, Benson Y. "The Social Ideals of the Churches for Agriculture and Rural Life," *Christian Rural Fellowship Bulletin No. 73,* June, 1942.

Lowdermilk, Walter C. "The Eleventh Commandment," *Christian Rural Fellowship Bulletin No. 74,* September, 1942.

Mills, W. H. "The Church and the Land," *Christian Rural Fellowship Bulletin No. 71,* April, 1942.

Price, Frank W. "The Kingdom of God in a Rural Community," *Christian Rural Fellowship Bulletin No. 33,* June, 1938.

Raper, Arthur. "Ethics of Land Tenancy," *Christian Rural Fellowship Bulletin No. 26,* November, 1937.

Scaff, A. E. "The History and Interpretation of the Doctrine of Christian Vocation." Unpublished B. D. thesis, Chicago Theological Seminary, 1940.

Chapter III. CHRISTIAN ACHIEVEMENT AND WITNESS: THROUGH THE WHOLE OF LIFE

Hodge, J. Z. "The Missionary and the *Ryat*," *International Review of Missions,* XVIII (1929), 518-528.

Hogg, A. C. "The Function of the Christian College," *International Review of Missions,* XXIII, p. 116.

Jacks, L. P. *Education Through Recreation,* New York: Harper and Brothers, 1932.

Lacy, Mary G. "Religious Significance in Rural Handicrafts," *Christian Rural Fellowship Bulletin No. 30,* March, 1938.

Patten, Marjorie. *The Arts Workshop of Rural America.* New York: Columbia University Press, 1937.

Rohrbaugh, Lynn. *Handy-Kit.* Delaware, Ohio: Cooperative Recreation Service.

Uganda, J. J. "Presentation of Christianity to Primitive Peoples," *International Review of Missions,* IV (1915), 382-395.

Washington, Booker T. *Working With The Hands.* New York: Doubleday Page and Co., 1921.

Chapter IV. THE FAMILY AND THE CHRISTIAN COMMUNITY

A. THE CHRISTIAN FAMILY

For bibliography on Christian Family Life, refer to the forthcoming report on Home and Family Life by the Foreign Missions Conference.

B. THE CHRISTIAN COMMUNITY

Church Conference on African Affairs, *Christian Action in Africa.* New York: Foreign Missions Conference, 1942.

Greene, Shirley. "A Church Program for the Rural Community," *Christian Rural Fellowship Bulletin No. 62,* May, 1941.

Mackay, John A. *A Preface to Christian Theology.* New York: The Macmillan Co., 1941.

Morgan, Arthur E. *The Small Community.* New York: Harper and Brothers, 1942.

Price, Frank W. "The Kingdom of God in a Rural Community," *Christian Rural Fellowship Bulletin No. 33,* June, 1938.

Rapking, Aaron H. *Building the Kingdom of God in the Countryside.* New York: Methodist Book Concern, 1938.

Sanderson, Dwight E. *The Farmer and His Community.* New York: Harcourt Brace and Company, 1924.

Smathers, Eugene. "A Rural Church Program That Makes Religion the Qualifying Factor in Every Experience of Life," *Christian Rural Fellowship Bulletin No. 66,* November, 1941.

Tripp, Thomas, A. "Rural Poverty and Rural Morale," *Christian Rural Fellowship Bulletin No. 44,* September, 1939.

Visser't Hooft, W. A. *None Other Gods.* New York: Harper and Brothers, 1937.

Chapter V. ACTIVITIES OF THE CHRISTIAN RURAL PROGRAM

INTRODUCTION

Allen, Harold F. *Come Over Into Macedonia.* New Brunswick: Rutgers University Press, 1943.

Butterfield, Kenyon L. *The Christian Mission in Rural India.* New York: International Missionary Council, 1930.

Butterfield, Kenyon L. *The Rural Mission of the Church in Eastern Asia.* New York: International Missionary Council, 1931.

Edmiston, A. L. "Christian Farm and Home Program (Africa)," Agricultural Missions, Inc., Mimeograph Series No. 125.

Felton, Ralph A. *The Rural Church in the Far East.* Calcutta: Baptist Mission Press, 1938.

Hargreaves, J. Robert. "The Significance to Rural Religion and the Rural Church of So-called Secular Agencies Related to Agriculture, the Home and Rural Life," *Christian Rural Fellowship Bulletin No. 72,* May, 1942.

Hubbard, Hugh. "A Christian Approach to the Chinese Village," *International Review of Missions,* XXVIII (1929), 240-245.

Madras Conference Report, *Evangelism.* New York: International Missionary Council, 1939.

Matthews, Harold S. "A New Experiment in Rural Evangelism (in China)," Agricultural Missions, Inc., Mimeograph Series No. 118.

Mosher, A. T. "The Kingdom of God and Rural Reconstruction," *Christian Rural Fellowship Bulletin No. 56,* November, 1940.

Rupel, Paul W. "The Building of an Indigenous Christian Community in Africa," Agricultural Missions, Inc., Mimeograph Series No. 46.

Skinner, S. E. "The Characteristics of a Christian Rural Community," *Christian Rural Fellowship Bulletin No. 59,* February, 1941.

Smathers, Eugene. "The Characteristics of a Christian Rural Community," *Christian Rural Fellowship Bulletin No. 61,* April, 1941.

Tau, Ch'i Kuang. "The Joint Council on Extension Service to the Rural Church (North China)," Agricultural Missions, Inc., Mimeograph Series No. 103.

Wilson, Warren H. "The Second Missionary Adventure," *Christian Rural Fellowship Bulletin No. 77,* December, 1942.

Wilson, Warren H. *Rural Religion and the Country Church.* New York: Fleming H. Revell Co., 1928.

A. WORSHIP

Bowman, J. W. *Worship in the Village Church,* United Church Review, December, 1933, 388 ff.

Palmer, Albert W. *Come, Let Us Worship.* New York: The Macmillan Co., 1941.

Palmer, Albert W. *The Art of Conducting Public Worship,* New York: The Macmillan Company, 1942.

Price, Frank W. "The Kingdom of God in a Rural Community," *Christian Rural Fellowship Bulletin No. 33,* June, 1938.

Rich, Mark *Rural Life Prayers.* New York: Federal Council of Churches, 1941.

Rockey, C. D. *Village Worship Programs,* Lucknow: Lucknow Publishing House.

Senger, Nettie M. *Worship,* Chinese Recorder, LVIII (1927), 319 ff.

Ziegler, Edward K. "Guidance in Worship in the Rural Church," *Christian Rural Fellowship Bulletin No. 70,* March, 1942.

Ziegler, Edward K. *A Book of Worship for Village Churches.* New York: Agricultural Missions, Inc., 1939.

Ziegler, Edward K. *Rural People at Worship.* New York: Agricultural Missions, Inc., 1943.

Ziegler, Edward K. *Country Altars, Worship in the Rural Church.* New York: Federal Council of Churches, 1942.

B. PREACHING

No books or articles dealing with Preaching in the rural church were found by the Committee, indicating a dearth of materials in this field.

C. PASTORAL WORK

Atwater, Amy. "A Plain Farmer's Religion," *Christian Rural Fellowship Bulletin No. 19,* February, 1937.

Dawson, Marshall. *Oberlin, A Protestant Saint.* Chicago: Willett, Clark and Co., 1934.

Schroeder, Martin, and Galpin, C. J. "The Rural Minister and the Country Church," *Christian Rural Fellowship Bulletin No. 55,* October, 1940.

D. RURAL CHURCH SCHOOL EDUCATION

Booth, Newell S. *Serving God in the Sunday School.* London: Society for the Promotion of Christian Knowledge, 1937.

Harner, Nevin C., and Baker, David D. *Missionary Education in Your Church.* New York: Friendship Press, 1942.

Hartshorne, Hugh and Ehrhart, Earle V. *Church Schools of Today.* New Haven: Yale University Press, 1932.

Hartshorne, Hugh and Lotz, Elsa. *Case Studies of Present Day Religious Teaching.* New Haven: Yale University Press, 1932.

Highbaugh, Irma. "Relation of Religious and Mass Education," *Chinese Recorder,* LXIV (1933), 470 ff.

International Missionary Council. *The Life of the Church.* Tambaram Series, II. *Religious Education.* Report of Jerusalem Meeting, II.

Lew, T. T. "Christian Religious Education Must Help Find the Way Out," *Chinese Recorder,* LXV (1934), 19-25.

McKibben, Frank M. *Improving Religious Education Through Supervision.* New York: Methodist Book Concern, 1931.

Miao, Chester S. "Extend the Boundaries of Religious Education," *Chinese Recorder,* LXV (1934) 27 f.

Myers, A. J. William. *Teaching Religion Creatively.* New York: Fleming H. Revell Co., 1932.

Price, Frank W. "The Significance for Religious Education of the New Rural Reconstruction Movement in China," Agricultural Missions, Inc., Mimeograph Series No. 47.

Vieth, Paul H. "A Program for Adults" in "Christian Education and World Evangelism," Report of the International Conference on Christian Education, Mexico. 1941.

Weigle, Luther A. "A Total Program of Christian Education for Children" in "Christian Education and World Evangelism," Report of the International Conference on Christian Education, Mexico, 1941.

Young, E. Mae. *Educating for Missions in the Local Church.* New York: Methodist Book Concern, 1936.

E. GROUP ACTIVITIES

Boyd, Neva L. "Social Group Work: A Definition and a Methodological Note," *Division of Social Work Bulletin, Vol. I No. 1.* Chicago: Northwestern University, 1937.

Coyle, Grace L. "Casework and Group Work," *Survey Graphic,* April, 1937, 102-104.

Dimock, H. and Hondry C. *A Professional Outlook on Group Education.*

Felton, Ralph A. *The Rural Church in the Far East.* Calcutta: Baptist Mission Press, 1938.

Hatch, D. Spencer. *Up From Poverty in Rural India.* 1932.

Hawkins, Gaynell. *Educational Experiments in Social Settlements.*

Higgins, Mrs. W. B. "Girls' Clubs For African Girls—'The Daughters of Africa,'" Agricultural Missions, Inc., Mimeograph Series No. 122.

Kilpatrick, W. H. *Group Education for Democracy.*

Makanya, Sibusisiwe. "The Bantu Youth League," Agricultural Missions, Inc., Mimeograph Series No. 65.

Moreno, I. L., M.D. *Who Shall Survive,* Washington, D. C.: Nervous and Mental Disease Publishing Co., 1934.

Page, Kirby. *Living Prayerfully.* New York and Toronto: Farrar and Rinehart, 1941.

Suggestions for Group Discussion and Suggestions for Panel Discussions (leaflets). Bureau of Agricultural Economics, U. S. Department of Agriculture.

Tead, Ordway. *Creative Management.* New York: Association Press, 1935.

Williamson, Ralph L. "Spiritual Development Through Neighborhood Fellowship Groups," *Christian Rural Fellowship Bulletin No. 79,* February, 1943.

F. THE RURAL SCHOOL

"A Rural Curriculum in a Christian Middle School," *Chinese Recorder,* LXIII, 1932, 326-327.

Booth, Newell S. *Teaching a Bantu Community.* Thesis, Hartford Seminary Foundation, Hartford, Conn., 1936.

Collins, Emma J. "Relating Subject Teaching to God," Agricultural Missions, Inc., Mimeograph Series No. 161.

Colonial Office. *Memorandum on the Education of African Communities.* London: Colonial No. 103, 1935.

Cook, Katherine M. *The House of the People.* Washington, D. C.: U. S. Government Printing Office, 1932.

Cooley, Rossa B. *School Acres.* New Haven: Yale University Press, 1930.

Cooley, Rossa B. "Education in the Soil," an account of Penn Normal Industrial and Agricultural School, St. Helena Island, South Carolina. Agricultural Missions, Inc., Mimeograph Series No. 45.

Counts, George I. *Dare the School Build a New Social Order?* New York: The John Day Company.

Foreign Missions Conference. *Christian Action in Africa.* New York, 1942.

International Missionary Council. *Missions and Rural Problems.* Report of the Jerusalem Meeting, VI, 249 ff.

Liang Shu-Ming. "Methods and Principles of Peasant Schools," New York: Agricultural Missions, Inc., Mimeograph Series No. 33, 1934.

Nelson, Erland. "Putting Culture into Agriculture," *Christian Rural Fellowship Bulletin No. 21.*

Olcott, Mason. *Better Village Schools.* Calcutta: Y. M. C. A. Publishing House.

Reisner, John H. "Rural Betterment in Africa." New York: Agricultural Missions, Inc., Mimeograph Series.

Ross, Emery. *Out of Africa.* New York: Friendship Press, 1936. Chapter IV.

Schairer, R. "Human Character and World Order," Lecture in *Christian Bases of World Order.* New York and Nashville: Abingdon-Cokesbury Press, 1942.

Williams, F. G. "Responsibility of the Rural Boarding School to the Community." New York: Agricultural Missions, Inc., 1939, Mimeograph Series No. 108.

Williams, Fred G. "Learning Through Labor" (Vocational Opportunity for Boys in School), Agricultural Missions, Inc., Mimeograph Series No. 109.

Williams, Mrs. Fred G. "Character Building in the School," Agricultural Missions, Inc., Mimeograph Series No. 138.

Works, George A. and Lesser, Simon O. *Rural America Today.* Chicago: University of Chicago Press, 1942.

G. HEALTH ACTIVITIES

Bridgman, Mrs. C. A. "Child Welfare Work in Junghsien, West China," New York: Agricultural Missions, Inc., Mimeograph Series No. 136.

Bulletins of the Christian Medical Council for Overseas Work, Nos. 1, 2, 3, 4.

Butterfield, Kenyon L. *The Rural Mission of the Church in Eastern Asia.* New York and London: International Missionary Council, 1931.

Chang, Fu-liang, "Program for a Rural Church," *Chinese Recorder,* LIX, 1929.

Christian Action in Africa. Report of the Church Conference on African Affairs, Africa Committee of the Foreign Missions Conference of North America, New York, 1942, Chapter VI.

Clark, Eric Kent, M.D. *Mental Hygiene for Community Nursery.* University of Minnesota Press, 1942.

Felton, Ralph A. "What is Right with the Rural Church," *Chinese Recorder,* LXII, 1936.

Fisher, Galen M. "Kagawa Returns to Japan," *Christian Century,* June 9, 1937.

Frazer, Agnes R. "The Place of Missions in Spreading the Knowledge of Health and Hygiene in Village Life," *International Review of Missions,* IX, 1930.

Gilbert, Ruth, R. N. "The Public Health Nurse and Her Patient," New York: Commonwealth Fund, 1940, p. 13.

Hatch, D. Spencer. "The Broader Basis for Health in Eastern Countries." Review in *National Christian Council Review,* LX, 1940.

Hiltner, Seward. *Religion and Health.* New York: The Macmillan Co., 1943.

Hodgson, Violet H. *Supervision in Public Health Nursing.* New York: The Commonwealth Fund, 1939.

Hoffman, R. E., M.D., F.A.C.S., "Efficiency in the Task of Medical Missions," Reprint from the *Journal of the Christian Medical Association of India, Burma and Ceylon,* January, 1940.

Hubbard, Mrs. Hugh. *New Life in Fan Village, North China.* New York: Missionary Education Movement (no date).

Hume, Edward H., M.D. "Christian Medicine in a New Day in China," *Chinese Recorder,* LXVI, 1935.

Hume, Edward H., M.D. "New Challenge of a New Day," *Chinese Recorder,* LXVI, 1935.

Hume, Edward H., M.D. "The Medical Missionary's Attitude," *Bulletin of the Christian Medical Council for Overseas Work,* July 3, 1941.

Hume, Edward H., M.D. Book Review, "Ten Years in the Congo," Davis, W. E., *International Review of Missions,* XXIX, 1940.

International Missionary Council, March 24 - April 8, 1928, "The Christian

Mission in Relation to Rural Problems," Vol. VI of the Report. New York and London, 1928.
International Missionary Council, "The Christian Ministry of Health and Healing," Section IX-B of the Madras Meeting.
Ma Teh Yin, *Village Life in North China.* Master's Thesis, Drew Theological Seminary, Drew University, Madison, N. J., 1943.
Next Steps in Public Health. Milbank Annual Report, 1936.
Phelps, P. M., R.N. and Puffer, Mrs. F. A., M.A. "Health Work in Villages Near Yeotmal, Berar," *United Church Review,* III and IV, 261-263.
Price, P. S. "A Philosophy of Rural Work," Agricultural Missions, Inc., Mimeograph Series, No. 93.
Rodger, John, M.D. "Family Limitation for Rural Families," Address for the Birth Control Federation of America at the National Conference of Social Workers, May 28, 1940.
Sanderson, Dwight. "Disadvantaged Classes in Rural Life," *Christian Rural Fellowship Bulletin No. 36,* January, 1939.
Shields, R. T. "Medical Missions in China," *Chinese Recorder,* LXVI, 1935.
Thompson, D. W., M.D. "Remarking the Rural Church," *Chinese Recorder,* LXVI, 1935.
Trowell, H. C. "Public Health in British Tropical Africa," *International Review of Missions,* XXVIII, 1939.
Tsurumi, Yusuke, "Toyohiko Kagawa," *Japan Christian Quarterly,* 1935, p. 111.
Walker, Rollin H. *The Modern Message of the Psalms.* Abingdon Press, 1938.
Wong, K. C. "The Future of Christian Medical Work in China," *Chinese Recorder,* LXXI, 1940.

H. TRAINING FOR HOME AND FAMILY LIFE

Dahlenberg, Edwin T. *Youth and the Homes of Tomorrow.* Philadelphia: The Judson Press—Revised 1940.
Editorial Division of the Board of Education of the Methodist Church. *Child Guidance in Christian Living.* (A magazine for teachers and parent education.) Nashville, Tenn.
Federal Council of Churches. *Family Life—Parenthood and Young People's Relationships* (a selected book list 1941).
Hamilton, Lulu Snyder. *God Lives in Homes.* St. Louis: The Bethany Press, 1942. (Meditations for mothers—Prayers of a modern family.)
Keiser, Armilda B. *Come Everyone and Worship* (Ages 6-8). New York: Friendship Press.
Munro, Harry C. *Parents and Teachers.* New York and Nashville: Abingdon-Cokesbury Press, 1940.
National Council of Parent Education *Handbook for leaders of parent education groups* in emergency education programs. Prepared under the direction of the advisory committee on Emergency Education Programs in cooperation with the Office of Education, U. S. Department of the Interior, 1934. The Council—60 East 42nd Street, New York.
Peery, Agnes Junkin and Werner, Emily J. *The Child and the Book.*
Book I What is God Like?
Book II The Bible.
Book III What Christ Means to the Present-Day World.
Book IV The Christian Citizen.
New York: Island Workshop Press Cooperative, Inc., 1942.
Rand, Winnifred, Sweeny, Mary E., and Vincent, E. Lee. *Growth and Development of the Young Child.* (Written by three members of the Merrill-Palmer Staff, Detroit, Mich.) Philadelphia: W. B. Saunders Co., 1938.

Staff of St. George's School for Child Study, Parent Education Division, Toronto University. *Outlines for Parent Education Groups.*

Williams-Ellis, Amabel. *How You Began.* (A child's introduction to biology.) International Bureau of Education. London: Gerald Howe, Ltd. ("Tells side by side the stories of animal evolution and of embryology—tracing life from a single-celled organism both in the child and in ordinary animal life.") Excellent for leaders in parent education groups.

Williamson, Mary Heald. *The Countrywoman and Her Church.* New York and Nashville: Abingdon-Cokesbury Press. (All parent educators in rural areas should have this.)

Wilson, Isabel, M.D. *How You Work* (with drawings). International Bureau of Education, London, England. London: Gerald Howe, Ltd.

(See also the forthcoming report on Christian family life by the Foreign Missions Conference)

I. METHODS OF ADULT EDUCATION

Butterfield, Kenyon L. *The Christian Mission in Rural India,* New York: International Missionary Council, 1930.

Butterfield, Kenyon L. *The Rural Mission of the Church in Eastern Asia.* New York: International Missionary Council, 1931.

Campbell, Thomas Monroe. *The Movable School Goes to the Negro Farmer.* Tuskegee, Alabama: Tuskegee Institute Press, Tuskegee Institute, 1936.

Chinese Recorder. Shanghai: Presbyterian Mission Press, 1936. p. 663.

Christian Action in Africa. New York: Foreign Missions Conference, 1942.

Community Drama, the Playground and Recreation Association of America. New York: The Century Co., 1926. Vol. VII.

Cook, Katherine Margaret. *House of the People.* Washington, D. C.: U. S. Government Printing Office, 1932.

Davis, J. Merle. *Modern Industry and the African.* London: The Macmillan Co., 1933.

Felton, Ralph A. *The Rural Church in the Far East.* Calcutta: Baptist Mission Press, 1938.

Galpin, C. J. *Life Story of a Great Country Pastor—John Frederick Oberlin.* New York: Home Missions Council of North America, 1941.

Hanna, P. R. and Research Staff. *Youth Serves the Community.* New York: D. Appleton-Century Company, 1936.

Hatch, D. Spencer. *Further Up in Rural India.* New York: Oxford University Press, 1938.

Hatch, D. Spencer. *Up from Poverty.* New York: Oxford University Press, 1936.

Hu Shih. *The Chinese Renaissance.* Chicago: University of Chicago Press, 1934.

Hubbard, Mrs. Hugh. *New Life in Fan Village, North China.* New York: Missionary Education Movement, 1940.

Landis, Benson Y. and Willard, John D. *Rural Adult Education.* New York: The Macmillan Co., 1933.

Laubach, Frank C. "Help a Million Blind to See." *Christian Century,* Nov. 19, 1941.

Laubach, Frank C. *Silent Billion Speak.* New York: Friendship Press, 1943.

Laubach, Frank C. *Toward a Literate World.* New York: Columbia University Press, 1936.

North, Eric M., editor. *The Book of a Thousand Tongues.* New York: Harper and Brothers, 1938.

Scully, Michael. "Mexico's Medical Revolution." *Reader's Digest,* March, 1943.

Shaw, Mabel. *God's Candle Lights.* New York: Friendship Press, 1932.

Tabb, W. E. *Visual Education in Rural and Foreign Communities.* New York: Agricultural Missions, Inc. Mimeograph Series No. 63.

Weiner, Philip Paul. "Visual Education," *Handbook of Adult Education in the U. S.* New York: American Association of Adult Education in the U. S., 1936.

Wiser, William H. and Charlotte Viall. *For All of Life.* New York: Friendship Press, 1943.

Yen, Y. C. James. *Tinghsien Experiment in 1934.* Peiping: Chinese National Association of the Mass Education Movement, 1934.

J. RESEARCH

Latourette, Kenneth S. "Research and Christian Missions," *International Review of Missions,* XXI (1932), 532-546.

Lindsay, A. B. "Extension and Research," *International Review of Missions,* XXII (1933), 415-421. Additional note on proposals made by the Commission on Christian Higher Education in India.

Puxley, H. L. "An Experiment in Research at an Indian Christian College," *International Review of Missions,* XXV (1936), 206-215.

"Research in Rural Chinese Evangelism," *Chinese Recorder,* LXV (1934), 330-332. A project carried on by the Peiping Presbyterian Technical School and Apprentice Trade School over a three-year period.

"Research," Section VIII of "The Report of the Central Board of Christian Higher Education (India) for the Year Ending March 31, 1939." *National Christian Council Review,* LX (1940), 52-54. "Sixteen colleges undertook research studies in the economic and social environment of the Christian community around them." Their names are given and the names of many of the projects also.

Chapter VI. LEADERSHIP OF THE CHRISTIAN PROGRAMME IN RURAL AREAS

TRAINING RURAL MEDICAL SPECIALISTS

Cabot, Dr. Hugh. "The Place of Nursing in Health Service," *Public Health Nursing,* April, 1943.

Chapman, Owen H., M.D. Reprint from *Chinese Recorder.* LIX (1929).

Chesterman, C. C. *In the Service of Suffering.* London: Edinburgh House, 1940.

"The Council's Statement," Jerusalem Conference of the International Missionary Council Report, 1928.

Felton, Ralph A. *The Rural Church in the Far East,* Department of Social and Industrial Research, International Missionary Council. Calcutta: Baptist Mission Press, 1938.

Harley, George Way, M.D. *Native African Medicine.* Cambridge, Mass.: Harvard University Press, 1941.

Lerrigo, P. H. J., M.D., D.D. "The Next Steps in Medical Missions," *International Review of Missions,* XXI (1938) .

Shih, Margaret. "The Church and Rural Health," *Chinese Recorder,* LXVIII (1937).

Welch, Janet, M.D. "Medical Missionary Training," *International Review of Missions,* XXIX (1940).

Wolf, Lulu (Mrs. R. N.) and Hubbard, Mrs. R. N. "Comments on Dr. Cabot's Article," *Public Health Nursing,* April, 1943.

TRAINING RURAL TEACHERS

Anderson, C. J. and Simpson, I. J. *The Supervision of Rural Schools.* New York: D. Appleton & Co., 1932.

Baker, Frank E. "Educating Teachers by the Experience Method," *Childhood Education,* December, 1935. 101 ff.

Booth, Newell S. *Teaching a Bantu Community.* Thesis, Hartford Seminary Foundation, Hartford, Conn., 1936.

Colonial Office, "Memorandum on the Education of African Communities," *Bulletin No. 103,* 1935.

Cook, Katherine M. *The House of the People.* Washington, D. C.: U. S. Government Printing Office, 1932.

Davis, Jackson. *The Jeanes Visiting Teachers.* New York: The Carnegie Corporation, 1936.

Fishman, A. T. "A Functioning Rural Community Training School," New York: Agricultural Missions, Inc., Mimeograph Series No. 53, 1935.

Foreign Missions Conference. *Christian Action in Africa,* and recommendations on education. New York, 1942, 90-94.

Hugh, Paul C. "Christian University Afield," *Chinese Recorder,* LXXI (1940), 413f.

Olcott, Mason. *Better Village Schools.* Calcutta: Y. M. C. A. Publishing House.

Sanderson, Dwight. *Leadership for Rural Life.* New York: Association Press, 1940.

Secretaries of British Mission Boards, "Training of Village Teachers in Africa," *International Review of Missions,* XVIII (1929), 231-249.

Steytler, J. C. *Educational Adaptations in Reference to African Village Schools.* London, 1939.

Chapter VII. THE RURAL CHURCH

"A Plan for Extension Service of the Rural Churches," Director's Report on the Country Church, to the Department of the Rural Church of the Nanking Theological Seminary, Exhibit A.

Bicksler, Harry E. "In Defense of the Small Rural Church," *Christian Rural Fellowship Bulletin No. 42,* May, 1939.

Davis, J. Merle. *The Economic and Social Environment of the Younger Churches.* New York: International Missionary Council, 1938.

Felton, Ralph A. *The Rural Church in the Far East.* Calcutta: The Baptist Mission Press, 1938. Especially 169-180.

Foreign Missions Conference. *Christian Action in Africa.* New York: 1942. Chapter VII, "The Comprehensive Approach to Rural Africa."

Galpin, C. J. "The Rural Church," *Christian Rural Fellowship Bulletin No. 37,* December, 1938.

Greene, Shirley E. "A Church Program for the Rural Community," *Christian Rural Fellowship Bulletin No. 62,* May, 1941.

Hargreaves, J. Robert. "The Significance to Rural Religion and the Rural Church of So-called Secular Agencies Related to Agriculture, the Home, and Rural Life," *Christian Rural Fellowship Bulletin No. 72,* May 1942.

Jones, Thomas Jesse. "Church and Community," *Christian Rural Fellowship Bulletin No. 78,* January, 1943.

Morse, Hermann N. and Dawber, Mark A. "The Rural Church and World Christian Unity," *Christian Rural Fellowship Bulletin No. 48,* January, 1940.

Mosher, A. T. "The Kingdom of God and Rural Reconstruction," *Christian Rural Fellowship Bulletin No. 56,* November, 1940.

Price, Frank W. "A Philosophy of Christian Rural Work," Agricultural Missions, Inc., Mimeograph Series No. 93.

Rich, Mark. "Effective Techniques in Developing Unity and Cooperation Among Rural Churches," *Christian Rural Fellowship Bulletin No. 49,* February, 1940.

Rich, Mark. "A Basic Philosophy for Promoting Cooperation Among Rural Churches," *Christian Rural Fellowship Bulletin No. 63,* June, 1941.

Rupel, Paul W. "The Building of an Indigenous Christian Community in Africa," Agricultural Missions, Inc., Mimeograph Series No. 46.

Smathers, Eugene. "A Rural Church Program That Makes Religion The Qualifying Factor In Every Experience of Life," *Christian Rural Fellowship Bulletin No. 66,* November, 1941.

Smith, Rockwell C. "Some Basic Implications in the Development of a Vital Rural Church Program," *Christian Rural Fellowship Bulletin No. 84,* September, 1943.

Sun, T. H. "The Church in China's Rural Reconstruction," *Christian Rural Fellowship Bulletin No. 54,* September, 1940.

"The Rural Church and Rural Life in the South," *Christian Rural Fellowship Bulletin No. 83,* June, 1943. Sections of the Report of the Southern Rural Life Conference, Nashville, Tenn., January 27-29, 1943.

Vogt, Paul L. "The Resources of the Country Church," *Christian Rural Fellowship Bulletin No. 87,* December, 1943.

Wilson, Warren H. "The Second Missionary Adventure," *Christian Rural Fellowship Bulletin No. 77,* December, 1942.

Wilson, Warren H. *The Farmer's Church.* New York: Century Co., 1925.

Wilson, Warren H. *Rural Religion and the Country Church.* New York; Fleming H. Revell Co., 1928.

Ziegler, E. K. "A Christian Rural Life Philosophy," *Christian Rural Fellowship Bulletin No. 67,* December, 1941.

PAPERS RELATED TO CHAPTER V:

Activities of the Christian Programme in Rural Areas

Any of the following papers may be obtained from Agricultural Missions, Inc., 156 Fifth Avenue, New York 10, N. Y., on request.

"Program of the Rural Church" from "Training and Guiding Lay Leadership in the Village Church," by Alice E. Murphy. M.S. No. 157, pp. 4-6.

"Goals for the Rural Church," Extension Service to Rural Churches in East China Nanking Theological Seminary, Nanking, China. M.S. No. 83.

"The 'Farm' Village Experiment—Toward a Christian Village," by a rural missionary. M.S. No. 75.

"Implications (of the Need for Parent Training) for the Individual Missionary" from "Village Homes and Christian Homes Training," by Glora M. Wysner. M.S. No. 115.

"Better Health in the Comprehensive or Larger Parish Program," by Henry S. Waters, M.D. M.S. No. 131.

"The Contributions to Better Health by Doctors, Nurses, Preachers, Teachers and Lay People in the Homes, the School and the Wider Community," by Helma J. Fernstrom. M.S. No. 153.

"Christ and Village Education," by Mason Olcott, *The International Review of Missions,* Vol. 29, p. 249, 1940.

"Putting Culture into Agriculture," by Erland Nelson, *Christian Rural Fellowship Bulletin,* No. 21.

"Cooperation and Religion," by M. M. Coady, *Christian Rural Fellowship Bulletin,* No. 50.

PAPERS RELATED TO CHAPTER VI:

Leadership of the Christian Programme in Rural Areas

"Training and Guiding Lay Leadership in the Village Church," by Alice E. Murphy. M.S. No. 157.

"A Plain Farmer's Religion," by Amy Atwater, *Christian Rural Fellowship Bulletin,* No. 19.

"If I Were a Rural Minister," by Charles Josiah Galpin, *Christian Rural Fellowship Bulletin,* No. 55.

"The Country Church Is Different," by Martin Schroeder, *Christian Rural Fellowship Bulletin,* No. 55.

"A Plan for Extension Service to Rural Churches in Operation by the Joint Council on Extension Service to the Rural Church of North China," M.S. No. 104.

PAPERS RELATED TO CHAPTER VII:
The Rural Church

"Findings of a Conference on Rural Work," held under the auspices of the National Christian Council at Nagpur, India, on September 25-26, 1934, M.S. No. 49.

"The Kingdom of God and Rural Reconstruction," by Arthur T. Mosher, *Christian Rural Fellowship Bulletin,* No. 56.

"A Philosophy of Christian Rural Work," by Frank W. Price, M.S. No. 93.

Index